Hidden Histories in the United Church of Christ 2

HIDDEN HISTORIES IN THE UNITED CHURCH OF CHRIST 2

edited by

Barbara Brown Zikmund

UNITED CHURCH PRESS
New York

Library of Congress Cataloging-in-Publication Data
(Revised for added volume)

Hidden histories in the United Church of Christ.

Includes bibliographies and indexes.
  1. United Church of Christ—History. 2. United
churches—United States—History. I. Zikmund,
Barbara Brown.
BX9884.H53 1987   285.8'34   84-152
ISBN 0-8298-0753-5 (pbk. : v. 2)

United Church Press, 132 West 31 Street, New York, NY 10001

For
my father
Henry Daniels Brown
1910–1970
who taught me to love history
and to look beyond the
obvious

Contents

INTRODUCTION

UNITY AND DIVERSITY

Barbara Brown Zikmund

THE UNITED CHURCH OF CHRIST is a case study of religious pluralism in twentieth-century America. Not only does it carry on the traditions of the German Reformed, Congregational, German Evangelical, and Christian denominations, but it also seeks to embody more flexible understandings of church unity in the face of diversity. It is a good example of the complex developments that make American religious history so unique.

The first volume of *Hidden Histories in the United Church of Christ* made the case that the history of the UCC cannot be adequately defined in terms of four denominational "streams" becoming one. When such "historical orthodoxy" dominates, parts of the history get lost, methods for preserving materials become too narrow, historical interpretations may be biased, and past events are treated out of context. An adequate history of the UCC must be nourished by "hidden histories" that seldom surface within the traditional fourfold approach.

It is important, therefore, to move beyond UCC historical orthodoxy and examine the history of special movements, women, and ethnic communities. The earlier book contained material on native Americans, blacks, Hungarians, Armenians, German Congregationalists, Schwenkfelders, and Japanese-American churches, along with an examination of laywomen's ministries and information about theological variety in Reformed history.

All these histories show that the United Church of Christ has been wrestling with pluralism for a long time. An adequate history of the UCC must retrieve and assimilate these histories. Then those who have been lost or slighted by standard interpretations of the past may experience justice. Unity in diversity requires that the United Church of Christ locate, preserve, and freely share all these histories.

A second volume of hidden histories is important for two reasons. There is need to redress some of the obvious omissions in the first collection. Chapters on the Christians, the Evangelical Protestants, and the Chinese Congregationalists explore more of the confessional, ecclesiastical, and ethnic variety of UCC history. This second volume also examines more deeply what it means for the United Church of Christ to celebrate its "unity in diversity." What are some of the historical pressures and experiences leading toward unity in the UCC? What instances of diversity and differentiation have helped the UCC define itself more precisely in a pluralistic age?

The first six chapters in this book show ways in which the history of the United Church of Christ and its historical antecedents moves from particularity toward unity. The efforts of peoples of faith to share sacred space, preserve liberty of conscience, get beyond sectarianism, combine intellectual rigor and popular piety, streamline denominational structures, and cultivate communication networks have shaped the unity of the United Church of Christ.

At the same time, there are other stories that show how unity has been broken, redefined, and stretched by diversity. The last four chapters of the book lift up two controversies leading to denominational fragmentation and clarification, efforts to provide special training for women's ministries and an example of ethnic church experience. They show how unity in diversity must reckon with theological, ecclesiastical, gender, and ethnic differences.

2

EXPRESSION OF UNITY

The interplay of unity and diversity within United Church of Christ history has, on the whole, been a healthy experience. Part One explores various ways in which particular histories have shaped UCC understandings of unity. When the founders of the UCC came together under the biblical hope that "we may all be one," they built on earlier experience. Evangelical, Reformed, Christian, and Congregational people grounded their ecumenical vision in concrete experiences.

The first chapter in this collection takes a closer look at what are known as "union churches." Eighteenth-century Europe was plagued with wars, unstable governments, and deplorable economic conditions. As German Reformed and German Lutheran immigrants arrived in colonial America, there were so few people of either religious tradition that the two groups found it easy to share church buildings. Both groups already had experience with common facilities in Germany. Besides, cooperation on the rural frontier was a way of life. In time, churches developed traditions, official guidelines, and policies whereby two congregations could build and maintain one church structure for their mutual benefit.

What originally began out of expediency, because of the scarcity of educated ministers, the poverty of the people, and desires to share their common German language and culture, became a way of life. These positive experiences of denominational cooperation at the grassroots level showed members of UCC churches that ecumenical understanding can begin with the very practical matters that emerge when two congregations share the same sacred space.

Another experience of unity is found in the development of a small but progressive group of German churches in the Ohio River valley. Chapter 2 explores the origins of the Smithfield Church in Pittsburgh, Pennsylvania, during the American Revolution. It explains how a movement spreading from that city eventually established a group of churches that cherished religious freedom, welcomed diversity of opinion, and respected the right of individual conviction.

These churches were fiercely independent. As a matter of principle they had no creed, allowing members to fashion their

3

faith for themselves, based on their own thinking and experience. They also insisted on the autonomy of each congregation, for fear of opening the door to "outside control." And finally, they emphasized the authority of the laity, not the clergy, to "work out" any problems in the churches.

Although these churches were wary of all ecclesiastical organizations, by the late nineteenth century they had organized themselves into a loose federation known as the German Evangelical Protestant Church of North America. Evangelical because it was grounded in the gospel (the *evangel*), and Protestant because it protested against any compulsion in matters of faith and conscience. Their small size, however, led them to seek a wider fellowship with the National Council of Congregational Churches in 1925, and through that connection they became part of the United Church of Christ.

The third chapter takes a longer look at the history of the Christian denomination. Although the Christians are technically one of the "four streams" within standard United Church of Christ history, their story is seldom adequately treated. This is because Christian origins are found in North Carolina and Virginia, on the Kentucky-Ohio frontier, and in New England. They are also divided into separate black and white developments.

Chapter 3 looks especially at the "Christian Connexion" in New England, showing how its antisectarian stance, its attitudes toward women in ministry, its expansion beyond New England, its definitions of ministry and theology, and its ecumenical tenacity continue to strengthen the UCC. Over the years Christian principles became denominational beliefs. They remained broad enough, however, to invite other Christians into mutual fellowship and cooperation. In 1931 the Christians joined with the Congregationalists, and in the 1950s most New England Christian churches became part of the United Church of Christ. Always deeply committed to church unity beyond sectarian labels, the Christian legacy strengthens UCC ecumenical identity.

Another way of seeing how historical experiences have shaped the United Church of Christ is examined in the fourth chapter. Within the history of the Evangelical Synod of North America, the little-known heresy trial of Karl Emil Otto in 1880

4

presents a unique example of theological leadership and the struggle for denominational integrity. Otto was initially condemned for his use of German scholarship and its challenge to biblical authority. His case was one of the earliest to raise this issue among American Protestants.

In defense, Otto pointed to the 1848 confessional statement of the Evangelical Church. It stated that where the resources of the Lutheran and Reformed traditions disagreed, Evangelical believers "adhered strictly to the passages of Holy Scripture bearing on the subject" and "the liberty of conscience prevailing in the Evangelical Church."

Although Otto was initially condemned, he was later informally vindicated. As the years went by, his approach to scriptural authority, learning, individual conscience, and willingness to allow missionary-like accommodation to American life prevailed. The Evangelical Synod learned how to live with a creative tension between sound biblical criticism and flexible churchly pietism. This legacy has become part of the United Church of Christ.

Chapter 5 approaches the issue of unity from the standpoint of ecclesiastical structures. It describes the ways in which women's mission work in the Congregational churches was developed during the nineteenth century by four independent women's mission boards. The boards came into being to support women missionaries and facilitate outreach to women. They worked cooperatively with male-dominated mission boards, but they raised their own funds and maintained control over their own projects.

By the early twentieth century, however, the ideal of bureaucratic efficiency, the increasing centralization of Congregationalism, pressure from missionaries to get beyond embarrassing divisions in the mission field, a general concern for cooperation, and the desire of younger women not to have separate women's organizations called for change in women's relationship to the mission boards. Great energy was expended to consolidate structures without losing the strengths of women's work. Finally, in 1927, three of the four women's boards were absorbed into the American Board of Commissioners for Foreign Missions.

In retrospect this consolidation was probably not in the best interests of women. The women tended to thrive when there was cooperation among separate organizations and when they could continue to control their own money and mission priorities. Pressure from the central Congregational bureaucracy and women's own desires to enter the mainstream of church and national life were instrumental in bringing about the merger. This story shows the ambiguity of unified structures in relationship to genuine unity in the church.

Finally, chapter 6 addresses the importance of communication for church unity by examining the legacy of religious journalism from the Christian denomination. From the publication of the *Herald of Gospel Liberty* in 1808 (the first religious newspaper in the world) to the *UCC News* in the 1980s, the health of the United Church of Christ has been nurtured by newspapers and magazines.

Herald founder-editor Elias Smith argued that liberty with respect to one's duty to God was essential. As the Christian movement grew, newspapers shaped and supported its identity. Newspapers provided "the unifying force of the whole church" and directed the energy of the church toward common purposes. Furthermore, the commitment of the Christian Church to justice was reinforced and enabled by a network of helpful publications. An understanding of the importance of journalism within the Christian tradition is but another way to explain the commitment of the United Church of Christ to unity.

The first six hidden histories should be read, therefore, as evidence defining and supporting unitive forces at work within the United Church of Christ. Taken together they show how a self-defined "united and uniting" church, which only came into being in 1957, can draw on concrete historical experiences to strengthen its ecumenical commitment.

DEALING WITH DIVERSITY

In the midst of these experiences that have supported and produced the strong commitment of the United Church of Christ to unity, there are also histories of brokenness and fragmentation. Through theological and ecclesiastical controversy,

6

through efforts to set up separate programs for women, and through the evolution of ethnic church life, the United Church of Christ has coped with diversity.

The results have not always been constructive, but they have shown the church that a vision of unity can be enriched through awareness of diversity. Part Two examines four histories that highlight issues of diversity in UCC history.

Chapter 7 shows this process by examining the impact of the life and work of an eighteenth-century German Reformed pastor, Philip William Otterbein. Otterbein was a German Pietist who tried to remain faithful to the church of his heritage, while at the same time responding in innovative ways to the spiritual needs of the people. On the American frontier he became a leader in the Methodist-oriented German Brethren movement. Although he supported classes for spiritual nurture in the local church, he did not ask those in the movement to leave their churches. Otterbein continued to serve German Reformed churches and claimed that the United Brethren movement was an "unsectarian" development. In time, however, the United Brethren organized into a separate denomination, becoming part of the Evangelical United Brethren Church and more recently finding a place in the United Methodist Church.

Otterbein's work is important for the United Church of Christ because, despite his concern for local church life and the "experience" of salvation, he refused to ignore the larger bond of unity among all Christians. Questions of polity never dimmed his vision of a common life in Jesus Christ. He always held the *Heidelberg Catechism* in high regard, and even as a charismatic leader of an evangelical movement that later became a separate denomination, he remained a minister of the German Reformed Church until his death in 1813.

In the early twentieth century the United Brethren and the Reformed Church in the United States sought reconciliation. Plans were formulated for a united church, which would have included the Evangelical Synod of North America. Although this "United Church in America" never materialized, those ecumenical conversations shaped the later Evangelical and Reformed union.

The story of Otterbein is not the only controversy grounded in

German Reformed history to produce another denomination. Chapter 8 presents the history of John Winebrenner and the Churches of God.

In this controversy John Winebrenner, a German Reformed pastor influenced by New Measures revivalism, was dismissed by his church and the synod in the 1820s for his views on the Bible, the church, free will, baptism, the Lord's Supper, and foot washing. His followers officially organized, forming a denomination known as the Churches of God, General Conference.

In the 1840s John Winebrenner became an antagonist of John Williamson Nevin, professor at the German Reformed seminary in Mercersburg, Pennsylvania. The dialogue between them about revivalism and evangelistic techniques led to early expressions of "Mercersburg Theology." Although both men lamented the low level of piety in mid-nineteenth-century America, they had different solutions. Winebrenner stressed the importance of individual regeneration through new birth. Nevin stressed a deeper knowledge of what it means to be a Christian through catechism and confirmation. Winebrenner saw the true church as a gathering of regenerate people. Nevin emphasized that the church was established by God through Christ.

The controversy with Winebrenner made the German Reformed Church more aware of its theological boundaries. Although today the UCC may not find itself comfortable with the Winebrenner theological legacy, the way in which Winebrenner combined a progressive commitment to social reform with evangelical conviction is a useful model.

Chapter 9 approaches the issue of diversity with regard to women. Although women have shared their gifts in the church for many years, and the first woman was ordained to the Congregational ministry in 1853, efforts to establish special channels for women's ministries within the denominations that make up the United Church of Christ did not take shape until the late nineteenth and early twentieth centuries.

The first volume of *Hidden Histories* noted the ways in which the deaconess movement supported and channeled women's gifts. Chapter 9 in this volume documents the history of the Chicago Congregational Training School for Women.

The CTSW was established in 1909 through the efforts of

Florence Amanda Fensham. Although women could receive a regular ministerial degree in several theological schools, there was need for a separate institution dedicated to theological education for women. At the school, young women who were eager to do something with their lives prepared for missionary service, social work, teaching, and the demanding career of a minister's wife. The school was especially committed to promoting professional stature for salaried women workers in the church. Its focused approach on women's education, however, did not last. In 1926 it was assimilated into the Chicago Theological Seminary.

Nevertheless, the Congregational Training School for Women was a creative response within its own time to the issue of women's preparation for church leadership. Although its assumptions about gender differences in the church are no longer appropriate, it did take seriously the implications of gender diversity in church and society that remain important to the United Church of Christ.

Finally, chapter 10 uses the history of Chinese Congregationalism to emphasize issues of ethnic diversity within the United Church of Christ. Beyond its English and German ethos, the UCC has included—and continues to attract—other ethnic groups. Stories of native American, Hungarian, Armenian, and Japanese UCC church life were included in the first volume of hidden histories. This chapter on the Chinese churches documents another group with longstanding connections to the UCC. In the future, histories of Hawaiian, Mexican, Samoan, and Filipino churches will need to be written. It may be necessary to delay the work, however, in order to get historical distance on recent events. Nevertheless, it is important for the United Church of Christ to define its unity in a manner that includes ethnic diversity.

Chinese Congregationalism in the United Church of Christ dates its origins from schools established by the American Missionary Association to serve the needs of Chinese immigrants in California, and from mission work authorized by the Hawaiian Evangelical Association to evangelize Chinese plantation workers in Hawaii.

In California, AMA superintendent William C. Pond supported Chinese members in his own church and worked as an agent for the California Chinese Mission. The CCM eventually founded and supported forty-nine Chinese mission schools. Only three of these remain as self-consciously Chinese churches related to the United Church of Christ: San Francisco, Berkeley, and San Diego.

In Hawaii, Chinese immigration patterns were different. Although Chinese mission churches and schools were started on all the islands, only four churches continue—three self-consciously Chinese churches in Honolulu, and one in Hilo, which recently dropped its Chinese name.

The situation of Chinese-Americans has dramatically changed during the latter half of the twentieth century. The old Chinese communities in major cities have matured, and recent waves of immigrants from Taiwan and Southeast Asia have led to the establishment of several new UCC Chinese churches since 1970.

Furthermore, denominational affiliation is only one part of what it means to be part of an ethnic Chinese church in the UCC. Increasingly UCC Chinese people relate ecumenically to other Chinese churches through organizations like the National Conference of Chinese Churches in America and to other Asian ethnic churches within the UCC through the UCC Pacific and Asian American Ministries. The story of the Chinese in the UCC shows how ethnic diversity itself becomes another force for the unity of the Christian church.

Hidden histories in the United Church of Christ can be interpreted in many ways. If it is possible to sustain denominational integrity in a pluralistic world, the United Church of Christ provides an interesting case study. Its diverse history contains examples and resources that promote church unity. At the same time, its diversity highlights issues that forever divide the Christian community: theology, ecclesiology, gender, and ethnicity (including race). Only time will tell if Paul's words about seeing in part—but someday seeing face to face—will be fulfilled in the United Church of Christ.

PART ONE

Unity

THE UNION CHURCH: A CASE OF LUTHERAN AND REFORMED COOPERATION

Horace S. Sills

REPRESENTATIVES OF THE nine participating denominations involved in the Consultation on Church Union stated in 1985: "Christians must find a way of being together in such a way that the very form of the Church in the world will communicate its message to the world, and still make room, within consensus, for a great range of theological points of view, practices in worship, and forms of organization."[1] Such a need has always been present in the church, but it becomes imperative in a pluralistic world to achieve this new form with strength enough to influence world society with the message of Christ. Churches need to reexamine their own theological histories, their structures, their strengths, their weaknesses, and be willing to open their thinking to more creative possibilities for inclusive action.

Within the Lutheran and Reformed traditions there is a bit of history that, although localized, is not far removed from the kind of church witness projected by the Consultation on

Horace S. Sills recently retired (1985) as Conference President of the Penn Central Conference of the United Church of Christ.

Church Union. This history began when immigrants arrived on American soil from the war-torn and poverty-stricken countryside of the German Rhine valley, called the Palatinate. It is a history of a proud people who sought to escape many years of war in their native land, a people with determined faith who were not afraid of hard work or easily discouraged. It is the history of the *Union Church*, a unique form of church cooperation in eighteenth-century America that started 250 years ago.

EUROPEAN BEGINNINGS

The Reformation was strongly supported by peasants in Germany and Switzerland. The people were glad to break away from the Roman Catholic hierarchy and follow men like Luther, Zwingli, Calvin, Knox, and other workers for religious freedom. Martin Luther led the way with his writings on the Doctrine of Grace and the Doctrine of the Sacraments. Luther convinced many people to open their minds to new possibilities in their relationship with God as revealed in scripture. His confessional statements maintain a prominent place within all Protestant groups today.

Ulrich Zwingli, sometimes called the "Father of the Reformed Church," worked diligently for church reform in Switzerland. If Luther and Zwingli could have agreed on the divine aspects of Holy Communion, separate church bodies would not have developed around their teachings. Luther maintained that Christ's body and blood existed in, with, and under the elements of the bread and wine. Zwingli and others taught the symbolic presence in these elements. At a conference in Marburg in 1529, fifteen articles were discussed and Luther and Zwingli agreed on fourteen and a half of them. They differed only on the part of the fifteenth article concerning the real presence: "And although at present we can not agree whether the true body and the true blood of Christ be corporeally present in the bread and wine, yet each party is to show to the other Christian love, as far as conscience permits, and both parties should fervently pray to Almighty God that by his Spirit he may strengthen us in the true understanding. Amen."[2] Zwingli was prepared to accept this statement and extended his hand to Luther as evidence of his willingness to be in fellowship. Luther, however, refused to acknowledge the gesture.

A calming and mediating influence on both Luther and Zwingli came through Philip Melanchthon, renowned Greek scholar, native of the Palatinate, counselor in reorganizing the University at Heidelberg, and good friend of Luther. Melanchthon worked to achieve church union. Although Luther did not always agree with Melanchthon's theology, the two men remained fast friends and defended each other's positions. Melanchthon, more than any other, opened the way for Reformed believers to be respected in Germany. Melanchthon was consulted by Frederick III when he became Elector of the Palatinate in 1559. Melanchthon counseled peace, moderation, and biblical simplicity.

Eventually Frederick aligned himself with the Reformed movement and called Zacharias Ursinus and Caspar Olevianus to Heidelberg to prepare an evangelical catechism. The *Heidelberg Catechism,* which became the primary confession of the Reformed Church, was the result of their work.

Frederick III died in 1576 and was succeeded by Louis VI, who introduced the Lutheran Creed to the Palatinate. Ursinus and 600 Reformed ministers and teachers were deposed and exiled from Heidelberg. In the year that Ursinus died, 1583, John Casimir, brother of Louis VI, second son of Frederick III, succeeded to the Electorate. He was in agreement with the tenets of the Reformed Church and recalled the exiled ministers to reestablish the Reformed Church in the Palatinate.[3]

During the Thirty Years' War, however, the district was taken over by Roman Catholics from Spain and Bavaria. Protestants suffered greatly. Although the Reformed faith was again established when the war ended, the people were so impoverished that they were unable to keep up their church and school properties. The properties fell into the hands of Jesuits who had been sent to the Palatinate to regain control for the Church in Rome. When the last Electorate favorable to the Reformed Church died in 1685, the Palatinate fell into the hands of the Roman Catholics of the House of Neuburg.

The years that followed were difficult for both Lutheran and Reformed people. In some cases the loss of buildings to the

Roman Catholics made it necessary for Lutheran congregations and Reformed congregations to share facilities. These were the first union churches, although in most cases no formal written agreements were executed. Such arrangements were called *Simultankirchen,* and they opened the way for further development in America.[4]

THE EXODUS

By the early 1700s the people of the Palatinate were ready for a change. There was no stability in the economy, in the rulers, in the religion, or even in the weather. The winter of 1708–9 was so severe it was reported that when birds landed, their feet froze to the ground. Many people suffered. Wars continued to rage. The Rhine valley was a major thoroughfare for armies moving to and from battle. The people began to leave the Palatinate at an overwhelming rate to escape from war, poverty, and religious persecution.

The Palatinate was near enough to France to be easily overrun and yet too far from Vienna, the capital of Germany, to receive aid quickly. The war of 1688–89 left the region a wasteland. King Louis XIV of France instructed his forces to "ravage the Palatinate." His orders were effectively obeyed. Twelve hundred towns and villages went up in smoke. In 1693 he sent his army in again to complete the desolation.

Wars did not cease. Between 1701 and 1713 European powers united against France and the Palatinate became the scene of marching armies going to or from battles in Bavaria, Italy, and the Netherlands. The catechism of the Palatines, published in London in 1709, reported that Marshal Villars, who led a French army through the region in 1707, "reduced the Palatinate to a perfect wilderness, not leaving the poor Reformed so much as a house to hide their heads in or hardly clothes to cover their nakedness."[5] War became a powerful inducement for the people to leave their homeland.

War also led to poverty. The wars fought in the early 1700s caused great poverty because the armies had to live off the country through which they passed. The failure of crops and the harshness of the winter, plus destruction by soldiers, left the people very poor. When they appealed to the Electorate, there was little relief. The people could not go on, so they chose to leave and seek a new life in the New World.

Finally, people left because of religion. Because each Elector had the power to decree what confession would become that of the population, the religion of the region changed four times in as many changes of Electorates. The people were expected to accept the religion of the prince. Those who refused could either leave their native land or conform to the decrees of the state. French rulers, being Catholic, oppressed Protestants as heretics and took away their churches. Such persecution contributed greatly to the dissatisfaction of the people.

TO AMERICA

When people left the region of the Rhine, they went first to Holland and then to England. They began moving into London in early May 1709, and by the end of June many thousands were crowding limited facilities. They were without funds or personal belongings, beyond what they could wear or carry. At first they were encouraged by reports that an earlier group of Palatines, led by the Rev. Joshua Kocherthal, a Lutheran minister, had been aided by the queen in obtaining transportation to New York for 41 persons—26 Reformed and 15 Lutheran. But the people arrived in London in such great numbers soon thereafter that the city could scarcely handle them. A committee was set up to try to care for the needs of these people and help determine what to do with them. Collections were taken, but the funds were insufficient to cover the cost of care. The committee decided that the people had to be resettled, some to Ireland, others to the New World. Three thousand were sent to New York, where they were expected to produce naval stores for the government. They landed in the summer of 1710.

In New York, far removed from their homeland, Lutheran and Reformed Christians found that there were so few in number of either religious persuasion that there was no need for separate church buildings. One building would suffice. Besides, they had been sharing worship facilities in the Palatinate since the Roman Catholics took away some of their buildings.

The first Union Church was located in what was called Rhinebeck, Dutchess County. The pastor who had led them from England, the Rev. Joshua Kocherthal, ministered to the Lutheran people and the Rev. John Frederick Hager (of whom little is known) cared for the Reformed group, which later affiliated with the Dutch Reformed Church. A church building was erected and was owned and maintained jointly by the two groups. In 1729 the Lutheran congregation sold their interest in this property to the Reformed congregation in amicable fashion.

Although the church at Rhinebeck is the first Union Church for which definite records have been maintained, it is possible that an earlier church may have been established by these same two pastors at West Camp or Newtown, in Catskill County. William Hill and Frank Blanchard, writing in the *Tercentenary Studies, 1928, Reformed Church in America* (pp.336ff.), state that the people arrived at West Camp in October 1710 and

> here they built log houses for protection from the winter's cold. They had come from a land of school houses and churches; to them these were necessities, and in three months a school house and a log church had been built. . . . Newtown was what is now West Camp. It was here the church was built and for eight years Rev. Joshua von Kocherthal, a Lutheran, and Rev. John Frederick Hager, a Reformed (at East Camp), worked together in harmony.

Those who settled in New York were soon discouraged. A dispute arose over land rights, and although the people contested the claims of the government to lands that had been purchased from the Indians, they eventually had to relinquish possession. There appeared to be no other choice but to move to Pennsylvania. William Penn had received from Charles II of England territory in the New World that extended west of the Delaware River between New York and Maryland. This territory was given in payment of a debt that Charles II owed to Penn's father. The territory was known as Pennsylvania (Penn's Woods), and it became a haven for thousands who sought to begin a new life in the New World. Soon a group consisting of thirty-three families left New York, in the spring of 1723. In care of an Indian guide they came to the headwaters of the north branch of the Susquehanna River. They traveled down the Susquehanna to the mouth of the Swatara Creek and up the creek until they reached Tulpehocken, near Lebanon. They wrote to their friends who remained in New York about their journey and the place they had found. Others followed soon after.[6]

Before the people who first went to New York reached Pennsylvania, others from the Palatinate had already started homes and churches there. They arrived in Philadelphia and moved into the surrounding communities to begin their new life. The majority of Pennsylvania immigrants had not come to carry out a religious life according to peculiar tenets or to organize themselves into separatistic religious communities. Rather, they merged themselves into the common life of the province and retained their old membership in Lutheran and Reformed churches.[7] They had a need, however, to be together. This need grew out of loneliness, poverty, language, and protection. Consequently, these German immigrants formed German communities wherever they settled. And wherever there was a community, there was also a church.

Not all churches were established as *Union Churches*. The first Reformed Church officially organized came into being when Holy Communion was celebrated on October 15, 1725, at Falkner Swamp in the Perkiomen valley. A congregation had gathered there before this date, but there was no ordained pastor available for the conduct of the sacrament. John Philip Boehm, a schoolmaster employed by the families to teach the children, agreed to act as Reader in leading religious services. He was so well liked that the leaders prevailed on him to administer the sacrament. Reluctantly, realizing his unordained status, he agreed. He was later ordained and became effective as a church organizer for German Reformed people throughout the territory.

WHAT IS THE UNION CHURCH?

Simply stated, a Union Church occurs when two or more congregations of differing denominations agree to use the same facilities. The statement, however, is the only simple thing about such an organization. In some communities as many as four congregations use the same facilities according to some formal schedule. Most Union Churches, however, have been (and are now) Lutheran and Reformed (United Church of Christ).

19

In the early pioneer days of settling on the land, the number of Lutheran or Reformed people in any given community was not large. There was a tremendous reliance on neighbors. People helped one another to build houses, clear land, plant crops, harvest, mend, repair, and start schools and churches. German people placed a high priority on education. Usually the first community structure erected in a new settlement was a school building, which could also be used for worship. Lutheran and Reformed people gave time and energy to the construction. The buildings were simple, usually made of logs, with a dirt floor. In some cases a structure was primarily built as a church and secondarily used as a school. Cooperation was a pattern of life and did not end when the building was finished.

These Christians who had suffered so much in the homeland and who looked to the future in this new place with much confidence believed that they could live together in harmony, not only as neighbors, but also as companions in worship. The use of the same facilities was not a new experience for them. They had accomplished this, in some cases, in Germany in the *Simultankirchen*. In America the need and the opportunity again opened the way for them to live a faith embracing visual cooperation.

Land on which church structures were erected was usually either given by one of the member families or purchased through the contributions of all members. In most circumstances the deed would be recorded in the name of both (sometimes more) congregations. Some records, however, indicate that only one congregation owned the property and permitted the other congregation to have equal use. Early deeds often describe the Reformed congregation as part of the "German Presbyterian Church." This referred to the form of government rather than to their confession of faith.

Although a deed was important as a legal instrument denoting ownership, the most important agreement had to do with the care, maintenance, and use of the facilities. Sometimes there was nothing more than a handshake on a verbal agreement reached by leading laypersons from each congregation. As time went on, however, those involved in Union Churches learned the value of written Articles of Agreement that detailed schedules of use by various organizations, as well as the congregations, assigned oversight responsibilities, described times and methods of payment of utilities and maintenance costs, and established procedures for dealing with other practical matters. Occasionally the Articles of Agreement translated into a Union Constitution requiring joint congregational meetings to decide such matters as giving the pastor an increase in salary. This meant that, in such churches, if the Lutheran congregation wanted to give its pastor an increase in salary, the Reformed congregation had to vote on the matter as well, even though it made no contribution to the payment of that salary.

The care, maintenance, and use of facilities in a church are generally entrusted to a group of trustees. In a Union Church this group comprises an equal number of persons elected by the respective congregations (usually three each). The trustees are responsible for inspecting the facilities, recommending maintenance care or repairs, and, when approved, overseeing their accomplishment. Recommendations are made to the Joint Council and Consistory for approval. The Council is the official board of the Lutheran congregations. The Consistory serves the same function in the United Church of Christ in Pennsylvania. If the recommendation is of major significance with a high price tag, the Joint Council and Consistory must bring it to the respective congregations for approval and funding.

Generally speaking, Union Churches did not jointly own parsonages (these were provided by each congregation or denominational parish); however, they did own the homes for the sextons. Such facilities were usually located near the Union Church and the sexton had free use of a home as compensation for keeping the church and grounds clean. More often than not, the grounds included the Union Cemetery, an important facility for the early churches. Until recently those who wanted to bury a loved one in a church cemetery were not charged. The care of such places was considered part of a church's ministry. As the cemeteries grew larger and care and maintenance became costlier, charges for burial plots or annual maintenance fees were instituted.

Union Churches were prominent in Pennsylvania and nearby states in the eighteenth and nineteenth centuries. They responded to housing patterns, the language spoken by the residents, the dominant confessions of faith, and the mode of transportation. Although the locations of some churches appear to us today as haphazard, unplanned, and ineffectual, it was not so for the settlers. The church needed to be close enough to the homes of the parishioners so that it would not take all day to get there by horse and buggy or by walking. The church was the major place for social gathering, as well as for worship. People came early and visited before and after the worship experience. Location was an important consideration.

At one time there were more than 500 Union Churches in existence. Most of these were in Pennsylvania, but there were also Union Churches in New York, Ohio, West Virginia, Maryland, Virginia, and North Carolina. Wherever the German Lutheran and Reformed people migrated, they founded Union Churches. In the mid-1980s Union Churches still numbered 103; however, there is no record of any Union Church being established after 1913.

REASONS FOR ESTABLISHING UNION CHURCHES

Although there is no single reason for the establishment of Union Churches, certain definite factors prevail. For instance, both the Lutheran and the Reformed settlers placed great emphasis on an educated ministry. They also maintained high regard for the ecclesiastical process leading to ordination. Because few missionary pastors accompanied the early settlers, those who did divided their time among churches in several communities. Marriages were performed, Holy Communion administered, and baptisms accomplished only when the pastor could make the circuit of the congregations for which responsibility was carried. Sometimes months passed before an ordained person was available. Because both the Lutheran and the Reformed congregations faced this difficulty, they saw no need for having two separate buildings. By sharing facilities they could also share pastors. If the Lutheran pastor could be there once each month and the Reformed pastor once each month, the people could take advantage of two worship experiences in the month. This would not have been so easy if they had been separate.

Another reason for the Union Church was economic. German

immigrants were poor. They had given up home, property, and family to come to the New World. Many of them had indentured themselves to sea captains, landowners, business concerns, for passage to America. For many it took two, four, or even six years to repay the debt. There was little left to provide a home and support a church. One building housing two congregations was cheaper than one congregation having to bear the full cost.

A third reason for the Union Church was language and so-cialization. Having come from the same regions in Germany and settled in the same regions in America, there was a closeness among these people that went beyond religion. Differences that are prominent among many religious groups today were not so important to the early settlers. The German language contributed to their community spirit and aided in their socialization. Church was the gathering place for many social events. Intermarriage was common between the two groups. Occasionally a Reformed person who married a Lutheran changed denominational affiliation, but usually the uniting couple felt no need for such a change. Traditions started quickly and endured a long time in Union Churches. For example, a girl who was born to a mixed marriage usually became a member of the congregation to which her mother belonged. Likewise, boys followed in the footsteps of their fathers.

In the eighteenth century, denominational consciousness was the exception rather than the rule in many places. In 1752 there was one Lutheran church and one Reformed church in Reading, Pennsylvania, but in the remainder of Berks County there were fifteen Union Churches and no separate Lutheran or Reformed churches.[8] Most congregations found it necessary to share a pastor with another congregation. The shortage of pastors and the poverty of the people meant that Lutheran and Reformed pastors served the same circuit of Union congregations consisting of from two to eight churches.

Furthermore, the church provided important opportunities to gather the community. Sunday was a day to rest from one's labors. It was a time to meet friends, discuss the events of the past week, and plan new events or solve problems that might arise in the future. People arrived at the church long before the time for services and stayed long after the services were over. Young boys and girls met and established relationships that sometimes resulted in marriage. The business of the community was conducted and decisions of charity as well as business were made. The Union Church was not only a place for worship, but also a forum for community decision making.

REASONS WHY UNION CHURCHES DID NOT LAST

The oldest continuing Union Church in existence today is the Old Goshenhoppen Church in Woxall, Montgomery County, Pennsylvania. Early records indicate that the Reformed congregation came into being in 1727, and a Lutheran congregation started three years later. The first house of worship was a log structure completed in 1732. It was a *Gemeinhaus*, used as a schoolhouse, a place of worship, and quarters for the schoolmaster. The records state that in 1737 thirty-eight and one quarter acres of church land were purchased in the name of both congregations. The deed was recorded on January 12, 1738. A large stone church building was erected in 1744. The present church was built in 1858. When the church was built it had two front doors, and by tradition, one door was used by the Lutherans to enter the sanctuary and the other was used by the Reformed congregation. This was not an unusual arrangement in Union Churches.

Even though there was (and still is in some places) a great affinity for the Union Church, the Union relationship did not always work. In some cases the creation of the Union relationship was convenient for a while but ended when expansion became necessary. Expansion was difficult in the Union relationship. Furthermore, other factors brought about dissolution of Union Churches: for example, community growth, the availability of more pastors, better economic conditions, greater emphasis on theology, Christian education expectations, dissatisfaction with lack of control of facility use, and confused identity in the community.

At the beginning, German communities were small and congregations had few members. No strain or demand was placed by the population on the Union Church to effect a change in the relationship. As the population grew, however, Union Churches discovered that their buildings were no longer adequate. Some churches evaluated their situation and ended the Union relationship, deciding to have two church buildings instead of one. In such cases one congregation usually purchased the equity in the Union property owned by the other congregation. The selling congregation erected a new church building. Often that congregation located the new church adjacent to, across the road from, or near the old Union Church building. Frequently the architecture of the new structure resembled the old building.

Along with community growth came population mobility. If a family moved from a home area that had no Union Church to an area in which there was a Union Church, they hesitated to join that kind of church, especially if the hour of worship changed weekly. However, when members of a Union Church moved to other communities, they had no difficulty uniting with a congregation that was unattached to another in a Union relationship.

Community growth and population mobility reached a high point after World War II. People who had gone to war or served the country in defense work began settling down in communities that were far removed from their hometowns. New churches were built in the new communities, and they were not Union. Union Churches, some of which were caught on the fringes of rapid population growth, found it necessary to make adjustments and even to dissolve the Union relationship altogether.

The shortage of pastors in the early years had helped to bring about the Union Church. When ecclesiastical bodies opened colleges and seminaries to train ministerial leaders, making more pastors available to congregations, Union Churches no longer seemed necessary. Change came slowly, however. Early missionary pastors founded and built many churches, including many Union Churches. With the increased number of pastors, existing pastors served fewer congregations and provided more worship experiences for each congregation. Yet as time went on, the availability of more pastors actually led to decisions to separate Union Churches.

The availability of more pastors also opened up theological questions that had been dormant in many Union Churches for years. The new pastors had never experienced a Union Church.

They received no special training in their seminaries to help them understand the peculiarities of a Union Church. Some clergy began to stress denominational theology and compared one theology with the other, implying that one was more accurate or better. Laypersons who had been existing in harmony in Union Churches for years without fear of theological inappropriateness began thinking differently about their heritage and questioned the advisability of continuing in a Union relationship. Some pastors pressed hard for Union dissolution because they did not see any denominational advantage in the relationship. They were not enamored with ecumenical possibilities, although in some instances the pastors in Union Churches developed close working friendships that enhanced local ministries and became models of ecumenical accomplishment.

All this created confusion as to the true identity of Union congregations. What were these churches? Were they Lutheran? United Church of Christ? Were the loyalties of people situated in Union relationships sustained at the expense of denominational loyalties? Even denominational leaders raised questions and encouraged congregations to consider separation.

As mentioned earlier, German people placed great emphasis on education. The parochial school was as much a part of a pioneer settlement as the church. There, children were taught the basics in education: reading, writing, and arithmetic. They were also instructed in the Bible and the Confessions of Faith. The church and school were important and cared for in the community.

The Sunday school was born in the late eighteenth century when a greathearted printer in Gloucester, England, assembled a few poor children in the front room of a house for instruction on Sunday. No one could possibly have foreseen that from this friendly gesture would spring a worldwide Sunday school movement. However, Sunday schools were a mixed blessing in Union Churches. The people considered them competitive with parochial schools already in operation. Pastors were not wholeheartedly supportive of the Sunday school either, partly because it was basically a lay movement. Yet the Sunday school thrived and grew at a phenomenal pace. It eventually became part of every church's program. In Union Churches, however, the Sunday school created a problem.

It must be remembered that each congregation in the Union relationship conducted its own worship service, maintained its own pastor, and recruited its own members. This did not mean that the people ignored each other's worship experience. On the contrary, many Lutherans attended Reformed services and vice versa. When the Sunday school movement finally caught on in Union Churches, it became fully Union in every respect but functioned like a third congregation.

Sunday schools were lay oriented and lay operated. People from both congregations gladly participated. Teachers were selected on their teaching abilities, not on the basis of the congregation to which they belonged. The Sunday school was organized separate from either congregation. It elected its own officers and teachers, maintained its own records, collected and expended its own funds. In many Union Churches the Sunday school contributed as much as one third of the operating expenses for the facilities. There have been (and still are) occasions when the members of a Sunday school controlled votes about remodeling facilities or changing worship and education schedules.

SCHEDULING

The schedules required for efficient use of Union Church facilities were (and are) difficult to manage. Consider the schedules of three Union Churches located within ten miles of one another.

The schedule of St. Paul (Dubs) Union Church (Hanover, Pennsylvania) is on an alternating basis week by week. The Lutheran congregation meets for worship at 8:00 A.M. on one Sunday. The Sunday school meets at 9:00 A.M. The United Church of Christ congregation meets at 10:15 A.M. The next Sunday the hours of worship are reversed; Sunday school does not change. Union services of worship are planned for midweek lenten services, Maundy Thursday, Good Friday, Easter dawn, and Easter morning. The pastors take turns conducting these services on alternate weeks during Lent and on alternate years for the others.

The St. Jacobs Union Church (Broadbecks, Pennsylvania) follows another pattern. Both congregations had been yoked with other Lutheran and UCC congregations in other Union arrangements. When the congregations in that church decided to merge, the two St. Jacobs congregations called new pastors of their own. Each pastor is available to conduct a denominational worship service each Sunday, but the congregations have chosen to retain the every-other-Sunday schedule. Each congregation worships every other week at 10:15 A.M., whereas the Sunday school meets weekly at 9:00 A.M. On this schedule each pastor is responsible for preaching twenty-six Sundays a year, minus time away for vacation. Although few parishioners attend the services of the other denomination, there are Union services for World Day of Prayer, Lent, Holy Week, and Christmas Eve. The pastors alternate in leading such worship.

The Bethlehem (Steltz) Union Church (Glenn Rock, Pennsylvania) follows a still different arrangement. It is characterized by "shared ministry." This means that both congregations are served by the same pastor and the congregations worship together as one. At present the pastor is affiliated with the Lutheran Church but has dual standing in the United Church of Christ. Worship services are conducted at 10:15 A.M. and the Sunday school, which is also Union, meets at 9:00 A.M.

In the shared ministry model (there are five examples of such models in Pennsylvania), congregations do not change every other week, nor do the pastors change every other week. However, they do change hymnbooks and the order of worship. The Lutherans have one kind of benevolence envelope and the UCCs have another. Benevolences are kept separate and the programs of each denomination are supported. Although each congregation has its own official board that meets monthly, there is a joint board that meets as required to make decisions about property and program.

It has been traditional in Union Churches to use non-denominational Christian education literature, such as David C. Cook publications. Other programs use UCC literature for some ages and Lutheran literature for other ages. Some schools alternate the use of denominational literature on a three-year cycle.

There are a wide variety of schedules among Union Churches and no congregation can completely control the use of the facilities. Churches usually settle on a plan that divides the time for meetings, special events, weddings, and so on as equally as possible. For example, both congregations use the facility on Sunday, giving the Lutherans exclusive use on Monday, Wednesday, and Friday and the UCC congregation exclusive use on Tuesday, Thursday, and Saturday. Funerals take priority over other events. Frustration with schedules and the need on the part of some to control all activities have led to the dissolution of many Union Churches.

THE COMMISSION ON THE WELFARE OF THE UNION CHURCH

Most Union Churches that end their cooperative relationships do so without difficulty. Sometimes, however, there are problems. The people may have been able to agree that separate organizations and church facilities would be desirable, but they cannot agree on how this can be achieved. The story is told of a Union Church in 1858 that agreed to dissolution. The Council and Consistory could not agree on how much the church structure was worth. In the final analysis they demolished the building and the members gathered at the site to chip the mortar off the bricks and divide them between the two congregations. The Lutheran congregation used their bricks to rebuild on the old site. The Reformed (UCC) congregation took their bricks a mile down the road and built a new church.

Over the years pastors and denominational officials questioned the advisability of having Union Churches. In 1948 Dr. Paul J. Hoh, president of the Lutheran Theological Seminary in Philadelphia, charged a group of clergy to grapple with this situation. As a consequence, an open meeting of Lutheran and Reformed pastors and laypersons was held at Zion Union Church (The Red Church), near Schuylkill Haven, Pennsylvania, November 4, 1948. Some people felt that the Union Church was the best living example of local ecumenicity and others felt that what the Union Church needed most was to be "torn asunder regardless of consequences."[9]

After the heat of the "battle of the Red Church" subsided, a meeting was held in Reading, Pennsylvania, on November 23, 1948, to evaluate what had happened. Out of the pros and cons, discouragements and promises, a new organization emerged: the Commission on the Welfare of the Union Church. Five representatives were appointed from among the Reformed (Evangelical and Reformed) synods in Eastern Pennsylvania and an equal number from the Lutheran Ministerium of Pennsylvania. In 1950 the Central Pennsylvania Synod of the Lutheran Church entered the Commission.

The intent of the Commission was to search for better ways to negotiate Union Church difficulties, provide an arena for discussing Union Church problems between representatives of each communion, and offer guidance to Union Church pastors and congregations for the enhancement of local ministries. The Commission drafted Proposed Policy statements on the Union Church that were submitted to the respective denominational synods for consideration. Two drafts of such proposals were rejected by several of the synods. The third draft, completed in 1957, was accepted and recommended to the churches. This policy, although not enforceable in all congregations, proved invaluable among Union congregations. It also helped Union congregations gain a new appreciation of their history. It suggested, among other things, that before any Union Church undertook major construction programs, representatives of the denominational offices should be called into the discussion.

The Commission caused the Lutheran and the Reformed synods to appoint consultants for Union Church negotiations. Two persons from each communion were appointed.

Close working relationships developed between these individuals and lasting friendships were made. The consultants developed procedures for planned change that they recommended to each Union situation. The process worked well. In fact, the Commission on the Welfare of the Union Church proved to be so effective that consultants were used far more than originally expected.

During the 1960s and early in the 1970s churches felt pressure from rapidly changing population and rising economic standards. Union Churches made adjustments that brought forth new and stronger congregations, more effective programs, and greater harmony among members. Many Union Churches discontinued the shared use of property and now have their own church facilities. Some Union Churches merged to form one congregation affiliated with one denomination. Still others agreed to share the services of one pastor and meet as one congregation. Many Union Churches, however, continue to share buildings, programs, and leadership, and they see no reason to stop. Not all these churches are small, weak congregations without potential for growth. In the largest Union Church, in Neffs, Pennsylvania, both the Lutheran and the UCC congregations have more than 1,200 members.

Although the Commission on the Welfare of the Union Church no longer meets, its influence is felt throughout the area where Union Churches are located. Consultants trained to guide the people through discussions to responsible decision making are still available.

AN ECUMENICAL LEGACY

The Union Church is a unique local expression of ecumenical cooperation in America. In a Union Church early pioneers saw no divided loyalties when they shared a church building with more than one congregation. They saw no disrespect for a particular denominational creed when they participated in worship conducted by a pastor of a denomination different from their own. They saw no confusion of theological thought when they attended church school classes in a Union Sunday school. These mothers and fathers, grandmothers and grandfathers knew how to make allowances and adjustments.

Those who began the Union Church felt that it was enough to agree on property, its ownership and its use. How different history might have been if they had considered agreements on the mission of the church. National denominational leaders who strive for greater ecumenical expression today would do well to reconsider history. This ecumenical movement at the grassroots level started with all the ingredients it takes to work together in harmony. The Union Church had the potential for more than it ever achieved; it was just ahead of its time.

CHAPTER
2

THE GERMAN EVANGELICAL PROTESTANTS

Curtis Beach

IT IS OFTEN SAID that the United Church of Christ was the first union of two American denominations with quite different histories and backgrounds—the English roots of the Congregational Christian Churches mixing with the German traditions of the Evangelical and Reformed Church. Actually, a similar merger, on a much smaller scale, took place in 1925, when the Evangelical Protestant Church of North America joined the National Council of Congregational Churches.

The Evangelical Protestants were an indigenous American denomination, originally German-speaking. In 1925 there were twenty-seven churches, mostly in the Ohio River valley. Dedicated to religious liberty, Evangelical Protestants stood for freedom of thought, an open mind, and respect for those whose beliefs were different.

Curtis Beach is a retired UCC minister living in Maine. From 1959 to 1975 he served as pastor of the Smithfield Church, Pittsburgh, Pennsylvania, the oldest and largest church in the Evangelical Protestant tradition.

PITTSBURGH BEGINNINGS

The first German Evangelical Protestant church was founded in Pittsburgh in 1782. At that time Pittsburgh was only a hamlet on the frontier.[1] Twenty-five years earlier no village was there at all, only Fort Duquesne, a French military outpost located at the point where the Allegheny and Monongahela rivers came together to form the Ohio River.

In 1758, during the French and Indian War, Fort Duquesne had been captured by a British colonial militia and renamed Fort Pitt, in honor of William Pitt (senior), the leader of the British government. Soon thereafter log cabins began to appear outside the military compound, built by people who wished to trade with the soldiers or the Indians. Pittsburgh was also the gateway to the West, populated by fur trappers and pioneers. In 1782 the village consisted of about thirty-five houses, most made of logs, and probably numbered less than 250 souls. Many of them were Germans. In fact, one third of the inhabitants of Pennsylvania in the 1780s spoke German.

In Pittsburgh, German settlers established the first church in the town during the American Revolution.[2] Its initial membership roll listed forty-two men. (After the German custom of that time, women were not voting members.) This early German church was completely independent, not connected with any synod or denomination. Its roster included both Lutherans and German Reformed members, as well as persons who belonged to no particular group. From the beginning it was a church that cherished religious freedom, welcomed diversity of opinion, and respected the right of individual conviction.

This attitude of tolerance was remarkable in 1782. In that period, churches in Germany were severely divided over theology. In New England, Congregational parishes were being torn apart by controversies: unitarianism and trinitarianism, liberalism and orthodoxy. Yet, in the wilderness of western Pennsylvania, a church developed that encouraged private thought, was cordial to diverse points of view, and honored the rights of personal conscience.

In 1782 the German church had organized and found a place to meet, a log cabin that it rented, but it had no minister. So the congregation sent a letter to the German Reformed Synod in eastern Pennsylvania, saying, in effect, "Please send us a preacher."

The man who was sent was a most unusual person named Johann Wilhelm Weber. From his diary we have knowledge of his life and of the infant church.[3] He was born in Germany in 1735 and came to America (Pennsylvania) with his young wife in 1764, at the age of twenty-nine. For several years he taught school, and then he decided to enter the ministry. He was examined and ordained by the German Reformed Synod. Although he served a parish near Philadelphia for a time, he was compelled to leave because the congregation felt that he was "too political." He was an ardent supporter of the War for Independence. When the synod received the request from Pittsburgh for a preacher, Weber responded. He says in his diary; "In May 1782 I was sent by the synod in Reading to western Pennsylvania to visit the congregation there and given a permit to be their pastor if they should call me." It took him a month to make the 400-mile trip on horseback, crossing the Allegheny Mountains. He preached in the Pittsburgh church and in other German-speaking villages in the area. As a result he received a joint call to serve the Pittsburgh congregation and three German churches near Greensburg, thirty miles away. All this for a total annual salary of "116 pounds in money, 100 sheaves of wheat, free lodging, and firewood." Weber accepted and went back to get his family, planning to return the next summer.

In June 1783 Johann Wilhelm Weber crossed the mountains in a wagon with his wife and six children. The four parishes provided them with an old house, in which, he wrote, "my family almost perished from the cold during the winter." The next summer he bought a tract of land near Greensburg, built a more adequate dwelling, and added farming to his pastoral duties. When his wife died in childbirth, he soon remarried, and his second wife bore him twelve more children. There were twenty mouths to feed at the family table.

For eleven years Weber served four parishes, riding on his horse at least eighty miles a week. Pittsburgh was thirty miles from his home and his other churches. Travel was not easy on poor roads, through dense woods, and over swollen rivers. He had to be armed with a gun, a knife, and a hatchet, in case of attack by the Indians. He was "a strongly built man, blessed with a constitution of iron." He needed to be, to keep up such an arduous schedule.

In 1787 John Penn Sr., and John Penn Jr., the grandson and great-grandson of William Penn, gave the Pittsburgh congregation a plot of land on Smithfield Street. It was large enough for a meetinghouse, a parsonage, and a cemetery. The parishioners did not build on this land immediately because it was so far out of town. Today it is in the heart of downtown Pittsburgh, surrounded by skyscrapers. Over the years five church buildings have been erected on the site.[4]

Planning and raising money for the first meetinghouse began in 1791, and the building was finished in 1793. It was a simple rectangular wooden structure, with no decoration and no steeple, only a chimney; it seated a hundred persons.

A year later, in 1794, Weber resigned from the Pittsburgh church, probably feeling that once the meetinghouse was completed, he could reduce his travel. He was fifty-nine years old and continued to serve the three parishes near Greensburg until his death, at the age of eighty-one.

After the resignation of Weber, the Pittsburgh church deteriorated. There was discord between the Lutherans and other members. For several years there were two separate church bodies, Lutheran and non-Lutheran, holding separate services in the same building. Eventually, however, the breach was healed, and in 1812 the two groups reunited. They reaffirmed the principle on which the church had been founded—as a fellowship in which all varieties of Christian thought were welcomed and the rights of individual belief respected.

At the 1812 meeting the name *Deutsche Evangelische Protestantische Kirche* (German Evangelical Protestant Church) was officially adopted. The word evangelical is derived from the Greek word *evangelion* (gospel). *Evangelische* was the term commonly used in Germany to designate non-Catholic churches. The word Protestant was used in Britain and the United States to express the same thing. By using both these terms the Pittsburgh Germans tried to make the character of their church clear to everyone, no matter what language they spoke.

The church again petitioned the German Reformed Synod in eastern Pennsylvania to send a minister. In 1813 a young man named Jakob Schnee moved to Pittsburgh with his family, and the congregation engaged him as its pastor for $200 a year. "Under his active and energetic leadership, the scattered congregation quickly reassembled, and by the year 1814 the number of members had grown to about 100." This did not count women, so the membership was probably twice that number, plus the children.

GROWTH

During the years since the first German meetinghouse was built, Pittsburgh had grown from a small village to an industrial town. By 1793 a constant stream of homesteaders passed through Pittsburgh on their way to find a new life in the Ohio River settlements of Ohio, Kentucky, Indiana, and Illinois. They stopped in Pittsburgh to buy boats, farm equipment, clothing, and supplies. Shipbuilding became a major industry. The town had iron and brass foundries, a textile mill, glass works, tool and nail manufacturing, and factories making all sorts of household items, such as soap and candles. In 1816, when Pittsburgh incorporated as a city, it had a population of 6,000. It had eight churches: one German, two Presbyterian, one Methodist, one Episcopal, one Catholic, and two smaller sects.

As the German church grew to about 200 members, it needed a larger and more dignified edifice. So, in 1815, under Schnee's leadership, the original building was torn down and a new structure of brick was constructed on the same site. It seated about 200, with a gallery holding 20. Three years later Schnee resigned and moved back East, leaving the church greatly strengthened.

Pittsburgh continued to grow. The city lay between two rivers, the Allegheny and the Monongahela. Soon settlements were begun on the farther side of the rivers. Across the "Ally" grew the town of Allegheny and across the "Mon" was an industrial area called Birmingham. The original Pennsylvania turnpike, completed in 1820, reduced the 400-mile journey from Philadelphia to Pittsburgh to less than two weeks. Because of the availability of coal and iron, Pittsburgh became a city of iron foundries. In 1830 its population was 12,500, and the town of Allegheny had nearly 3,000. There were churches of many kinds, but only one German church: the Evangelical Protestant Church on Smithfield Street.

As the city grew the church grew also. In 1826 a young German Reformed minister named David Kammerer came to town. He was intending to go as a missionary to frontier settlements farther west. When he preached in the German church, however, he was so well liked that the congregation asked him to become their pastor. Kammerer was twenty-five years old, a man with a kind friendly manner, boundless energy, and great vision. Under him a Sunday school was started, modeled on those in the English-speaking churches and using lay teachers and graded classes, rather than only offering confirmation instruction by the minister. He also organized a daily elementary school for the children, conducted in German by a trained teacher. It was 1828, seven years before Pittsburgh had public schools. Before long it became evident that the church building was not big enough for all these activities and a growing congregation. In 1831 the members began making plans for a new structure.

The same year a dissident group of the church members of Lutheran background withdrew and started their own church, the First Lutheran Church of Pittsburgh. Although this was a momentary loss in numbers to the Evangelical Protestant congregation, it was also a blessing. It relieved the tension that had always existed between the Lutheran and non-Lutheran members and permitted the church to develop its liberal traditions freely.

As the church celebrated its fiftieth birthday, in 1832, it had about 300 worshipers. It was strong and healthy, ready to give leadership in the development of other German Evangelical Protestant churches.

NEW CHURCHES

When the Pittsburgh church was planning for its new building, it realized that many of its members lived across the river in the town of Allegheny. So it decided to start a new congregation there, contributing members and money to the project. A man named Voegtly donated land. A new meetinghouse in Allegheny, known as the Voegtly Church, and a new (third) building for the Pittsburgh church were completed in 1834.[5]

As Pittsburgh grew, more and more German people came to the area. Other German Evangelical Protestant churches were established in the city and in the mill towns around it. Members of the Pittsburgh church helped to organize a congregation in industrial Birmingham, across the Monongahela River, in 1846. A church was begun in McKeesport, farther upstream, in the same year. A few miles up the Allegheny River, in Etna, a church was founded in 1849 and another one, in nearby Tarentum in 1873. Additional Pittsburgh churches were started: West End in 1864, Manchester in 1865, Baum's (Bloomfield) and Mount Washington in 1873, Homestead in 1890, Spring Hill in 1895, and Duquesne Heights in 1900. Farther down the Ohio River, churches were established in Beaver Falls in 1888 and Saxonburg in 1895. There was also a church, St. John's, in Wheeling, West Virginia (date unknown).[6] With all the new Evangelical Protestant churches in and around Pittsburgh, the original church on Smithfield Street needed a more specific name. It decided to call itself "Smithfield Church," as it still does today.

Evangelical Protestant churches were not limited to the Pittsburgh area. The highway of mid-America was the Ohio River and from Pittsburgh it flowed westward to the Mississippi and south to the sea. From colonial times boats sailed down it, bearing pioneers to the virgin wilderness on its shores. Many settlements had grown up along the Ohio River, and one of the largest of these was Cincinnati. Founded in 1788, Cincinnati was for many years a struggling village. With the coming of steamships, however, the town grew rapidly, and by 1830 it was bigger than Pittsburgh. Cincinnati was a thriving trading and manufacturing metropolis, proudly calling itself "the Queen City of the West."

Many of the inhabitants of Cincinnati were Germans. Like Pittsburgh, it was a center of German life and culture. As people from the Evangelical Protestant churches of the Pittsburgh area moved to Cincinnati, they found new neighbors in Ohio who favored a free approach to religion. Out of these relationships new Evangelical Protestant churches were born.

The first German Evangelical Protestant church established in

Cincinnati was St. Peter's, founded in 1832. Thirty-four men signed its roll as charter members. Its first meetinghouse was a small unused church building that it purchased for $350. Two years later, when that part of the city was threatened by floods from the river, the congregation moved the structure, section by section, to higher ground. In 1845 another Evangelical Protestant church, St. Paul's, was founded. Many years later these two congregations united to form the present Cincinnati church of St. Peter and St. Paul.[7]

Between 1845 and 1860 German immigration to the Cincinnati area was especially heavy. Many Evangelical Protestant churches were started: St. John's, across the river in Newport, Kentucky, in 1857; St. John's on Neeb Road in 1850; St. Mark's in 1864; and St. John's of Mount Auburn in 1866. The church in Bridgetown, adjacent to the city, began in 1870, and St. Paul's in Barnesburg (Mount Healthy) in 1874. Across the river in Kentucky, St. John's in Johns Hill was gathered in 1876 and St. John's in West Covington, in 1892.

The Ohio River did not stop in Cincinnati. It flowed on to the Mississippi and carried German settlers to other towns. The United Evangelical Protestant Church in Madison, Indiana, was founded in 1842; St. Peter's in Osgood, Indiana, in 1850; and the Independent Evangelical Protestant Church in St. Louis, Missouri, in 1856.[8]

SHARED PRINCIPLES

What were the characteristics of these churches? First, and most important, was their freedom of thought. As a matter of principle they had no creed. They allowed members to fashion their faith for themselves, based on their own thinking and experience. Some parishes adopted a statement like this one, found in the first constitution of St. John's on Neeb Road, Cincinnati (1850): "We join together to know the will of God as taught in the Holy Scriptures, allowing freedom of conscience and freedom of interpretation in points of doctrinal difference. We unite for the purpose of serving God and our fellow men [and women]."[9]

A second characteristic of these churches was their insistence on independence—the autonomy of each congregation.

This resulted from their memories of life in Europe, where churches were too often dominated by the state. Evangelical Protestant congregations refused to join in any synod, fearing that it would open the door to "outside control." This desire for independence prevented the development of any denominational structure for a long time.

A third characteristic of these churches was the authority of the laity. It was the congregation, not the pastor, who made the decisions. When the churches had troubles, as they often did, they had no synod or denominational officers to appeal to for help. They had to solve their problems themselves. "Many times, when there were difficulties, the church continued to develop and grow because the congregation made the right decisions and kept it alive. The minister always played an important role, but the final responsibility for the working out of problems rested on the lay members. This was a source of strength."[10]

EARLY MINISTERS

Yet Evangelical Protestant ministers were outstanding clergymen. They left an important legacy.

One early pastor was Gustav Wilhelm Eisenlohr. Born in Germany in 1811, the son of a village pastor, he was educated at the universities of Heidelberg and Halle and then worked as an assistant in his father's parish. Later he became the minister of a church and the principal of a grammar school in Baden. He took part in the political revolution of 1848 and, to avoid being sent to prison, fled to America. For a year he served a church in New Richmond, Ohio, and then moved to Texas, where he held a pastorate in New Braunfels, a largely German community. While there he began contributing to a German religious periodical, *Protestantische Zeitblaetter* (Protestant Pages of the Times), published in Cincinnati. His articles so impressed the members of St. Paul's Evangelical Protestant Church in Cincinnati that in 1857 they invited him to become their pastor, without seeing or hearing him. For twenty-two years he served St. Paul's and became a leader in the Evangelical Protestant Ministers' Association. He retired in 1879 and returned to Texas, where he died in 1881.

A leading writer in the Evangelical Protestant fellowship was Gustav Schmidt. He was born in Germany in 1853 and studied at the universities of Berlin and Bonn. He came to Pennsylvania and was ordained to the ministry by the Pittsburgh Association of Evangelical Protestant Ministers in 1884. He served the church in McKeesport for forty-two years. When the Evangelical Protestant journal *Kirchenbote* (Church Messenger) was established in 1885, Schmidt became editor. For years he wrote articles on social issues, especially on the evils found in growing industries in the cities: long working hours, low wages, unhealthy conditions, child labor, the exploitation of women, and the accumulation of vast fortunes by the industrial "barons." He was a strong voice in the social gospel movement.[11]

Another distinguished minister was Friedrich Ruoff. Born in 1850 in Wuerttemberg, Germany, he graduated from the University of Tuebingen in 1870. He served in the Prussian army during the Franco-Prussian War. In 1873 he came to America to serve in St. John's Church of Mount Auburn, Cincinnati. Six years later he was called to the "mother" church in Pittsburgh (Smithfield). Ruoff was deeply concerned about people and helped countless German immigrants find jobs in the steel mills and other industries. He worked to establish two Evangelical Protestant social agencies in the Pittsburgh area: an orphanage in 1888 and a home for the aged in 1891. During his pastorate the Smithfield Church erected its fourth building. Ruoff was an outstanding preacher, admired not only by his parishioners, but also by the whole city. At his funeral in 1904, Smithfield Street, one of the main business arteries of the city, was closed to traffic to accommodate the hundreds of mourners who came to stand in silent tribute to him[12]

DENOMINATIONAL ORGANIZATION

For many years there was no denominational structure among the Evangelical Protestant churches, only the ministerial associations in Pittsburgh and Cincinnati. Gradually, however, people came to believe that some kind of federation was needed. Finally, in 1885, the pastors of both areas, fourteen from Pittsburgh and thirteen from Cincinnati, met at Smithfield Church in Pittsburgh to set up an organization. They called it the

German Evangelical Protestant Church of North America, even though it was not a church, just a fellowship of ministers. It had a central committee consisting of officers and three trustees. They started a denominational journal, *Kirchenbote* (Church Messenger), later renamed *Kirchenzeitung* (Church Gazette), and a children's paper, *Christlicher Jugenfreund* (Christian Friend of Youth). They published a yearbook of articles and reports, *Volkskalender* (People's Almanac), as well as Sunday school materials and hymnals for children and adults.[13]

Increasingly, however, they felt the need for an organization that included laypersons. In 1911 a meeting was held at St. Paul's Church in Cincinnati, and another in 1912 at the Mount Washington church in Pittsburgh. Plans were made for congregational representation, and the body was enlarged to include delegates from the parishes. It still bore the name Evangelical Protestant Church of North America; the word German was dropped.

In 1917 the organization adopted a Declaration of Principles, expressing the convictions that had governed Evangelical Protestant churches from their beginning:

> Our Church is called Evangelical because it accepts as the foundation and rule of faith and life the Gospel of Jesus Christ. . . .
>
> Our Church is called Protestant because it protests against any compulsion in matters of faith and conscience. . . . We expect our members to form their own convictions, based upon personal experience and deliberation. Differing opinions need not lead to discord as long as the spirit of true freedom and Christian love of neighbor prevails. . . .
>
> We look up to the God of omnipotence, justice and love, who is our Father. We recognize in Jesus our highest ideal and divine Master. We believe in the blessedness of loving service, in the power of prayer, in the victory of truth, and in life eternal.[14]

MERGER WITH THE CONGREGATIONALISTS

During the early decades of the twentieth century there were many social changes affecting the German-speaking churches in this country. The influx of immigrants from Germany, on which the Evangelical Protestant churches depended for growth, practically ceased. Churches could no longer obtain ministers from Europe. As the younger generation preferred to speak English, parishes became bilingual and eventually gave up the use of German altogether. Ultimately the churches were becoming American and losing touch with their German-American roots. The fact that the denomination had no theological seminary made it difficult to find ministers for Evangelical Protestant churches. And, as a small group of parishes, with no "home" or "foreign" mission boards, the churches felt unable to play an effective part in the wider work of the church.[15]

The answer to these problems pointed toward a union with some larger denomination, one that shared Evangelical Protestant principles of local autonomy and personal freedom of thought. Carl August Voss, minster of the "mother" church, Smithfield, in Pittsburgh, believed that they should consider the Congregationalists.

Voss was born in 1876 in Wheeling, West Virginia, and grew up in Cincinnati, where his father, Eduard Voss, was pastor of St. Paul's Evangelical Protestant Church (1879–1910). He went to Elmhurst College and Meadville Theological Seminary and did further study at Lane Theological Seminary and the University of Cincinnati. Ordained to the ministry in 1896, he served Immanuel Church in Cincinnati (an independent congregation) for nine years. In 1905 he was called to Smithfield Church in Pittsburgh, where he served for the next thirty-eight years. During his pastorate the church erected its fifth (present) building. Voss also served as the first president of the Evangelical Protestant Church of North America after its reorganization as a representative body, holding office from 1913 to 1920.[16]

As Voss and others considered the future of the denomination, they looked to the Congregationalists. Congregationalism had developed strong regional and national organizations, while preserving the autonomy of the local churches.

In 1922 Voss began informal conversations with the Congregational officers in New York. A year later the Evangelical Protestant Church asked Voss to chair a committee, enter into negotiations, and draw up a plan for union. Any vote to join the Congregationalists had to be made by the Evangelical Protestant Church as a body, as well as by each individual congregation. Finally, on October 20, 1925, the Evangelical Protestant Church of North America became part of the National Council of Congregational Churches at a meeting in Washington, D.C.[17]

In his address to the National Council on that occasion Voss said:

> While your institutions found their birthplace on a different soil from ours, we realize that it is the same spirit of tolerance, freedom, loyalty and devotion, so dear to our hearts, that prevails in your circles. The fact that our churches have always been congregational in their polity has made it doubly easy for us to affiliate with your body. Your history and ours reveal that, while independence is a great treasure, it is not to be confused with irresponsibility, and that only by organization, fellowship and interrelationship can this independence be safe-guarded.[18]

The Evangelical Protestant Church joined the Congregational fellowship as a separate, nongeographical conference, functioning like the Calvin (Hungarian) Synod in the United Church of Christ. It had two district associations: one in the Pittsburgh area, with fourteen churches, and one centered in Cincinnati, with thirteen churches in Ohio, Kentucky, Indiana, and Missouri. This status as a separate conference was only temporary. In 1935 the Pittsburgh Evangelical Protestant Association dissolved itself, and most of its churches became part of the Congregational Conference of Pennsylvania. Eventually they all did. The one Evangelical Protestant church in Missouri, the Independent Church in St. Louis, joined the Congregational Conference in that state. A separate Evangelical Protestant Conference, embracing only the churches in Ohio, Kentucky, and Indiana, continued to exist for a few years. But on May 17, 1947, at a meeting in St. John's Church in Newport, Kentucky, it voted to dissolve and become part of the Congregational Christian Conference of Ohio.[19]

After the United Church of Christ was formed, many of the formerly Evangelical Protestant churches joined it. The first of them to bear the new name was in Cincinnati. As mentioned earlier, St. Peter's and St. Paul's, the two oldest Evangelical Protestant churches in that city, combined in 1948 to become St. Peter and St. Paul United Church of Christ. This was nine years before the national merger. In the early 1980s the church had about 650 members.[20]

The largest UCC church that was originally Evangelical Protestant is St. John's UCC in Newport, Kentucky, across the river from Cincinnati. In the 1980s it has more than 1,300 members.

The oldest Evangelical Protestant congregation, Smithfield Church in Pittsburgh, still meets on the site of its first meetinghouse in 1794. When it joined the Congregational fellowship in 1925, it had more than 1,000 members. Membership has declined as people have moved from the city to the suburbs. In the late 1960s a small Methodist church federated with it, and the combined congregation, now called Smithfield United Church, had about 500 members in the mid-1980s. Its present building on Smithfield Street, erected in 1926, is the fifth church to stand on that spot. Unusual stained-glass windows, depicting historical events in the life of the city and the church, include one scene showing the first Evangelical Protestant pastor, Johann Wilhelm Weber, riding through the forest on his horse.

The Evangelical Protestant Church no longer exists as a distinctive movement. As one who grew up in it has said, "It was a noble effort on the part of many men and women to achieve freedom of mind and spirit, inspired by the Christian faith."[21] Its legacy has not been lost. The formerly Evangelical Protestant churches play an important role in the life of their communities and in the wider Christian fellowship. The United Church of Christ is a tapestry weaving together many strands and different religious traditions. The Evangelical Protestant heritage is a significant part of that tapestry.[22]

CHAPTER
3

ORIGINS OF THE CHRISTIAN DENOMINATION IN NEW ENGLAND

Elizabeth C. Nordbeck

THE PIONEERS OF New England's Christian Connexion, asserted the Rev. Austin Craig before a ministerial gathering in 1850, certainly "did not purpose the formation of a new sect." Nevertheless, he admitted, "moral affinities presently consociated them," while misunderstanding and opposition from other religious groups gradually pushed them toward a more theologically and structurally defined position.[1]

Some Christians* had begun to call their movement a denomination as early as the mid-1820s. As a whole, however, the group adamantly rejected such labels, advocating instead a broad and fundamental christian inclusivity and eschewing all "party names." Austin Craig's address, delivered on the eve of a historic convention at Marion, Ohio, effectively united the

Elizabeth C. Nordbeck is Associate Professor of Church History at Lancaster Theological Seminary, Lancaster, Pennsylvania.

*Hereafter this chapter will follow the Christian Connexion's own most common usage: the word Christian, upper case, will refer to the Connexion itself; "christian," lower case, will refer to the generic body of believers.

46

three distinct regional movements that "carried the name of Christ only," and was thus especially notable for its attempt to summarize the several "principles" generally held among them. Resolutely biblical, privatistic, antidogmatic, and revivalistic, most of the Christians—especially in New England—had steadfastly resisted attempts to systematize or codify what they believed or how they ordered themselves. On both pragmatic and theological grounds they insisted on a believer's right to private judgment and on the concomitant necessity for tolerance and cooperation among believers whose private judgments might differ.

Even in 1850, after fully half a century of growth, the Christians were difficult to define precisely. By far the least well-known of the United Church of Christ's four constituent traditions—the denominational textbook devotes barely three of fifty-eight pages of history to its origins[2]—the story of the Christian Connexion is undeservedly "hidden." Indeed, at a time when matters of justice, spirituality, creeds and confessionalism, biblical faithfulness, and women's rights continue to be at the forefront of the United Church of Christ's common life, the Christian radical witness in these areas, along with a warm and heartfelt piety, provides a usable tradition.

Why has this movement of both vitality and innovation drifted into obscurity over time? At least two factors are responsible. In the first place the Christians were not one movement, but three. Springing up almost simultaneously among New England Baptists, Virginia Methodists, and Kentucky Presbyterians at the turn of the century, Christian "converts" were theologically and regionally diverse. Despite important common understandings that led to cooperation—notably their insistence on "taking the name of Christ alone" and on the New Testament as a sufficient "creed"—the three groups differed in leadership, in their primary concerns and emphases, and on the process and speed with which their organizational structures came into being. Origins of the New England group are further complicated by the separate conversions to Christian principles of cofounders Abner Jones of Vermont and Elias Smith of New Hampshire—two men whose theologies and personal styles were distinct and not infrequently disharmonious. Moreover, regionally diverse publications, educational institutions, and record-keeping procedures have all contributed to a scattering of materials, making historical recovery difficult.

More important, though, the Christians' vehement anti-creedalism, uncompromising New Testament faith, and revivalistic style made them something of an anomaly even at the height of their strength and influence. Convinced that trinitarianism was a "doctrine of man," nowhere to be found in the scriptures, many Christians happily named themselves "unitarians"; William Ellery Channing himself looked on them "with singular pleasure because they 'stand fast in the liberty wherewith Christ hath made us free.'" The Christian churches, Channing wrote approvingly, "embrace a greater variety of opinions than can be found in any other. . . . Your denomination is practical proof that christians interpreting the scriptures for themselves may live in peace, and may join great fervor with great liberality of opinion."[3] Unlike Channing and his Unitarian colleagues, however, virtually all the Christians energetically promoted a fervent, "experimental" piety that found its source and expression not in theological abstractions or the academy, but in freestyle worship and personal experience of the living God. The Christians were colleagues and frequent collaborators with groups like New England's Free Will Baptists. They gladly supported "seasons of refreshment" and revival in many denominations. Assailed from the religious left as too emotional and from the right as too unorthodox, Christians clung determinedly to a kind of "middle way" that attempted to hold head and heart, unity and diversity in tension.

The balancing act cost them dearly. Not only were their "principles" often and widely misunderstood, but also more than a few of their numbers eventually defected to groups as theologically different as the Unitarians and the Millerite Adventists. Even within the loyal Christian fold, diversity was held in tenuous check by a common commitment to christian unity and "civility" and a common mistrust of uniformity. The net result, wrote denominational historian Milo T. Morrill in 1912, was a movement that was frustratingly hard for an outsider to comprehend:

> Readers will still press for categorical answers about Scriptural doctrines and theological dogmas. They will be answered perhaps that Scriptural doctrine should be care-

fully differentiated from theological doctrine; that Biblical language should be discriminated from philosophical formulae. . . . To elucidate the matter still further, suppose a minister of the Christians were asked to declare his views relative to the Trinity. He might answer in one of four ways. He might say, I know nothing about the Trinity; such a word does not appear in my Bible, but is a human invention. Or he might say, I neither affirm nor deny that upon which Scripture does not speak. Or he might say again, I believe in the Biblical Trinity but not in the theological. Or yet again, he might declare assent to the doctrine as commonly understood and might become a controversialist, handling metaphysical "essence" or "substance" or "three-in-one" speculative ideas incapable of conclusive proof, but capable of endless argument.[4]

With the exception of Morrill's history, no major work has been done on Christian origins in the past century. Nevertheless, in part because of their schismatic relationships with American Methodism and Presbyterianism, adequate material on both the Virginia and the Kentucky Christian movements is available. It is the New England group that remains virtually unchronicled. That movement—one that "kindled with new intelligence the countenances of the uneducated"[5] in rural New England—also produced the first religious periodical in America.

NEW ENGLAND BEGINNINGS

In the wake of the American Revolution the religious contours of New England underwent rapid and radical change. The hold of Puritan Calvinism, embodied in the Congregational or "Standing Order" churches, was more relaxed in New England's northern and western hill country. Even in these regions, however, Congregationalism was solidly established, subsidized by public taxation and supported by a network of Harvard- and Yale-trained pastors. During the Great Awakening, roughly from the late 1720s to the late 1740s, Congregational churches suffered numerical losses to Calvinistic (or "particular") Baptists. However, the changes precipitated by revolution—political, economic, and social, as well as religious— broke the grip of the Standing Order and pushed the region toward pluralism. From the 1770s on, Shakers, Free Will Baptists, and Universalists, in addition to larger groups like Methodists and Baptists, energetically challenged Congregational hegemony. By 1815 Shakers, Free Will Baptists, and Universalists constituted one quarter of New England's rural churches.[6]

Although there is no scholarly consensus on the origins of the late-eighteenth-century sectarian impulse in America, it is clear that the postrevolutionary ethos promoted new religious options that were experiential (or "enthusiastic"), antiauthoritarian, innovative, and populist. Out of this ferment New England's Christian Connexion emerged. The Connexion was a "sect" that disavowed sectarianism, advocating instead the emancipation of the common person from creeds, catechisms, "hireling ministers," and denominations. Two men are credited with its founding.

Abner Jones, youngest of five children of strict Baptist parents, emigrated from Massachusetts with his family to Bridgewater, Vermont, in 1780. The next year, at the age of nine, Abner had his first religious experience, the result of a neighborhood hunting accident that touched off a local revival. "I was fully convinced that I must be born again or damned," Abner recalled, and shortly thereafter he was converted. Despite this early episode, Abner's adolescent years were ones of doubt, spiritual turmoil, and career experimentation. A decade after his conversion he "reconsecrated" himself to God and was baptized. Although at this time he began to entertain thoughts of preaching, Jones remained unclear about *what* he should preach and undertook the study of medicine instead. A close reading of scripture convinced him that his spiritual confusion was the result of embracing "many things without proper examination"; therefore he resolved to preach and practice nothing that could not be found in the Bible.

Before long Jones began to question not only the discipline and practice of his inherited faith, but also many familiar Calvinist doctrines. His mind was "brought out of a dark narrow prison, into the sunshine of a free gospel offered to everyone." It now seemed clear that the gospel proclaimed few of the traditional doctrines that he had once accepted unquestioningly: the Trinity, Christ's expiatory atonement, eternal punishment for sins, the doctrine of election. Jones discarded them all as spiritually binding and pernicious.

Around 1797 Jones and his new wife settled in Lyndon, Vermont, where he took up the practice of medicine and put his religious calling aside. But soon a "reformation" in an adjacent town moved him to a public confession of his backsliding ways; and in 1801 he preached his first sermon. Thereafter "doors opened . . . on every hand." The same year Jones took a still more radical step: he and a dozen residents of Lyndon covenanted together to form a church, "rejecting all party and sectional names, and leaving each other free to cherish such speculate views of theology as the scriptures might plainly seem to them to teach." This was the first Christian church formally gathered in New England. In 1802, with three Free Will Baptist clergymen officiating, Abner Jones was ordained. During the next twelve months he began an active ministry, founding two more Christian churches at Hanover and Piermont, New Hampshire. Until his death in 1841 Jones exerted prodigious energy in support of the new movement, often preaching thirty to forty times a month in his travels across New England.[7]

A second founder, Elias Smith, was undoubtedly the most outspoken, theologically peripatetic, ideologically doctrinaire, and generally cantankerous of the Christians' early leaders. Smith was born three years before Abner Jones, in Lyme, Connecticut. Like Jones, he was the son of pious Calvinist parents— his father a Baptist and his mother a Congregationalist. Smith recalled a childhood filled with intense religious experiences. When Smith's family moved to Woodstock, Vermont, in 1782, he followed reluctantly, preferring less harsh and isolated circumstances. However, his schooling from a Baptist preacher and a conversion experience in the woods drew him "almost unconsciously" toward ministry. At twenty-one he joined the Baptist church; the next year he preached his first sermon; and thereafter he began a public ministry that eventually took him to Virginia.

Smith's view of ministry was iconoclastic from the start. He disliked the traditional black broadcloth of the clergy, was uncomfortable with the title "reverend," and objected to the use of notes in preaching. The doctrines of election and the Trinity were serious stumbling blocks for him. After his ordination in

1792 he got married and took a pastorate in Salisbury, New Hampshire. Yet he remained restless and uncomfortable in a settled position. His relationship with parishioners was as troubled as his theology. A brief lapse—the first of several during his lifetime—into the "heresy" of Universalism in 1801 was followed by a move to the comparatively sophisticated seacoast town of Portsmouth, New Hampshire. There, Smith crystallized his views on church and state. For the first time he ventured to say aloud that "the name CHRISTIAN was enough for the followers of Christ, without the addition of the word baptist, methodist, &c." In 1803 he and twenty-two others in Portsmouth covenanted "to bear the name of CHRISTIANS, leaving all unscriptural names behind." Inside of a year the new church had 150 members.

In June of 1803 Smith met Abner Jones, "the first free man I have ever seen." Before he came to Portsmouth, Smith wrote: "I considered myself alone in the world." Jones was instrumental in persuading Smith to abandon the last vestiges of his inherited Calvinism, as well as the "cumbersome" organizational structures of his church. Together both men began to preach—not without controversy—to receptive audiences in the Piscataqua area of New Hampshire and as far south as Boston. By 1804 Smith had become bold to denounce as "abominable in the sight of God" matters such as "calvinism, arminianism, freewillism, universalism, reverend, parsons, chaplains, doctors of divinity, clergy, bands, surplices, notes, creeds, covenants, platforms. . . ." To this litany of unscriptural things he soon added the necessity of a college education for ministry, missionary societies, and church councils for ordination and discipline.[8]

Smith's and Jones' active itinerancy earned the new movement converts and enemies. Strong at first in Massachusetts, Christian sentiments spread rapidly northward into the Maine and New Hampshire seacoast areas and more slowly into Vermont, Rhode Island, and Connecticut.[9] However, the publication of the *Herald of Gospel Liberty* in 1808 brought the Christian Connexion into a decade of solid growth. The *Herald*, conceived and published by Elias Smith at Portsmouth and later Portland, Maine, was significant as "the first religious newspaper in the world" and as a vehicle for Smith's own strident republican sentiments. More important, however, it provided a forum for news and theological discussion among Christians across the country as they began to define their movement and establish its boundaries. Through the mutual encouragement found in its pages, churches were planted in isolated areas of the north. By 1810 forty Christian churches had been gathered across New England, served by twenty preachers or "elders" who dutifully reported their gospel labors in the biweekly tabloid.

Growth of the movement in this early period was part of a larger "Second Great Awakening" that affected frontier and settled America after the turn of the century. In New England localized revivals swept like ripples over the rural landscape between 1800 and 1815, revitalizing old congregations and engendering new ones. To the Christians, these "quickenings" clearly represented "a glorious outpouring of the spirit of God in New England . . . perhaps beyond what has been known for many years," and a visible sign that their own cause was one whose time had come.[10] Every edition of the *Herald* brought new reports of "general reformations," many of them following an almost predictable pattern of events. An 1812 revival in Westerly, Rhode Island, was typical:

> At first but few attended; but after a few evenings the School-house was crowded in every part, and at last the windows were raised that people around the house might hear. In a short time they were obliged to meet in the Meeting-house, and frequently seven or eight hundred would attend an evening meeting. At some of the meetings a general sobbing has been heard through different parts of the Meeting-house; while an awful solemnity appeared through the whole. At certain times while the preachers and brethren were engaged in prayer, a great part of the assembly would be on their knees, and many like Peter's hearers were saying in bitterness of soul,—"What shall we do?" . . . When there is preaching, the people are very attentive to hear the word; after preaching, it is common for a very large number to speak one by one in exhortation . . . some not more than 12 or 14 years old.[11]

Many other religious groups shared the revivalistic zeal of the Christians, but few shared their ecumenical interests. As early as 1812 they were involved in serious union discussions with the Free Will Baptists of Maine and New Hampshire. Periodically they promoted local interdenominational meetings at which "all party distinctions, of names and other things" were temporarily laid aside.[12] Correspondence between northern and southern Christians began as early as 1808 in the pages of the *Herald*. And in 1811 Elias Smith was in Virginia representing the New England fellowship at a meeting "in order to attend to the important question so often asked,—'Can the Christian Brethren in the South be united with the Christian Brethren in the North?' "[13]

The elimination of "party distinctions" and the fostering of an irenic spirit of cooperation among religious groups were elusive goals. Christians encountered bitter opposition throughout New England, fueled by their own fervent evangelizing and Elias Smith's scathing attacks on "sectarian bondage" and "hireling" clergy "too lazy to work." Where the Christians did promote unity among "the sects" it was often in an ironic reversal of their own intent. For example, when Frederick Plummer, one of New England's earliest itinerant Christians, arrived in Chelsea, Vermont, in 1811, the "combined Sectarian parties" banded together to oppose him.[14] The next year, after calling a series of meetings to support orthodoxy, religious groups in Bristol, Rhode Island "declared themselves a Christian union of all denominations excepting the poor 'Christians!' " who were formally requested to desist.[15]

Christian itinerants and settled pastors were often subjected to harassment. Elias Smith was hounded by opponents from the beginning of his ministry in Portsmouth: irate mobs broke windows in the church, dumped vials of asafetida in the alley nearby, disrupted baptisms, and even attempted to haul the preacher bodily from his pulpit. Although few other Christian leaders suffered outright violence, many at one time or another endured verbal attacks and defamation of character. A letter from Frederick Plummer, for example, describes typical missionary trials during his labors in Woodstock, Vermont. The work of God has been great, he wrote to the *Herald* in 1812, but "the opposition has been great" as well: "Every false and base report, that bigotry, envy and malice could invent, have been circulated to injure my feelings and character."

This widespread antagonism was not simply a response to

the Christians' revivalism, biblicism, and anticreedalism—all of which had earlier characterized the Great Awakening of the 1700s. Rather, it was what one modern commentator calls their relentless "zeal to dismantle mediating elites within the church"[16] that set Christians at odds with the Congregational Standing Order and with Baptist, Methodist, Episcopalian, and Presbyterian leadership. "Venture to be as independent in things of religion," Elias Smith declared repeatedly, "as [in] those [things] which respect the government in which you live." Smith and his colleagues called for an ecclesiastical revolution that was fully as radical as America's political one had been. They insisted on "gospel-liberty" that demolished traditional distinctions between laity and clergy, elevated individual conscience over the authority and decisions of groups or councils, and rejected the recondite theological abstractions of the academy in favor of a believer's own interpretive insights.

WOMEN IN MINISTRY

The Christian ethos of equality and individualism offered grounds for innovations that in the early 1800s were uncommon, except among radical separatist and sectarian groups. Christians supported women's public ministries long before revivalist Charles Finney brought the issue into general debate; and nearly a dozen "female laborers" were in their graves before Congregationalist Antoinette Brown was ordained.

Exactly when women began preaching among New England Christians is unclear. Historian Milo Morrill indicates that as early as 1812, "women preachers were working and highly esteemed" in the movement at large, and that same year Christian women were "exhorting" at religious meetings in Vermont.[17] From the beginning the Christians' egalitarian thrust and inclusive worship practices encouraged women inclined toward public profession. The *Herald of Gospel Liberty*, October 1816, described a revival in Deerfield, New Hampshire. The writer noted what a difference there was between "an assembly of men improperly called *Divines*, who meet to make *compendiums of Divinity*" and a meeting of Christians, "where a large number of free brethren and sisters meet, to preach, sing, pray, exhort, and edify each other; where all serve by love,

was to be done with those perennially troublesome passages from 1 Corinthians and 2 Timothy? The answer lay in a clever distinction. "But where is it that Paul considers it to be a shame for a woman to speak, teach, and usurp authority over the man? I answer, 'in the church,'—not in meetings of public worship; and in no other way can Paul's declarations be reconciled."[27] By thus narrowing the meaning of "church" to encompass little more than the gathered body in its formal, organized sense, Christians could handily exclude women from the tasks of ordering and administrating and leave them free to accomplish the more important tasks of evangelizing, preaching, and teaching.

It is sometimes argued that it was precisely this fine distinction that kept preaching women—or "female labourers in the church," as they were usually designated—from formal ordination until a decade and a half after Congregationalist Antoinette Brown's ordination in 1853. Christians were willing to grant their females license to "prepare the soil" for the churches but not to hold structural power in them. Such an argument, however, misunderstands the Christians' own early and radical mistrust of church structure itself—a mistrust that was especially pervasive in New England, where the background of Christian converts from Baptist and Congregational origins was one of uncompromising independency. Christians considered themselves a movement or a "connexion" and not a church or denomination. Denying accusations of sectarianism, they created structures warily and gradually, and then only out of a growing need for permanence, order, and effective communication. Ordained Christian elders were notoriously casual about the sacraments, sometimes leaving it to the discretion of an individual convert whether he or she would choose to be baptized. Christian laypersons spoke publicly, interpreting the word and participating fully in decision making. It was scripture—the word preached with passion and taken to heart—that was the source of power and the center of faith. The exclusion of women from administrative positions in "the church," therefore, was a relatively minor, formal sort of limitation. In this way Christians were able to support women's public ministries and preaching and Paul's prohibitions concerning women in the churches. Ironically, their progressive stance did not lead them until much later to question the meaning of a gospel that declares spiritual equality and radical individual liberty but keeps some of its most powerful exponents from performing certain minimally important duties. Only with the opening of the frontier west of Pennsylvania, not in New England, did Christian women achieve full ministerial status. Unencumbered by old proprieties and recalcitrant social structures, women finally ministered with freedom and license that remained largely impossible in the old northeast until the turn of the century.

EXPANSION

Innovation, a freewheeling approach to structure and discipline, and apparent harmony in both worship and practice characterized much of the first two decades of the Christian Connexion in New England. Growth was rapid, if sporadic: in 1814 forty-nine men (forty-four of them ordained) presided over as many churches in the region; seven years later the number of preachers and churches had reached nearly eighty. In New York, under leadership that was drawn heavily from the ranks of New England-born converts, growth was remarkable: by 1820 fifty preachers, including three women, were itinerating or serving churches; fully one third of these were native New Englanders.[28] Close cooperation and communication existed between New England and New York well into the latter part of the century. Preachers routinely itinerated successfully throughout the entire territory.

From the beginning, however, the Connexion had problems. Elder Uriah Smith, during a swing through New Hampshire in 1813, reported with consternation that there were churches calling themselves "Churches of Christ" that had neither deacons nor records. "I think our travelling elders are deficient in not doing these things in the first naming of a company the *church of Christ*," he wrote. He promised to appoint officers wherever he baptized five or more persons.[29] Two years later the *Herald* noted similar difficulties in an article entitled "Churches Out of Order." By 1816 the paper suggested that there was need to consider the subject of proper ordination procedures because of disciplinary problems and irregular practices in western New Hampshire and Vermont.[30]

Two "scandals" shook the young movement. In 1816 the volatile Elias Smith lapsed into Universalism, this time for an extended sojourn of seven years. Although he later recanted, many of Smith's colleagues never forgave him. With his defection the Christians lost not only their most brilliant and visible spokesperson, but also their credibility with a public already predisposed to criticism. The *Herald of Gospel Liberty* was sold to Robert Foster, a layman from Portsmouth, who carried on publication in May 1818 under the new name *Christian Herald*. Although Foster continued the paper as an organ of "religious intelligence," he was no controversialist. Smith's grand purpose had been "to shew the *liberty* which belongs to men, as it respects their duty to God, and each other." But Foster's was significantly less ambitious: to promote "the cause of the Redeemer" and to "give an impartial statement of the spread of experimental religion."[31] The new *Herald* continued through a bewildering series of shifts in name and management until well into the twentieth century. It never again equaled the vision and power of the original publication.

Along with Elias Smith's heresy, controversy erupted in Connecticut over the alleged "sundry atrocious acts" of Elder Douglas Farnum, a charismatic and popular but eccentric itinerant from Vermont. Convicted of several charges—among them "naming obscene things in public" and "telling some if they wanted or would go to heaven with him to follow in creeping on the floor from room to room"—Farnum was formally disfellowshiped by a General Conference at Hampton, Connecticut, in 1819.[32] His guilt or innocence remained a subject of lively debate for years.

This departure of two influential leaders under questionable circumstances was embarrassing to the Christians. It gave credence to detractors' claims that the movement was both emotionally excessive and theologically unsound. To counter such opposition, and because of a growing need to safeguard young and isolated churches, by 1820 the Christians began to construct a rudimentary denomination out of their formerly loose fellowship.

In New England a tradition of congregational autonomy, shared by Baptists, Free Will Baptists, and Congregationalists, had long been coupled with systems of fraternal advisement and support among churches. As early as 1809 irregular local "elders' conferences" and "general meetings" were organized by Christians in Portsmouth, New Hampshire. Similar meetings were held in every New England state by 1820. These gatherings initially brought laypersons and ministers together for devotions, discussion, and mutual support. It was not long before they took on a more formal cast, dealing with matters of discipline, admonishment, and order. In 1816 a "General Conference" was called at Windham, Connecticut, with representation from Pennsylvania, New York, and all New England states except Rhode Island. A similar gathering, held at Portsmouth in 1819, recommended "a union of the several churches throughout the connexion in the United States" and advised that a United States Conference of Christians be established. One year later, albeit with limited participation from outside the northeast, the conference was formalized at Windham. Expressing dismay at the "impositions and havoc" wrought by interlopers "whose characters have been stained with immoral conduct, entering in among us under the name Christian," the delegates adopted recommendations minimally to regularize ministerial standards, church membership and financial practices, and record keeping. Their ultimate values, however, were uncompromising: "Be assured," they wrote to their absent colleagues, "that we do not mean to take away or abridge your liberties in the gospel."[33] Statistics collected at the Windham meeting were printed in the first *Christian Almanac and Register*, which continued to be published irregularly into the 1850s. Although its data were sometimes only minimally accurate, the *Register* was an important symbol of the movement's growing denominational consciousness and interregional solidarity.

MINISTRY AND THEOLOGY

The year 1820 marks a watershed for the Christian Connexion. After 1820 Christians confronted a dilemma as they attempted to articulate their principles and regulate their practices without wholly abandoning the "antisectarianism" that, paradoxically, united them. Two areas in particular—ministry and theology—felt the force of debate and change.

Massachusetts-born John Rand, a convert from Baptist beliefs, was the first person ordained among New England Christians. His consecration in 1806, presided over by elders Smith, Jones, and Joseph Boody, set a precedent. It was understood that individuals raised by recognition of their gifts could be ordained in the presence of three elders, a conveniently simple procedure in a movement that was rural and itinerant. The few elders and the demands of effective evangelism, coupled with the Christians' deep antipathy toward "hireling" clergy, whom Elias Smith believed lived high off the public coffers and worked precious little for the Lord, prohibited anything like a settled ministry. By 1819 state support of clergy had all but ceased, the sharp tongue of Elias Smith was silent, and the needs of the young movement were rapidly changing. Christians began rethinking their earlier attitudes.

Furthermore, men like Douglas Farnum alerted leaders to the need for minimal standards of membership and office. Organizing regular local conferences was one "special remedy" specifically aimed at expunging "those who say, they are apostles, but are not."[34] Other measures were taken: in Maine, for example, unordained persons wishing to preach were first to be recognized by their own churches and then approved by conference.[35] Increasingly, ordinations took place with a "respectable body of Christians" present, as well as the requisite three elders.

It was not discipline, however, but the plight of young churches—"planted and left by evangelizing preachers, which are now perishing through famine of the word"—that was most problematic.[36] During the 1820s and 1830s Christians further defined the nature of ministry. Evangelist and pastor were separate offices, the one for planting churches, the other to "take care of them after they are planted." The latter office, wrote two ministers from the field in 1826, "has been sadly neglected by us as a people."[37] By 1836 cofounder Abner Jones modified the equation of "settled pastorate" with "hireling." A hireling, he wrote, is simply one who agrees to preach for a stipulated time and a set salary. Admitting that he himself had served under such stipulations for a year, he emphasized the need for mutual support and liberty, without potentially burdensome contracts that were unequal in their demands on pastor and people. Ministers should not be hirelings, but they *should* have a living.

The way was cleared for Christians to assume, without guilt, the regular care of specific churches.[38]

Theologically, Christians experienced great change in the period after 1820. The "theologizing" process was even more protracted and more complex than the process of rethinking ministry. From the beginning, Christians had shunned the heady intricacies of "speculative theology," insisting on the sufficiency of the word itself and the combined power of the human heart and mind to grasp gospel truth. Elias Smith had articulated three foundational principles: no head over the church but Christ, no confession of faith but the New Testament, no name but Christian. The people veered little from these in more than half a century. Standards for church membership were based on action, not assent. Whereas proper christian life was essential, uniformity of belief was neither anticipated nor desired, since "genuine religion can breathe freely only in an atmosphere of freedom." To each individual believer, not just to an educated elite, the Bible offered up its full truth.

In one sense, little theological change occurred between 1820 and the final decades of the century. Christians remained wedded to the Bible as the center of their beliefs, adamantly rejecting anything that smacked of creedalism, including written summaries of their principles. They continued to insist on the precedence of piety over professional training. But the fact that theological issues—like the Trinity, a future state of rewards and punishments, and the Second Coming—were public issues represented an important step toward denominational consciousness. In the pages of the movement's several periodicals, in pamphlets, at conferences, in publications of the Christian General Book Association, established in 1834 "that the connection may assume a character,"[39] Christians pursued theological debate with energy and sophistication worthy of the most effete Harvard-trained Congregationalists. Like the first-century churches they sought to emulate, Christians discovered the need for clearer self-definition, while defectors and detractors carried off members and spread misinformation about the fellowship with impunity.[40]

On October 2, 1850, delegates from eleven states and Canada met at Marion, Ohio, for the largest General Convention held to date. Historian Morrill reckons it a milestone meeting for the denomination, expressive of a "new thrill of organic life . . . a new spirit and conviction dominating the people's thought."[41] New Englanders and southern Christians built on the groundwork for unity established a decade earlier, when extensive correspondence and debate had issued finally in a formal union between Christian conferences of the two regions. The *Christian Palladium*[42] of December 1841 announced the consummation, expressing its wish that the union might "serve as a living and convincing example to the divided sects, that Christians can be one in spirit and work, though a difference of sentiment may exist among them."[43] Not all Christians accepted these developments with equal joy, but the prevailing sentiment in New England was one of approval. In an environment where many religious groups had long vied for acceptance within a limited population, the inevitability of the Christians' sectarianism continued to be discussed. "The Christians are, and must be, a sect," one writer asserted. "It cannot and should not be avoided. . . . As a member of that connexion, I should prove recreant to honesty and consistency if I did not use the means and influence in my power to advance her denominational interest in preference to all others."[44]

At midcentury, after fifty years of common life as a "connexion," Christians began to recognize what their primitive forebears had discovered: in the living church, form and freedom, spirit and structure are not (and cannot be) mutually exclusive if a movement is to survive its founding generation. The gradual "institutionalization" of their Connexion, however, did not shake the Christians' firm conviction that the true church is broad and open, its doors wide enough for the admission of all christians "as christians simply." The center of the church is a person and not a proposition; therefore, no one formulation of the church can ever be absolutized as "true"; no simple intellectual assent to creeds or confessions can make an "obedient christian" out of one whose life is not an imitation of Christ. As "Christian principles" gradually became "denominational beliefs," they remained broad enough to invite other christians into mutual fellowship and cooperation, including the Congregational churches in 1931. A well-known New England pastor and educator, Elder Jasper Hazen, summarized the story well in a fitting verbal legacy for the United Church of Christ:

> To be an able disputant, on minor points, a powerful master, or an elegant dancer, may fix the gaze and command the approbation of an admiring and wondering crowd; but neither do much good to the souls or bodies of men. Then let us leave the arena of the theological gladiator, and say to our brethren in Christ, and to the world, "Our great objects are the unity of Christians and the conversion of the world. We labor for both objects, because of their high importance; and for one of them again, that by its accomplishment we may secure the other." "*That they may all be one—that the world may believe that thou hast sent me.*"[45]

EVANGELICAL PIETISM AND BIBLICAL CRITICISM: THE STORY OF KARL EMIL OTTO

Lowell H. Zuck

THE EVANGELICAL ROOTS of the United Church of Christ represent a unionist-pietist liberal approach to Christianity. Among most nineteenth-century immigrants on the Midwestern frontier, German Evangelicals stood in stark contrast to the doctrinal rigorism that was popular among Missouri Lutherans, Christian Reformed, and, to a lesser extent, Presbyterian, Congregational, Baptist, and Methodist revivalists.[1]

German Evangelicals in Missouri, Illinois, and other Midwestern states traced their roots unofficially to the Prussian Union Church, founded in 1817. On arrival in the United States, in 1840, they organized themselves into a church association (*Evangelische Kirchenverein des Westens*), making use of German confessions from both Lutheran and Reformed traditions. They also displayed a pietistic ability to pray, sing, form congregations, and train ministers, following the ecumenically open but conservative Lutheran-Reformed tradition. They started a church journal (the *Friedensbote*) and reshaped a new

Lowell H. Zuck is Professor of Church History at Eden Theological Seminary, St. Louis, Missouri.

catechism (*Evangelical Catechism*). But the most important institution for developing a new German Evangelical consciousness in America was a seminary, begun in 1850 at Marthasville, Missouri, and later moved to Webster Groves and renamed Eden Theological Seminary.[2]

The fourth president of this Evangelical seminary served from 1872 to 1879. His name was Karl Emil Otto (1837–1916).[3] The story of this immigrant clergyman, who was educated at the German university of Halle, illustrates how an immigrant church, loyal to German traditions, was able to maintain faith commitments in the face of rationalist intellectualism. It is a story of the struggle between the latest German critical biblical scholarship and a healthy religious pietism on the American frontier. Although Otto created a controversy involving parochial immigrant concerns, his life reveals the basically liberal characteristics of American German Evangelicals: a group that was unwilling to stay safely within narrow confessional limits, or to be restricted by fashionable theology and traditional institutionalism.

CONCERN FOR ORTHODOXY

In 1845 Philip Schaff, who had come to the German Reformed Seminary at Mercersburg, Pennsylvania, and who was also rooted in the same Prussian Union Church as Karl Emil Otto, had been unsuccessfully tried for heresy. He was accused of teaching a view of the Reformation that was too Catholic for his American Reformed audience.[4] The romantic German Mediating theology behind Schaff's teachings was also important to Otto. Karl Emil Otto, however, was more deeply involved with German historical critical scholarship than Schaff had been.

Karl Emil Otto was one of the first biblical scholars using German methods to be tried for heresy. Although he was unfavorably judged by the Evangelical Synod in 1880, the judgment did not permanently alienate Otto from the German Evangelical community. His story shows that German Evangelicals had a greater tolerance for German biblical scholarship than any other non-Unitarian American denomination at the time. The only groups in America that advocated more radical doctrines than Otto's were the Free Religious Association, formed out of Unitarianism in 1867, and the Society for Ethical Culture, begun in 1876 by Felix Adler as a reaction to narrow Judaism.[5]

Among liberal Protestants in the 1870s, conservatism dominated. Only the Congregationalists and Baptists, with their loose form of government, allowed liberal theology access to seminaries. Prof. Crawford H. Toy was forced to resign from the Southern Baptist Seminary at Louisville, Kentucky, in 1879 when his views seemed to impugn the plenary inspiration of scripture. The *Alabama Baptist* wrote: "The fortunes of the Kingdom of Jesus Christ are not dependent upon German born vagaries."[6] Toy had studied in Germany.

Andover Seminary clung to its Calvinistic creed until the 1890s. In 1891, Prof. Egbert G. Smyth, who had studied in Berlin and Halle in 1863, was able to have the Massachusetts Supreme Court overrule attempts to remove him for heresy from Andover in 1886.[7] Egbert's brother, Newman Smyth, who had also studied in Germany, was denied an Andover appointment in 1881 because of his opposition to eternal punishment.

In 1893 the celebrated Presbyterian heresy trial of Charles A. Briggs (Union Seminary) took place, resulting in his dismissal by the General Assembly.[8] A. C. McGiffert, a Marburg Ph.D. and Union colleague of Briggs, resigned from the Presbyterian ministry in 1900 to become a Congregationalist. H. Preserved Smith of Lane Seminary was dismissed from the Presbyterian ministry in 1892. All three had studied in Germany. Fundamentalism continued its hold over Presbyterians for another quarter century.

In 1904 a Methodist, Borden P. Bowne, was examined and acquitted of heresy at Boston University. And in 1906 Prof. Algernon S. Crapsey was deposed by the Episcopal Diocese of Western New York for not being creedally traditional.[9]

In retrospect, it is remarkable that a heresy trial regarding biblical criticism took place in 1880 at a remote German Evangelical Seminary in Missouri. This incident shows the sensitivity of the German Evangelicals to the latest scholarship and their capacity to handle controversy.

GERMAN ROOTS

Karl Emil Otto was born on January 7, 1837, in Mansfeld, Saxony, at the foot of the Harz Mountains.[10] His father, Karl Friedrich Otto, was headmaster of the school at Mansfeld where Martin Luther received his education. Soon after young Otto was confirmed at age fourteen, his father died. An older brother, who had already become a pastor, took charge of Otto's studies, preparing him for high school. For nearly six years Otto concentrated on ancient languages at the Saxon territorial Pforta school, where scholars spoke Latin in middle and upper classes. With the help of his brother, Otto enrolled in the University of Halle and studied there from 1857 to 1860.

At Halle, Otto studied with the notable Mediating theologians: August Tholuck in systematics, Julius "Sin" Mueller in biblical theology, and Hermann Hupfeld, in philology. Hupfeld's critical and philologically accurate method of studying Near Eastern languages was especially influential in forming young Otto's approach to biblical exegesis.[11] It is interesting to note that Prof. Heinrich Heppe, who prepared the way for the Wilhelm Herrmann-Rudolf Bultmann liberal tradition at the University of Marburg, had also studied (at Marburg) with Professors Mueller and Hupfeld.[12]

After Karl Emil Otto completed theology study and passed his first examination, he spent some years as a private tutor in a pastor's family and taught Latin to gifted students at the famous Francke Orphan's Institute at Halle. With his final examination Otto appeared to have a bright future as a theologian and pastor in Germany.

MISSIONARY TO AMERICA

In September 1864, however, Otto attended the Altenburg Kirchentag assembly. There he heard addresses by two American pastors from the Lutheran Wisconsin Synod and the Evangelical Synod in Missouri. Both spoke of the desperate need for well-trained theologians to minister to German immigrants on the American frontier. On the spot, Otto decided that he would go to America, if he could find a way. Before long he received a five-year appointment to the Wisconsin Synod from the Berlin

Missionary Society. He was sent to the Wisconsin Synod with the assurance that he could have a permanent position in Germany, if he should decide to return. In February 1865 Otto was ordained to the Evangelical ministry at Magdeburg, Germany.

Karl Emil Otto arrived in Milwaukee on April 29, 1865, where he was kindly received by Pastor Muehlhaeuser of the Wisconsin Synod. He was assigned to two Lutheran and one Reformed rural congregations in Dodge County, Wisconsin. In spite of primitive frontier conditions, Otto endeared himself to his people. He found, however, that the Wisconsin Synod, with its increasingly strenuous Lutheran confessionalism, was in conflict with his commitment to Evangelical unionism and a critical approach to scripture.

In a short time Otto became acquainted with the milder Evangelical Synod. The notable Evangelical traveling preacher Louis von Ragué persuaded him to travel to St. Louis in late 1865 to visit Pastor Louis Nollau, founder of the Evangelical *Kirchenverein*.[13] Nollau appreciated Otto's abilities and viewpoint and told him of a vacancy at St. Paul's Evangelical Church in Columbia, Illinois (across the river from St. Louis). Resigning from the Wisconsin Synod in 1866, Otto spent the next four years at Columbia, Illinois. He became an Evangelical minister in 1867 and married a relative from Germany, Amelia Otto, in the same year. They had seven children.

SEMINARY PROFESSOR AND PRESIDENT

By 1870 Otto's scholarship and pastoral gifts were well known, and he was called to a professorship at the Marthasville, Missouri, Evangelical Seminary. Otto had barely arrived at Marthasville in July when he learned of the sudden death of the school's forty-seven-year-old president, Andreas Irion.[14] When Irion's successor, Johann Bank, resigned in 1873, after little more than a year, because of ill health, Karl Emil Otto, at age thirty-eight, became president of the institution.

Under Otto's leadership a new educational spirit was introduced. Irion had powerfully represented the practical and old orthodox spirit of the mission houses, whereas Otto, less comfortably for the synod, taught the critical theology of the German universities. Irion had been a mission-institute Pietist,

70

teaching theology as a deep-going mystic; Otto was a critical theologian. Irion represented Wuerttemberg pietism, combining childlike religious feeling with a speculative spirit; Otto, on the contrary, was a North German, a believing Christian but less pietistic. Through his schooling he had been trained in historical-critical research, leading to positive results. Otto's strength lay in exegesis. He taught dogmatics, but it was not his main field. His greatest love was Old and, especially, New Testament exegesis.[15]

In 1873 the seminary and denomination started a new journal, the *Theologische Zeitschrift*. Already in March of that year Otto published the first of three installments on "The Exegesis of Romans 5:12–19." His intention was to acquaint members of the synod with what he was teaching. The articles were well received, and Otto was chosen editor in 1877.

Otto's difficulties did not come from his students. He possessed outstanding teaching abilities that aroused enthusiasm. The students had not previously heard such deep-going exegesis. Irion had presented the deep thought contents of biblical concepts; but Otto controlled Greek as if it were his basic language. He was able to contribute not only philological enlightenment, but also what his contemporaries called "the nutritious bread of living scriptural thought."[16] Moreover, Otto led his students into developing their own abilities to think and become earnest researchers themselves, thus reaching the highest goal of a teacher.

In 1879 Otto's popularity with students resulted in a student strike against the other seminary professor, K.J. Zimmermann, who appeared inadequate by comparison. As a result, Zimmermann resigned and Otto gave up the presidency but remained as professor. Twenty-two of the twenty-six strikers later returned. Louis F. Haeberle became president, showing tact and firmness until his retirement in 1902.

Meanwhile the students began telling their home pastors about the theological viewpoint of their favorite professor. Many pastors were startled. The old beliefs were no longer being taught at the seminary. The leader of the opposition was retired seminary president Johann Bank. Bank and his friends wrote a formal letter to the seminary board demanding that Otto's teachings be investigated. They referred to Otto's 1873–74 articles and questioned whether his views on sin as the wages of death, original sin, and atonement and justification were biblical.

The board was not convinced. Early in 1880 it passed a resolution of confidence in Otto, asking him to continue teaching. It examined his dogmatics notes regarding the meaning of Christ's death and atonement, the death of humanity, the miracles of Christ, and the sacrifice of Isaac and found no problems.

In two resolutions the board fully supported Otto:

> (1) The Seminary Board has convinced itself that the doubts raised about Professor Otto's teaching have no basis in fact, and that therefore his further continuance at the seminary must be desired by the Board.
>
> (2) That Professor Otto shall be requested to forget what has happened and on the basis of strengthened confidence to continue his work with good cheer and courage.[17]

CENSURE

However, when four articles on the temptation story in Genesis 3 appeared in the *Theologische Zeitschrift* from May to August 1880, it became necessary to consider Otto's case at the fall synodical General Conference. Otto had not hesitated to have the articles published, even while he was being examined by the seminary board. He felt no need to seek the approval of any higher authority than his conscience.

Otto's symbolical method of scripture interpretation created a sensation among Evangelicals. At the September General Conference of the synod, the committee appointed to investigate his work declared that he had deviated from the synodical doctrinal position and demanded that he promise in the future to maintain true doctrine. Otto defended himself with dignity. He affirmed the basic confessions of the church and accepted the unconditional authority of scripture, but he insisted that a teacher be allowed latitude in interpretation. He questioned the competence of the synod to decide such matters.

By a vote of 47 to 9, however, the General Conference declared its lack of confidence in Otto. It also added a "Neological Paragraph" to the synodical Constitution, stating: "We must decidedly repudiate any neological [new] method of teaching and explanation of the scriptures, and insist firmly that in our seminary the Christian doctrine is presented in the manner of the positive believing direction, as it is done in the Evangelical Church of Germany."[18]

Otto had no alternative but to resign his professorship, as well as his membership in the synod. He became pastor of a non-synodical Evangelical Church in Darmstadt, Illinois, where he served until 1887. By 1885, however, Otto renewed his affiliation with the Evangelical Synod with no malice. Already in 1883 the St. Louis Evangelical publishing house issued Otto's 268-page *Bibelstudien fuer die gebildete Gemeinde (Exposition of Romans for Educated Congregational Members)*. It included a twenty-nine-page appendix exegeting the Genesis 3 temptation passage.[19] In 1887 Mennonites from Kansas invited Otto to teach in their preparatory school at Halstead, Kansas. But after only a year, Otto accepted the pastorate of an Evangelical church at Eyota, Minnesota, serving from 1888 to 1890.

APPRECIATION

In 1890 Otto accepted a call to become professor of ancient languages and history at Elmhurst College, Illinois. For fourteen years thereafter he prepared students to enter the Marthasville Seminary from Elmhurst. Samuel D. Press, later president of Eden Seminary, noted with pride that his immigrant father, Gottlob Press, had studied under Otto in 1874 and "stood by Otto after his dismissal, remaining loyal to him to the end." In turn, Sam Press studied under Otto at Elmhurst, saying of him:

> The only truly academically trained member of the Elmhurst faculty at that time was Prof. Emil Otto, an outstanding scholar, a man of unimpeachable character. . . . The mainstay of the curriculum at Elmhurst for me were the four years of Latin and the three years of Greek with Prof. Otto. His excellent lectures were too advanced for most of his students.[20]

Otto's teaching at Elmhurst included deep-going lectures on world history and German literature. In 1898 he published a story for young people about an American lad who was kidnapped in Connecticut during the American Revolution, an unusual theme for a German immigrant theologian![21] He also published a fictional history from ancient times, *The Bride from Damascus*, set in the Greek Orthodox Church of A.D. 633.[22] In 1897 he produced a 137-page German-language history of the life of George Washington, noting both Washington's success as a military commander and leader and his willingness to give up power and go back to civilian life. This may have reflected Otto's own renunciations as a theologian.[23]

Otto retired from teaching in 1904. For the rest of his life he struggled with defective hearing and the illnesses and deaths of his wife and eldest son. He returned to Columbia, Illinois, where he died in 1916 at the age of nearly eighty. Those twelve years as emeritus professor were active years, filled with preaching chores and regular writing for the *Theologische Zeitschrift*. The announcement of his death in that journal was followed by one of his own articles, "The Meaning of the Old Testament for Christian Preaching," written shortly before his death. The previous issue contained two Otto articles on "American Idealism" and an exegesis of Colossians 1:24.[24]

At the funeral Eden Seminary president William Becker used the text, "He that overcometh shall inherit all things" (Rev. 21:7, *King James Version*). Otto had overcome what he called his "catastrophe." Carl E. Schneider, Evangelical historian, wrote later: "In calmer moments it became apparent that the action [of the synod's excommunicating Otto] had been too hasty. Otto was vindicated not only by posterity but by many of his contemporaries, and never again was the question of confessional orthodoxy made the issue of serious discussion by any General Conference."[25]

OTTO'S METHOD

Otto's exegesis approached Paul critically. He believed that a great assignment had been given to proclaim the gospel, "to pave the way for a Christian unity of the faith between those who are influenced and those who are not influenced by the so-called modern view of the world." Paul needed to be brought nearer to the Christian church by a manner of interpretation that would "explain Paul purely out of himself, uninfluenced by the authority of doctrinal tradition."[26]

Otto discussed the origins of sin and its consequences by examining Paul and the dogmatic traditions. In exegeting Romans, Otto wrote with Protestant fervor:

> If we now compare verse 3:22 "Through faith in Jesus Christ for all who believe," with 1:17, "Through faith for faith," and combine these, then we have Paul's trilogy: Out of faith (God's faith), through faith (Christ's faith), to faith (the new mankind's faith), and the doxology concerning the depths of the richness, the wisdom, and the knowledge of God (11:33), which doxology refers to the perfection of the work of redemption; then we have essentially a substantiation of our interpretation.[27]

But Otto's lengthy discussion of the doctrine of the atonement bordered on heresy:

> Because God cannot forgive sins without a vicarious death, . . . therefore he himself had to finally furnish the perfect offering, which was to bear vicariously the suffering of punishment for all mankind. That God did by presenting Christ as the atonement offering. . . . One can tell at once by this "orthodox" interpretation, that it is not derived from exegesis, but from dogmatics. One would hardly have found this explanation in these two verses (Rom. 3:25–26), if one had not had beforehand this interpretation. And where did one get it? Not from the Bible, but from Scholasticism. . . . The theory of the atonement goes back in the first place to Anselm's attempt to construe the revealed content of the revealed truth about faith by the means available to human reason. This background should serve warning not to identify the outcome of this theory immediately with revealed truth itself.[28]

Even more sensational than his work on Paul were Otto's articles on the study of the Genesis temptation story (Genesis 3). He reviewed different types of exegesis (allegorical, literal, dogmatical, and theosophical), showing reasons for rejecting them all. His was a symbolic interpretation: "The tree of life is not actually a fruit tree; the tree of knowledge is not actually a tree; then too no serpent actually appeared. The appearance of the serpent symbolizes the fact that just that made itself felt which is symbolized by this picture." Otto argued that the serpent was a natural being, created by God as every other creature. It was not a creature of Satan. There was no trace that the serpent had its cunning from anywhere else except from God. "The serpent symbolizes the power that resides in nature and entices to evil. This power is not yet morally bad in itself." It is a power that dare not gain influence over humanity, if we do not want to become morally bad.[29] Otto supported a feminist interpretation of the fall: "The fact that the serpent approaches the woman first is generally associated with the greater lack of self-control and the greater temptability of the woman. But actually it rather points to the connection of the sinful fall with the sex relationship only to the extent that the sex discretion occurs earlier with the woman than with the man."[30]

Otto's basic point was that the story of the fall points to sin as grave disobedience to God. The tree, the serpent, and the conversations are merely a shell. Otto was concerned with practical teaching, recognizing two ways to grasp offered truths, either in the form of abstract truth or in the form of a graphic story. He did not believe that they needed to contend against each other as if they were enemies. Those who cannot yet free themselves from the story form to grasp the moral truths should stay with this form so that they will not lose the content of the same. But those who have the duty to impart religious truth to their times and companions should get clear in their minds concerning this truth.[31]

Nor did Otto pit science and faith against each other as enemies:

> The Scriptures should not be interpreted according to the demands of the natural sciences, but according to the Scriptures themselves. Exegesis must simply seek to find that which the Scripture passage intends to say. If it should happen that the passage should represent conceptions which are impossible to reconcile with scientific findings, then there will still be time to decide in favor of which side of the respective collision one might choose to stand.[32]

THE EVANGELICAL MIX

The synodical case against Otto rejected his statement that he was not asking for recognition of a "liberal interpretation," but of the "neological" (modern) method of exegeting scripture.

Such an argument, however, was in keeping with the confessional stance of the Evangelical Synod. Its 1848 confessional statement affirms

> the Scriptures as the Word of God and as the sole and infallible rule of faith and life, and accepts the interpretation of the Holy Scriptures as given in the symbolic books of the Lutheran and the Reformed Church, the most important being the Augsburg Confession, Luther's and the Heidelberg Catechism, in so far as they agree. But where they disagree, we adhere strictly to the passages of Holy Scriptures bearing on the subject, and avail ourselves of the liberty of conscience prevailing in the Evangelical Church.[33]

The confessional statement revealed the unionist confessional spirit of the Evangelicals, which allowed choice between Lutheran and Reformed confessions, while at the same time affirming the priority of scripture and appealing to individual conscience on points of disagreement. Although it could be criticized as contradictory, the paragraph nicely combined liberal individualism with conservative scriptural authority. Highly trained scholars leaned toward autonomy of conscience, while ordinary pastors and church members, grounded in conservative pietistic views, favored traditional scriptural authority.

Although Otto followed the confessional tradition of his predecessors, William Binner, Andreas Irion, and Adolph Baltzer, he did so with greater discernment, penetrating to more daring conclusions. Building on his excellent German theological training, Otto affirmed the authority of Holy Scripture without question. However, he also considered himself better qualified than many others to distinguish between favored interpretations of texts and their actual meanings. He insisted that the meaning "which according to my best knowledge is the meaning of Scripture constitutes for me the norm for my teaching."[34]

The censure of Karl Emil Otto at the 1880 synodical conference centered on what constitutes Evangelical freedom. Maintaining that he espoused scientific, theological truth, Otto urged that the synod could accept his position without fear of drifting from doctrinal moorings. Indeed, the contrast between

77

an orthodox and a more liberal position, which he admitted he held, was wholesome for the church. On the basis of the confessional paragraph, he demanded recognition and equal rights for both.

At the time the irenic spirit of the Evangelicals was overcome by fear of the dangers of "neology." When the vote went against Otto, he was dismissed from the synod. More orthodox Evangelicals tried to prevent any other professors with his views from becoming seminary professors. Yet Otto was not repudiated as a person, or as a teacher, although he was never invited back to teach at the seminary.

"Americanization" was a crucial issue for non-English-speaking believers, and the wave of the future for Evangelicals was on the side of Americanization. As early as 1874, when Otto was president at Marthasville, he had proposed that students who completed their work with honors at "Eden" should be sent to an English-speaking college or theological seminary for further work.[35] Conservatives responded that it would be far better for them to attend German universities. Yet Otto's flexibility on language issues was consistent with his critical and forward-looking theological views.

As the years went by, it was Otto's approach to scriptural authority, learning, individual conscience, and willingness to allow missionary-like accommodation to American life that prevailed in the Evangelical Synod. By the time of Otto's death in 1916, onetime student Samuel D. Press said of Otto that "not only his theology was Christocentric, but also his life."

Press expressed the prevailing Evangelical spirit when he went on to say:

> Professor Otto holds a distinctive place in our Synod. Through Otto's intellectual talents, God presented our Church with one of his richest gifts. . . . Otto was an untiring searcher for truth. . . . Completely unpartisan, Otto had the courage to present his theological positions freely and openly, without concern for personal consequences. . . . What a tragedy that our Church robbed itself of the services of such an outstanding theological servant! Nevertheless, this noble person continued to serve the Church faithfully until the end of his life.[36]

The little-known heresy trial of Karl Emil Otto before the Evangelical Synod in 1880 presents a unique example of theological leadership and the struggle for denominational identity on the American scene. The small German Evangelical denomination made an initial mistake but went on to recover its identity and its ability to grow amid struggle. Karl Emil Otto and the Evangelical Synod show how sound biblical criticism and flexible churchly pietism learned to live together.

WOMEN'S MISSION STRUCTURES AND THE AMERICAN BOARD

Priscilla Stuckey-Kauffman

DURING THE EARLY nineteenth century American Protestants sprang into missionary action, sending workers to countries around the world. Women played a significant role in this missions revolution. They organized local groups called auxiliaries to collect money and volunteers for a burgeoning foreign missions movement. Women's auxiliaries, however, worked under the supervision of the general church boards run by men.

WOMEN'S BOARDS ORGANIZED

After 1850, women organized mission societies that operated independent from male-led denominational boards. In each of five major Protestant denominations[1] women set up mission boards to channel resources specifically toward women and children in other countries. Women believed that the Christian gospel would improve the status of foreign women.

Congregational women led the movement toward indepen-

Priscilla Stuckey-Kauffman received her Master of Arts degree from Pacific School of Religion in 1985. This chapter is a condensation of her thesis. She is a Mennonite.

dent women's mission societies. Between 1868 and 1873 they set up four boards: the Woman's Board of Missions, located in Boston (WBM), the Woman's Board of Missions of the Interior, located in Chicago (WBMI), the Woman's Board of Missions for the Pacific, located in San Francisco (WBMP), and the Woman's Board of Missions for the Pacific Islands, located in Hawaii (WBMPI). The three mainland boards cooperated with the male-led American Board of Commissioners for Foreign Missions.[2] The women's boards chose their missionaries and raised the money to support them. The American Board then commissioned them, arranged for living situations, and supervised their work. Women missionaries were responsible in part to the American Board, but the women's boards remained structurally independent of the American Board and retained control over the money they raised. Directors of the women's boards viewed the relationship with the American Board as a cooperative, rather than a supervisory one.[3]

At the time of organization the women's boards set strict governing principles. Funds raised one year were not disbursed until the next year, thus avoiding unforeseen deficits. Only single women were employed as missionaries. Married women, working with their husbands, came under the jurisdiction of the American Board.

The women organized themselves into a system of boards, branches, and auxiliaries to educate local women in foreign missions and to secure funds. Boards were regional entities that covered several states and directed the activities of the branches organized along state lines. Local auxiliaries, the backbone of the organization, carried on missions study projects and raised money. They sent money to the branches, and the branches passed it on to the boards. The regional boards then applied the money to missions projects and dealt directly with the American Board. The women's boards' system of organization was recognized as extraordinarily effective in raising money, and its success was attributed to the close communication between the boards and local constituencies.[4]

By 1877, in nine years of existence, the Boston-based WBM (the largest of the women's boards) raised nearly $480,000 and published more than 40 million pages of missionary literature. Volunteer labor kept administrative expenses under 2 percent of board receipts over the same nine years. By 1918, after fifty years of independent work, the receipts of the three mainland boards (WBM, WBMI, and WBMP) totaled 20 percent of all the receipts of the American Board over twice as many years.[5]

The women's boards also increased the number of missionary recruits. In 1920 the American Board commissioned a new high of seventy-three persons for missionary service. Of this number, forty-seven were single women, nine married women; and seventeen were men. Of eight physicians, five were women.[6]

After fifty years of vigorous work the women's boards had made significant contributions to Congregational missions. They increased total missions receipts by thorough fund-raising efforts and low overhead costs. They supplied the majority of missionaries in the field and took full responsibility for financing them. Their fund-raising methods were highly personalized and recognized as models for the whole denomination. The system of women's boards cooperating with, yet remaining independent from, the American Board was an organizational success. It made possible women's contribution to the work of the denomination, without sacrificing the special concern women held to direct their resources toward other women.

In 1927 this cooperative venture came to an end. One by one the three mainland women's boards voted to merge their organizations into that of the American Board. Why did women in the 1920s choose to relinquish their autonomy? What persuaded them to allow their boards to be absorbed into the American Board, when the existing cooperative relationship seemed to work so well?

The full story of the absorption involves the relationship of the women's boards and the American Board in the 1920s, and the larger context of Congregational polity. Changes in American religion and society also influenced women to choose a unified mission endeavor with the American Board.

MOVEMENT TOWARD CONSOLIDATION

Independent women's mission boards in the post-Civil War era always felt pressure to consolidate with existing male-led societies. Women struggled against assumptions that they were not capable of running an organization, since "the idea of their conducting a business, keeping books, or carrying on the work of a large organization was unheard of." Opposition to women assuming public roles was common. The notion that women would speak or pray in public "just like any other minister" challenged traditional sex roles. Men feared that the women's missionary movement was a thinly veiled suffrage campaign. Women feared disapproving husbands and the taint of impropriety.[7] Some women's boards succumbed to these pressures and were taken over by the men.[8]

Despite early and continued opposition, women's boards were recognized as making valuable contributions to mission work. Women developed administrative techniques that appealed to their constituency of women and children. Requesting small amounts of money (because women did not have access to large sums), women's boards canvassed regularly and extensively. They enjoyed huge financial successes.[9]

Full treasuries spurred new rounds of opposition from male church leaders. Some feared that women's agencies would take over money available for mission work. Others complained that women collected their money at the expense of denominational treasuries. Both allegations had little basis in fact. Women continued to contribute to *all* mission boards, not simply women's groups. Women argued that they had tapped a source of funds not reached before: women's purses.[10] Yet pressures to absorb women into male-led structures mounted in the early decades of the twentieth century. By 1930 most major Protestant groups had effected such mergers. In some cases women participated in the decisions, in others women's organizations were simply confiscated.[11]

As Congregational leaders formulated plans to consolidate mission boards in the 1920s, the assumption that men should take rightful leadership over women exerted a subtle influence. Women made up only a small percentage of ordained clergy or membership on national committees. A commission investigating the 1.2 percent female clergy in Congregationalism reported in 1921: "Our ordained women are too few in number and too modest or at least inconspicuous in their form of service to appear at present to offer to our denomination any serious problem." It heartily endorsed women serving instead as church assistants in religious education, secretarial jobs, and social work. The report shows that in the early 1920s substantial feeling existed against women exercising full and independent leadership among Congregationalists.[12]

Yet the absorption of the women's boards by the American Board cannot be fully explained as the triumph of male dominance. Many factors influenced the final decisions. An examination of the broader context of American society and religion provides further clues.

THE IDEAL OF BUREAUCRATIC EFFICIENCY

Historians consider 1895 to 1915 the Progressive Era in American history. The period was characterized by reforms in many areas, from government policies to religious and social life. Reformers were driven by an unquestioned faith in "scientific" problem solving, which to Progressives meant dependence on bureaucratic solutions. The catchword was *efficiency*. Efficiency reigned when professional leaders headed well-organized structures that achieved clearly defined results.

Because organizations valued efficiency, certain patterns of decision making resulted. Progressives tended to centralize decision making nationally, rather than allow it to remain diffused in local, state, and regional bodies. Within the church this meant that denominational executives began to view administrative offices as the true center of the church's life. Legislative bodies, by contrast, were crude and cumbersome. Denominations followed the business community and moved toward a bureaucratic style of church government.[13]

Bureaucratic values of efficiency and centralization resulted in new fund-raising techniques. Mission and benevolent societies had proliferated during the nineteenth-century Protestant missions boom. By the twentieth century churches complained about the financial strain placed on them through duplicated giving and tried to centralize fund-raising systems. The "Apportionment Plan" and "Every Member Canvass" were two widely adopted schemes for increasing benevolent giving. Under the Apportionment Plan, mission agencies cooperated in assigning a quota to each church in a denomination. Motivated by a goal, local congregations increased their giving and enlarged the income of the agencies. Funds were collected through the Every Member Canvass, a local annual fund drive in which canvassers secured pledges from members door to door in a one-day campaign. These new fund-raising methods called for the cooperation of all mission agencies in a given denomination. They were carried out systematically and with the businesslike efficiency so highly prized during the Progressive Era.

CENTRALIZATION AND CONGREGATIONALISM

Congregationalists participated in the Progressive movement toward centralized decision making and unified fund raising. But forces toward centralization had already existed for many years within Congregationalism. During the nineteenth century Congregational churches had built stronger associations with one another, culminating in 1871 with the organization of the National Council of Congregational Churches. The National Council was an advisory body without administrative powers. It was established to foster the unity of the churches without endangering their individual liberty. Its constitution decreed, "This National Council shall never exercise legislative or judicial authority, nor consent to act as a council of reference."[14]

One of the reasons a national organization had been formed related to the number of Congregational mission agencies. By the 1870s Congregational churches were contributing to five agencies alongside the American Board and the three women's boards: the Education Society, for training ministers; the Congregational Home Missionary Society; the American Missionary Association, for ministry to people of color; and two publishing societies. To reduce the financial burdens placed on churches by these agencies, in 1871 the National Council made the first of many recommendations to consolidate mission and benevolent societies. However, the loyalty of individual mission board constituencies made such a move unthinkable.[15]

By 1907 the National Council had increased the scope of its jurisdiction and functioned as an administrative, as well as advisory, body. Again, a committee investigating the situation recommended that the mission boards and churches avail themselves of the National Council's services as a central clearinghouse. However, the independent spirits of the mission agencies prevented them from agreeing.[16]

Recommendations that mission boards should connect themselves more closely to the National Council reflected growing tensions between the churches and mission societies. The churches viewed the mission boards as a threat to the democracy of Congregational polity. Mission boards had been established by individuals, rather than by representative groups from the churches. This tension was heightened by dissatisfaction over the financial askings of the boards. It confirmed the need felt by the churches for centralized fund raising.[17]

By 1913 Congregationalism took steps to integrate the mission boards into centralized denominational structures. The National Council adopted an Apportionment Plan and promoted the Every Member Canvass to simplify mission board appeals to local churches. A national committee, called the Commission on Missions (COM), brought together National Council appointees and mission board representatives to suggest a national missions budget. Local churches were informed of the suggested dollar amount to be raised each year. This new centralized system won many supporters, including members of women's boards. The treasurer of the WBMP lauded it as "a systematic plan for the co-operative, not competitive distribution of all funds. . . . Congregationalism united in purpose, effort, and giving."[18]

MISSIONARY PRESSURE

Pressure to merge mission boards came from directions other than the churches and the National Council. The first group to suggest the consolidation of the women's boards with the American Board was a missionary group in China. The Council of the North China mission station, in their 1920 annual meeting, recommended "that the American Board and the three Woman's Boards be combined in a single organization which will assure a more unified and efficient administration of foreign missionary interests both in the United States and upon mission fields, and secure a larger recognition and more adequate support for woman's work."

Missionaries observed that the American divisions, besides

causing administrative problems, were difficult for the Chinese to understand. Noting that "at this time . . . so many former methods of organization are being overhauled and reorganized and made to give account of themselves and their reasons for existence throughout the world," the missionaries urged the American Board and women's boards to discuss merger at their next annual meeting.[19]

Initially the American Board expressed surprise at the North China vote and assured the women that it considered the missionaries' action "rather beyond their jurisdiction." The American Board left the women free to close the issue at this point. The women discussed the matter briefly and then dropped it. The seeds of consolidation had been planted, however, by missionaries—the very people the mission boards existed to support.[20]

COOPERATION

Throughout the 1920s momentum toward merging mission societies increased. The various mission agencies cooperated more fully, led by the women's boards. In 1921 the three mainland women's boards, feeling that their administrative work overlapped and sometimes conflicted, formed a cooperative council to unify procedures and advise the separate boards. The women chose a cooperative council as a middle way between the extremes of merging into one body, or functioning on a case-by-case basis. The women demonstrated their preference for greater cooperation but did not destroy individual board identity through merger.[21]

As the women's foreign mission boards increased cooperation among themselves, they also began to break down the boundary between foreign and home mission work. Among Congregationalists, the two activities had been carried on by separate and sometimes rival boards. Each board had its own independent structure, so that local auxiliaries of the women's foreign mission boards existed alongside local auxiliaries to the home mission boards. In the late 1800s women in the Far West had integrated some home and foreign mission board activities, planning joint projects and sometimes even sharing state officers. The women preferred cooperation to consolidation, pooling efforts but retaining individual board identities. Western women took pride and pleasure in cooperation, noting that they were pointing the way for the rest of American Congregationalism. "It may be that the Pacific Coast is destined to demonstrate the feasibility and desirability of closer relationships along these lines," commented the WBMP secretary.[22]

While Congregational women cooperated freely among themselves, especially in the Far West, tensions increased in the relationship of the women's boards to the American Board. Male decision makers were reluctant to open the door to women's participation. In January 1921 the Woman's Boards' Council voted to ask the Prudential Committee (executive committee of the American Board) if a representative of the women's boards might sit with them. But it was not until ten months later that an invitation actually appeared. In October, Letitia Thomas Evans, chair of the Woman's Boards' Council, reported with some asperity to the WBMP president, "I am going to be in Boston for the Prudential Committee meeting on the 25th, in response to the *first* of its 'frequent invitations to attend one or another of its meetings.' " She reported some trepidation before the meeting:

> I feel that history is in the making and I am experiencing a "thrill" at the thought of being a part of it. I trust the realization will be as full of thrill. I am afraid I will have stage fright and that my brain will not function in the presence of this conservative, august body. It will take some time before we can expect to win the confidence of the members but I will be as quiet and humble and receptive, as I can be on occasions!! That always makes a hit with men!![23]

Apparently it did, because cooperation between the women and the men intensified. By 1923 the three Woman's Boards and the American Board were discussing the corporate membership of women on the American Board.[24]

The American Board was not alone in opening its proceedings to women. The Commission on Missions, the overseeing committee from the National Council and the mission boards, had always included a few women. It was intended to be a representative body.[25] However, no woman served on its executive committee. At the end of 1921 the executive committee invited one secretary from each missionary and benevolent society to participate in its meetings, without vote. The three women's boards together were allowed one representative. It was a meager gain, but a real one.[26]

At the same time the American Board and the women's boards moved toward cooperation in another venture—publication. Before 1922 each of the four foreign boards published independent periodicals. The American Board's *Missionary Herald* was the oldest and carried the largest circulation. In 1922, in the interests of unifying foreign missions activities in the churches, the women's boards merged their publications into the *Missionary Herald*. They did so reluctantly, since it meant losing a special means of communication with their constituency. The minutes of the WBMP note that they discontinued publishing the *Bulletin* only for the sake of "playing fair with the other Boards who are giving up their magazines."[27] In the *Missionary Herald* each women's board was given a small number of pages each month and editorial representation. An article in the first issue revealed what had prompted the new joint venture:

> Beyond question it is a right step forward, an adjustment that meets the temper of the times; that makes for consolidation and co-operation, and that recognizes the entire and united life of the churches that are behind the enterprise. . . . The call is to get together, to move forward in step, to rally all the forces for a more adequate advance.[28]

The "temper of the times" calling for cooperation and efficiency made such a move necessary.

CONSOLIDATION

While Congregational women worked for greater *cooperation* among mission boards, national Congregational leadership explored the *consolidation* of the boards. In January 1923 Charles E. Burton, secretary of the National Council and ex officio general secretary of the Commission on Missions, presented a proposal to the COM that accelerated the process of consolidation. Referred to as "Dr. Burton's Plan," the proposal called for making the Commission on Missions the central and sole fundraising agency for all benevolent and mission societies. Burton thought that the Apportionment Plan failed to solve the problem of mission board competition for funds. As many as eleven societies appeared on the list of apportionments every year—boards for foreign missions, home missions, church extension, education, plus the three women's boards. The Apportionment Plan had centrally organized fund-raising, but it did not address the problem of multiple requests for contributions. Burton proposed that the Commission on Missions become the central promotional agency.

Women responded promptly and negatively to Burton's proposal. The Woman's Boards' Council wrote in February 1923 that it favored cooperation but opposed a central promotional agency, since it would have a "disastrous" effect on the work of the women's boards. The women's boards would have to sacrifice more for the proposed system than either the American Board or any of the home mission societies because the women's boards had their own promotional system. Under Burton's plan for unified promotion the state branches—the intermediate agencies between local auxiliaries and the regional boards—would cease to exist. This would eliminate the boards' primary channel of communication with local women. In addition, since supporters of women's boards contributed twice to missions—once to the general church fund and once to their own mission projects—the women warned that Burton's plan would eliminate independent giving and decrease funds available for women's mission work.[29]

As a result of discussion raised by Burton's plan, in 1924–25 the Commission on Missions took steps to consolidate the mission societies. It appointed a Committee of Twelve (including four women) to investigate the possibilities of merging. The committee was asked to set guidelines to help the church spend money "in a way that produces the largest results for the Kingdom; one that will bear the closest scrutiny of keen-minded businessmen; one that the new generation, used to cooperation, will not be impatient of on account of an unnecessary number of organizations."[30] The times had changed; Congregationalists, emphasizing businesslike efficiency, could no longer tolerate wasted money or multiple agencies. A "new generation" had grown up during the Progressive Era that demanded new church structures.

The Committee of Twelve reported back to the Commission on Missions in January 1925, recommending the reorganization of mission societies into four boards: (1) foreign missions (consolidating the women's boards with the American Board); (2) home missions (consolidating women's groups into churchwide agencies); (3) education; and (4) ministerial pensions. Each of the four new boards would be composed of "not less than one third women." The committee asked all mission and benevolent societies to group themselves into the four categories, to study the possibilities for merging and present proposals for consolidation to the committee. The women's boards and the American Board were instructed to work out their consolidation so that "the splendid effectiveness of the Woman's Boards as educational and collecting agencies be not impaired."[31]

The mission boards responded in various ways to this radical proposal. The home mission societies strongly resisted the idea of merging. But the foreign boards, although wary of losing their independence, agreed to consider consolidation. The Woman's Boards' Council met with the American Board Cabinet in February 1925 for a three-day conference to formulate a merger proposal.

The resulting "Tentative Plan"[32] was a carefully considered and highly specific outline for consolidation. It listed eight stipulations drawn up by the Woman's Boards' Council. The women's boards would agree to consolidate on two conditions: if the women's home missions unions merged with the male-led homeland societies, and if the Prudential Committee (executive committee) and the corporate membership of the American Board included at least one third women.

Following these stipulations the boards outlined the structure of the merged organization. Women were given one third of the membership on all committees. Fifteen of the forty-five directors would be women, as well as seven of the twenty members of the Prudential Committee. Women would make up one third of the corporate members at large. Women would hold at least one third of the departmental secretary posts. In some departments that plan called for near parity of men and women officers.

Appended to the detailed outline was a statement by the

women discussing the advantages and disadvantages of consolidation. The statement provides clues to their attitudes toward consolidation. The women agreed that the first advantage of the new arrangement would be eliminating confusion in the churches by merging the homeland societies as well as the foreign boards. The women's insistence that the home missions societies merge indicates that the women's boards did not want to be alone in sacrificing their independence. The women acknowledged that now that mission work for women was integrated into the system of church benevolences (by way of the Apportionment Plan), there was less need for separate women's collecting agencies. Foreign missionaries would approve of simpler methods of promotion and administration. They believed that younger women would support the integrating of men and women in organizational life. Finally, they indicated that women's participation might improve the quality of administration, especially if women's efficient methods were used by the whole organization instead of only by the women's part of it.

On the one hand, all the advantages listed by the women benefited the women's boards themselves only indirectly. Major beneficiaries were the *constituencies* of the women's boards—missionaries, local churches, and the denomination as a whole.

Disadvantages, on the other hand, affected the women's boards and the whole denomination. In the new structure women might lose their sense of ownership of mission work without a separate budget and the close working relationships cultivated by the women's boards. Alongside this danger lay the possibility that if women entered the mainstream, men would no longer do their share.

Other disadvantages listed by the women show keen insight into administrative procedure. They feared that reorganization would decrease the level of giving for the period of readjustment. They felt that "a larger organization with more machinery" would not be more efficient, as the national leadership believed, but less effective. They suspected that reducing the number of administrators could diminish efficiency in the long run, since a corporate sense of ownership would be harder to maintain. They also opposed increasing the centralized power of the Commission on Missions, fearing that mission boards would lose autonomy.

After the hard work of hammering out a plan acceptable to both the Woman's Boards' Council and the American Board Cabinet, the "Tentative Plan" was circulated to each of the women's boards and the full American Board. Each of the three women's boards carefully reviewed the document and in April 1925 approved the substance of it.[33]

BETRAYAL

In May 1925 the American Board and the women's boards reported their findings to the Committee of Twelve. However, the document presented was not the carefully outlined "Tentative Plan," but a more general statement drawn up by the Prudential Committee of the American Board. It seems that the Prudential Committee had unilaterally decided it was unnecessary to go into such detail in the report to the Committee of Twelve. At the last minute they had discarded the "Tentative Plan" and had drawn up an alternative and less detailed summary of agreement among the boards. The boards had barely enough time to review the document before reporting back to the Committee of Twelve.

The new document, the "Report to the Committee on Missionary Organization,"[34] was less attentive to women's concerns than the "Tentative Plan." It did not list the women's eight stipulations regarding merger (although some of them were incorporated in a list of five conditions at the end). It did not discuss advantages and disadvantages, as did the first document. The "Tentative Plan" had specified the numbers of women and men to be elected to each office, approaching parity. The new report avoided detail.

Despite these changes, the women's boards accepted the new document as necessary for coming to agreement with the American Board. They trusted the Prudential Committee's word on the appropriateness of the statement because they had to report to the Committee of Twelve in less than three weeks. Helen B. Calder, secretary of the Woman's Boards' Council, mailed the statement to the women's boards for approval. "I hope you can have time for unhurried consideration of this proposal," she wrote. "We do not want to approve of anything because the time is short, but it is important that we have a united statement to present, and that may mean for all of us some compromises."[35] The compromising done with the revised statement fell heavily on the women.

Although all three women's boards approved the new report on time, when Calder and a representative from the American Board met with the Committee of Twelve, they reported that opposition to the merger was growing on their boards. The American Board felt that plans for consolidation were being forced. They thought present levels of cooperation with the women's boards were adequate. Calder reported fears that the new organization might lose the distinctive efficiency of women's work. She added that women who supported a merger felt that the reluctance of the men would keep the process from working. Calder later said, "I testified to the unselfish attitude of all the women who have discussed the matter, expressing my conviction that they have been considering it with the thought in mind of the best good of the work, not of maintaining their own organizations."[36]

Eight days after the meeting with the Committee of Twelve, Letitia Evans, chair of the Woman's Boards' Council, wrote to Helen Calder of the Boston Woman's Board. She voiced her discouragement with the process of consolidation. "More and more I realize that our men, even the friendliest, have to travel a long long way before they include women in their thinking."[37]

During the summer of 1925, before the National Council meeting in October when the Committee of Twelve would make its final proposal, the women's boards considered pros and cons of consolidation. The discussion in the Woman's Board of Missions for the Pacific provides clues to the attitudes of the women toward merger.

Letitia Evans, former president of the WBMP, traveled from Boston to take part in WBMP discussion. She reported that the Prudential Committee of the American Board "was not at all keen to take women on its board. It would mean losing members that the secretaries feel they cannot lose." She advised refusing to merge unless the women's home missionary groups also merged with the homeland societies. She said that in a merger, the mission societies would come more directly under the National Council, and she did not want this to happen to the women's boards, if the home missions women retained their independence. "If we merge with the American Board we come under the National Council; cannot lift a finger unless the National Council let us do it. If the Home Boards do not merge, the [Woman's Home Missionary] Federation is a free lance."[38]

Evans' principal opponent was Mrs. J. H. Lash. Lash was president of the Southern California Women's Missionary Society, a group resulting from the merger of the WBMP branch and the corresponding women's home missions union. Because of the happy cooperation experienced between home and foreign missions women in her district, Lash did not believe that confusion would be caused by merging foreign boards and not home societies. Further, Lash reported that to the rank-and-file women of southern California, consolidation meant only working for the full Congregational apportionment figure (instead of only the women's boards' share). Because they were already doing this, merging mission boards would not change activities on the local level. Lash concluded, "I am all for merger every time."[39]

The WBMP discussion highlights the differences between women at the national level and in local groups. National leaders of the women's boards tried to protect the rights of their boards, especially vis-à-vis the home societies. Women on the West Coast, especially the rank-and-file women, saw no need to compete with the home missions agencies, since a great deal of cooperation already existed. The national women's leaders, perhaps because of their awareness of and contact with prominent denominational leaders (most of whom were men), tried to protect the independence of their boards against encroachment by centralized bureaucracy. Local women, especially those in the Far West who seldom came into contact with the leaders located in the East, did not see the possible threats to their status and were less protective of their individual organizations.

FINAL APPROVAL

In October 1925 the Committee of Twelve reported to the National Council the results of its yearlong probe into merging benevolent societies. The final recommendation was even more radical than the fourfold consolidation it had proposed in January. It called for bringing all existing agencies together into two mission societies, one home and one foreign. When the home societies opposed this recommendation, it was modified to unify the home societies only at the level of boards of directors.[40]

The American Board and the women's boards, however, were challenged to consolidate completely. A new Prudential Committee would include "at least one-third women," who "should be co-ordinate with the men in every respect as an integral part of the management, in order that the values of the Boards may be conserved." Women were to be considered as departmental secretaries. However, the proposal retained local women's auxiliaries, "existing because of the basic fact that many more women than men have free time for church work." This rather patronizing comment, added to the proposal after discussion by the National Council, showed how the council assumed that women would continue to do the majority of the work on the local level while holding a minority of official posts in the organization. The council also approved of the merger because it "would place the women unitedly back of all church interests and responsibilities instead of behind only part of them." There was an underlying fear on the part of national church leaders that if women were allowed to retain separate organizations, they would channel resources away from the national budget.[41]

The National Council approved the Committee of Twelve's proposal for complete consolidation of the women's boards with the American Board and the partial unification of home mission societies. Each mission board met separately to discuss the proposal, and within a year all had voted to accept them.[42] In November 1925 the WBM (Boston) and the WBMI (Chicago) voted to merge. The WBMP (San Francisco) waited until its annual meeting in September 1926.[43]

When that historic vote was cast . . . which made the Woman's Board of Missions for the Pacific one with the American Board, there was a finality about it similar to the feeling which possesses one upon handing in an examination paper. . . . This was the end of opportunity offered through the W.B.M.P. and the door was closed never to be reopened.

A brighter vision soon dispelled this disheartening

one. . . . These fifty-three years marked not the extent of life of the W.B.M.P., but instead a time of *sowing* whose resultant harvests should continue through years never-ending.[44]

The women acknowledged that contemporary trends toward streamlining organizations had influenced their decision. "The new movement is in the development of unity—all the boards coming together . . . men and women working side by side in the churches [and] national organizations. This spirit of unity is the adventure of the new day."[45]

Actual consolidation took effect on January 1, 1927, as each board began transferring funds to the new merged American Board. Each board retained a holding corporation to look after assets that could not be disbursed immediately.[46] The era of separate and independent Congregational women's mission boards came to an end.

IMPACT

Women's predictions about the disadvantages of consolidation proved accurate in the years after 1927. By 1929 income had decreased and the new American Board reported that "the merger has laid an extra burden upon the treasury of the American Board.[47]

The merger placed extra strain on all Congregational missions structures as they adjusted to new arrangements. The secretary of the National Council acknowledged that "without doubt some momentum was lost in turning aside for a little to repair the machinery."[48]

The lost momentum was never fully recovered. In fact, the "improved organization" never became satisfactory to the mission boards or to the denomination as a whole. By 1927 the Commission on Missions reported that eight mission boards had rescinded their 1925 votes to approve unification. Furthermore, the Commission on Missions, a prime mover behind the plan to consolidate mission boards, lost favor because the boards continued to mistrust centralized authority. A new Missions Council took its place, composed entirely of mission board members.[49]

Women working for missions suffered a serious loss of morale. By 1939 the treasurer of one of the women's boards' holding companies wrote sadly to the American Board treasurer; "Another Board year is ending. For us it is almost as if it had not been, for we have had only one or two small meeting[s] and no business of importance to transact."[50]

Although consolidation integrated the American Board, it did not guarantee women an equal voice in administrative affairs. Women gained only one third of the decision-making seats. Consequently, they were never able to exercise power greater than that of a sizable minority. If American Board decisions had been made by consensus, a ratio of one-third women might have represented a democratic settlement, since the financial portion related to women's work totaled about one third of the American Board.[51] Board decisions, however, were made by majority vote. Women did not have the ability to outvote male board members. The fact that women were legally guaranteed one third of the American Board seats, however, did have a positive influence in subsequent years.

WHY?

Why did the women agree to merge their independent boards into the American Board? Pressure from denominational leaders certainly influenced them, especially the Commission on Missions as an arm of the National Council. Yet under democratic Congregational polity the women's boards were free to depart from the wishes of national leadership, as did the home missions societies, who successfully resisted consolidation.

Male dominance over women in church leadership played a part. The American Board and the National Council were reluctant to admit women to men's committee meetings. The American Board unilaterally dismissed the "Tentative Plan" and substituted a document that was less sensitive to women's concerns. Finally, the American Board agreed to give women only one third of the positions in the new merged board. Had men seriously intended to bring women's agenda into the new structures, they would have agreed to full parity between men and women in all aspects of American Board management.

The Congregational women, however, did possess the right to

accept or refuse consolidation. What were their reasons for approving it?

In the first place, the women thought many of the circumstances that led to the formation of independent boards in the nineteenth century had changed. Women were beginning to be included in the decision making of the American Board. Women's concerns were no longer excluded from the missions budget. Through the Apportionment Plan women felt fully integrated into the denominational budget. In the minds of some women this nearly equaled consolidation.

In the second place, many missionaries requested consolidation. The women's boards took seriously the wishes of the people they existed to support.

Third, women were open to consolidation because of the changes taking place nationally in the status of women. The Nineteenth Amendment giving women the vote passed in 1920. Women, especially the younger generation of women, were eager to join the ecclesiastical mainstream. The era of separate organizations seemed over. Those who continued to prefer them appeared conservative in a new era of cooperation.

Finally, women were influenced by the American turn toward bureaucratic solutions for social and political problems. The nationwide emphasis on businesslike efficiency led Protestants—both men and women—to trust in organizational procedures for curing religious ills.

Yet ideal organizational life took different forms for Congregational men and women. National leaders (mostly men) pursued consolidation, whereas women preferred *cooperation* among separate organizations. The women celebrated cooperation because they believed it led to ecumenical and world unity. By working together peacefully with other women and men within the same denomination, they hoped to further the cause of world peace.[52] But they consistently drew back from centralized and consolidated organizations. In 1921 women chose to unify their three boards, not by creating a central structure, but by adding a joint council with advisory powers. In 1923 they opposed Burton's plan for a centralized promotional agency. Except for some women in the Far West who welcomed mergers, the women's boards favored cooperation but opposed consolidation. Yet, in the end, pressure from the central Congregational bureaucracy and women's desires to enter the mainstream of church and national life persuaded them to merge.

Unfortunately, consolidation did not accomplish the positive goals that Congregational leaders had promised. Rather, it reinforced trust in bureaucratic solutions, and it furthered a system of male-dominated leadership in the church. Women gave up autonomy, and their unique contributions to foreign missions strategy were lost. It was a high price to pay.

CHAPTER
6

RELIGIOUS JOURNALISM: A LEGACY FROM THE CHRISTIAN CHURCH

J. Martin Bailey

RELIGIOUS NEWSPAPERS AND magazines have played a formative role in the development of many American denominations. This was especially true among the Christian churches that eventually joined together to form the Christian denomination. The United Church of Christ draws a deep appreciation for the importance of communications in our contemporary world from this source. Newspapers, magazines, radio, television, film, and other audiovisual productions supported by the United Church Board for Homeland Ministries (e.g., United Church Press), and the news and public relations efforts of the Office of Communications are building a legacy deeply rooted in the history of the Christian denomination.

Although the publications of the Congregationalists, the Evangelical Synod of North America, and the Reformed Church in the United States were significant to denominational identity, especially certain German and Hungarian periodicals, the

J. Martin Bailey served from 1963 to 1982 as the editor of *United Church Herald* and *A.D.* He is the Associate General Secretary for Media and Member Services of the National Council of the Churches of Christ in the U.S.A.

power of religious journalism to shape and strengthen discipleship and community is exhibited most clearly among the Christians. As that denomination matured, the expectations of its publications changed, but the centrality of its journalistic witness remained extremely important.

THE FIRST RELIGIOUS NEWSPAPER

The earliest publication in the Christian tradition was *The Christian's Magazine*. It was first issued in 1805 from Portsmouth, New Hampshire, by Elder Elias Smith, soon after he decided to forsake his Baptist origins for Christian principles. Smith organized a Church of Christ in Portsmouth in 1803, "owning Him as their only Master, Lord and Lawgiver, and agreeing to consider themselves Christian without the addition of any unscriptural name." The same year Elder Abner Jones, another important Christian leader, visited Portsmouth. Smith later said that Jones was "the first free man he had ever met."

The Christian's Magazine, published quarterly, cost twelve and a half cents a copy, payable on delivery. As its editor, Smith held his pen in one hand and a battle-ax in the other. He used the journal to attack the established ministry of the church, criticizing powdered wigs and useless church paraphernalia.[1] He wrote on many subjects, "historical, doctrinal, experimental, practical and poetical." With the encouragement of friends, including a member of the U.S. Congress, he decided to publish a more frequent periodical in which to report religious events. On September 1, 1808, Elias Smith began publishing the *Herald of Gospel Liberty*, claiming that it was the first religious newspaper in the world.[2]

Smith published the paper from his house near Jeffrey Street in Portsmouth every other Thursday evening. He charged one dollar a year, exclusive of postage, fifty cents to be advanced when the first number was delivered and the other fifty cents when twenty-six numbers were delivered. He arranged for the four-page *Herald* to be "punctually forwarded to any part of the United States where conveyance is practicable."[3]

From the beginning, readers of the *Herald of Gospel Liberty* were primarily pastors and members of the Free Christian Churches in the New England states. They were pleased with the pioneering journal. Soon the model that Smith created was copied by others. His work was noted with pride throughout the Christian Church, when a century later an impressive leather-bound volume was published to mark *The Centennial of Religious Journalism*.[4] During the negotiations that led to the union with the Congregational Churches in 1931, Christian Church leader Warren H. Denison identified the publication of the "first religious newspaper in the world" as a major contribution of his church.[5] Today members of the United Church of Christ who know the heritage of the Christian Church speak of the *Herald of Gospel Liberty* with family pride.

The claim to be the first religious newspaper in the world is disputed. American Baptists, who trace their journalistic history back through *Missions* to the *Massachusetts Baptist Missionary Magazine*, which was launched in 1803, also make that claim. William B. Lipphard, editor of *Missions* for fifty years and executive secretary of the Associated Church Press, knew of "no other church publication on this continent or in Europe"— and therefore in the world—as old as *Missions*. Lipphard believed that UCC claims to pioneering journalism dated back to 1820 and the *Missionary Herald*, published by the American Board of Commissioners for Foreign Missions, now the United Church Board for World Ministries.[6] Because of this competition for the distinction of being first, the Christian Publishing House included Smith's *Christian Magazine* among the historical facts mentioned in a booklet printed sometime before 1931.[7]

THE THEME OF LIBERTY

The *Herald of Gospel Liberty* began out of a deep concern to nourish the new freedoms enjoyed by citizens of the young United States. The Constitution, with its Bill of Rights guaranteeing religious freedom, was fresh in the minds of thoughtful people. Yet, Smith noted, "it is not now a tyrannical government which deprives us of liberty; but the highly destructive principles of tyranny which remain in a good government." He quoted Isaac Wilbur, a member of Congress: "The people in this country are in general free, as to political matters; but in the things of religion, multitudes of them are apparently ignorant of what liberty is." The design of the *Herald of Gospel Liberty* was "to shew the *liberty* which belongs to [all], respects their duty to God, and each other." Smith had no doubt but that "many will be displeased at what may appear in this paper from time to time, unless they own that *right is equal among all.*"[8]

The idea for the newspaper had come originally from Smith's Congressional friend Isaac Wilbur. Wilbur offered Smith generous financial support for a publication dedicated to religious liberty. Although Smith's first *Magazine* had struggled financially, and he knew that costs for a weekly newspaper were high, the thirty-nine-year-old preacher-editor declined the support. Smith feared that his own "liberty of utterance" would be abridged and that his friend might be unpleasantly involved.

In the first 146 issues of the *Herald* Smith wrote fifty-three articles on "Liberty." He wrote forcefully about religious liberty—"what I long for all [people] to enjoy." He affirmed that he was "bound as a lover of [humanity] to instruct them, and teach them the nature of it, according to my ability and the opportunity given to me to do it." Within the first year of publication the three principles of the Christian Church were identified: "1st. No head over the church but Christ. 2d. No confession of faith, articles of religion, rubric, canons, creeds, etc., but the New Testament. 3d. No religious name but Christians." Smith insisted, on January 19, 1810, that "every Christian hath an equal right to the peaceable and constant possession of what he believes to be the truth contained in the Scriptures . . . even though his principles may, in many things, be contrary to what the Revered D. D.'s call Orthodoxy."[9]

Relentless in his opposition to religious despotism, Elias Smith hurled bitter invectives against church polities, clerical trappings, ministerial titles, ecclesiastical associations, hireling preachers, creeds, and all the "isms" that lead to religious tyranny. Although his editorial successor believed that the time had come "when arguments instead of censure, and entreaties instead of the scourge may do more for the cause of truth than a host of censures and volumes of invectives," Smith had firmly established that the editor of a religious journal was free to express his or her own opinion and select the articles and news for publication. This concept, frequently tested and continually reaffirmed, became the foundation for all periodicals issued by those denominations that later came together in the United Church of Christ.

For example, editors of the Congregational Christian journal *Advance* frequently wrote about church politics and often raised the hackles, as well as the eyebrows, of some subscribers. It was one thing to espouse a nonecclesiastical cause (such as the welfare of laboring persons, or the United Nations), but it was another to argue about an issue coming before the General Council (specifically, union negotiations with the Evangelical and Reformed Church).

After the United Church of Christ was formed and had begun publishing the *United Church Herald*, Douglas Horton wrote: "The *Herald* is the organ of the denomination, though its editorial policy, expressing the individuality in fellowship that runs all through the United Church, is wholly in the hands of the editor."[10] Obviously, each editor must test that principle, and only when the concept of freedom of the press has been affirmed in some practical way is the liberty of the gospel available to a responsible editor. As the *United Church News* comes of age its editorial freedom tests the principle once again.

SUPPORT FOR IDENTITY

In the early days, when a visit from an itinerant preacher was the event of the year and second-class mail was delayed because a postmaster wanted to read the magazines, church periodicals provided the bonding agent for most denominations. The *Herald of Gospel Liberty* facilitated communication between conventions, conferences, and boards.

> The proceedings of our general convention, local conferences and various boards would be known to a limited number only, were it not for this avenue of information. And the same is true for the fellowship of the church. The church paper brings the whole [community] into fellowship. . . . Then, too, it is the unifying force of the whole church, and as such directs the energy of the church toward one common denominational purpose.

Elias Smith, more than any other person, held the conservation and preservation of the church's prosperity.[11]

In 1834 the *Christian Herald* (as the *Herald of Gospel Liberty* came to be known) had trouble paying its bills. Christians in New England, however, were determined to preserve their journal. On the first day of the new year an assembly of preachers and others met in Hampton, New Hampshire, to organize the Eastern Christian Publishing Association. Under a new name, the *Christian Journal*, the old *Herald* still served the church. By 1851 the name was changed back and the *Herald of Gospel Liberty* took a motto welcomed throughout the church: "In necessary things, unity; in non-essentials, liberty; in all things, charity."[12]

Elsewhere in the Christian Church journalism thrived. In 1843 Christians in North Carolina selected D. W. Kerr as itinerant preacher (superintendent) and as editor of a paper known as the *Christian Sun*, begun in 1844. By 1850 the Christian General Book Association published a weekly *Christian Messenger* and a semimonthly *Christian Palladium*. When North Carolinians considered union with some of the northern churches, they spoke of the Christian churches connected with the *Palladium* and wrote to its editor. So important did the *Sun* become to churches throughout the Southern Conference that biographies of clergy published in P. J. Kernodle's *Lives of Christian Ministers* frequently included references to articles published in the paper. In the discursive style common at the turn of the century it was recorded that such and such a pastor was "a regular contributor to the church paper, which owing to the death of the editor, Elder D. W. Kerr, had been moved to Raleigh, North Carolina."[13]

Loyalty to the *Christian Sun* did not die with church mergers. Christians from the Southern Conference continued to subscribe to the *Sun* long after their church had united with the Congregationalists and even with the Evangelical and Reformed Church. Its weekly editions, edited by F. C. Lester, were replaced by the monthly newsletter of the Southern Conference of the UCC in 1965.

The *Herald of Gospel Liberty* gradually absorbed more than a dozen papers, including the *Gospel Herald*, founded in 1843 by the Ohio Christian Book Association. In January 1868 the offices of the *Herald of Gospel Liberty* moved to Dayton, Ohio, and the paper became the general denominational organ. Its most distinguished and energetic editor was Alva Martin Kerr, a man who suffered for forty years from an incurable bone disease. Kerr encouraged the Christian Church to look beyond its small size and struggle with important issues in the decade that followed World War I. His editorials and the articles he selected convinced people that the newspaper was the "greatest factor binding the people of the Christian Church as a fellowship."[14]

That conviction about the importance of a church journal led those who shaped the United Church of Christ to agree that the first agency of the new church should be its periodical, *United Church Herald*. In an introductory editorial Theodore C. Braun and Andrew Vance McCracken expressed their agreement that the "united journal must provide concrete, visible evidence that the United Church of Christ is in the process of becoming a reality." Historian Louis H. Gunnemann noted that "the birth of the *United Church Herald* was not only of symbolic importance but also proved to have immeasurable influence in giving the United Church a sense of unity and identity."[15]

In the early years editors were intentional about the selection of authors and news, believing that the pages of the magazine must introduce members of the new and larger church family to one another.

As the United Church of Christ discovered its identity in a courageous struggle for justice and peace, the *Herald* reflected and led churches in their response to the turbulence of the 1960s. The concern for identity was not lost in 1972, when the *Herald* and *Presbyterian Life* merged to form a unique ecumenical journal called *A.D.* A widely reprinted article by Oliver Powell described the United Church as a "Beautiful, Heady, Exasperating Mix."[16] One issue attempted to answer the question, "What does it mean to belong to the UCC?"[17] Another celebrated the twenty-fifth anniversary of the United Church of Christ.[18]

COMMITMENT TO UNITY

The identity of the Christian Church was closely tied to the goal of Christian unity. From its earliest editions the *Herald of Gospel Liberty* argued that the division of Christians was both weakness and sinful. In July 1840 the Rev. Ira Allen wrote in the *Christian Palladium:* "The principles upon which union is based are a matter of revelation, and not of human policy. It is not for Christians to say how, and for what purpose they will unite, for these things are fixed by a higher power. . . . Union is the *sine qua non* of the religion of Christ."[19]

When a hymn was written, to the tune of *America*, for the centennial of the founding of the *Herald*, its verses linked the paper and the cause of Christian unity:

> Our fathers' God, we raise
> To thee our hymn of praise
> For gospel light.
> It shines from sea to sea,
> Before it shadows flee,
> It sets the bondmen free
> From error's night.
>
> One hundred years have gone,
> The day begins to dawn
> When souls are free;
> The vision of the years,
> Delayed by doubts and fears,
> Within Thy church appears,
> Blest unity.
>
> Thou *Herald* of the right
> Long may the gospel light
> Illume thy page!
> For truth and unity,
> For love and liberty,
> May all thy witness be—
> From age to age.[20]

Alva Martin Kerr, longtime editor of the *Herald*, was a staunch advocate of Christian unity. In an editorial he wrote: "The door of the church has been made narrower than the gate of Heaven, and the church has cast out those whom Jesus received." After he addressed the Ohio Pastors Association in 1924, A Columbus newspaper reported: "Ministers from all over Ohio, many of them men of eloquence, listened enthralled for more than an hour last night while a little chap with the inspired logic of a prophet, condemned isolated denominationalism. . . . Crippled in body, he revealed to his listeners a flaming soul afire with the conviction that in union lies the true strength of the church."[21] It was no accident that the tradition of the *Herald of Gospel Liberty*, so committed to church union, merged with *The Congregationalist* in 1934 to form *Advance*. It was a step forward.

As the Congregational Christian Churches considered union with the Evangelical and Reformed Church, *Advance* editor John Scotford became a target of antimerger forces for his outspoken editorials and support for union. Malcolm K. Burton, a vigorous opponent of the merger, was named as part of a three-person "Forum on the Merger" in a 1947 issue of *Advance*. Burton stated that "the committee was appointed by the Executive Committee of the General Council in an effort to offset the one-sided treatment of the merger by the editor, Dr. John Scotford."[22]

Scotford's editorials built on the assumption that church union was part of the identity of the Congregational Christian Churches. In June 1948 he wrote:

We have prided ourselves upon being the most broad-minded, liberal, and progressive of American denominations. A proposition has been put before us which has been accepted by the other party and a majority of our churches and people. If we cannot unite with a church as reasonable, as gracious, and as Christian as the Evangelical and Reformed, what chances are there of reducing the divisions which plague Protestantism? The eyes of the world will be upon us at Oberlin; the hope of future unions depends on our decisions.[23]

This commitment to unity continued to shape UCC identity as defined in an August 1981 *A.D.* editorial. The editor wrote:

I hope that we will reclaim our ecumenical heritage and invest heavily in cooperative mission efforts. . . . We have turned inward during the last decade, feeling the need to build a United Church identity. . . . It is time to build on our new self-consciousness and to work selflessly for larger goals. I hope that we will use these years of conversation with the Christian Church (Disciples of Christ) to understand what it means to be a uniting church in the 80s. . . . We need to test with our Disciples friends how the Spirit is leading us to serve together. Perhaps our careful

work in the Consultation on Church Union will lead us to
an altogether new approach to unity.[24]

The '70s and '80s gave rise to a broader, if not altogether new,
approach to unity. It is not unity for the sake of unity, but unity
for the sake of mission and service. Describing "A Continuing
Search for Unity," on the occasion of the twenty-fifth anniversary of the UCC, Dorothy G. Berry quoted President Avery Post:
"United Churches have been created by God to birth the world's
new global people."[25]

ADVOCATE FOR JUSTICE

The quest for social justice and peace found expression in
many of the journals that are part of the history of the United
Church of Christ. When Elijah Shaw became editor of the *Christian Journal* in April 1835, he announced that "doctrinal subjects will find a place in our columns. Doctrine is the foundation of practice." During his editorship the paper was a
progressive advocate of measures "that promised success in
building the Redeemer's kingdom." The *Journal* was owned by
the Eastern Christian Publishing Association. It went to considerable lengths to prove that it was the successor to the *Herald of
Gospel Liberty* and, therefore, the oldest religious paper in the
nation. (The Association seemed especially eager to establish
seniority over the Congregational *Boston Recorder!*) In 1838 the
Association duly resolved "that the columns of the *Christian
Journal* be open for articles on the evils and sin of slavery, so far
as the same may involve the fundamental principles of morality
and religion."[26] Shaw, however, had not waited for the authorization of the Association. Soon after he became editor he
published an article that began: "We believe slavery to be a sin,
always, everywhere and only a sin."[27]

This subject was more difficult in the Southern Christian
Convention. In 1854, the year before he became editor of the
Christian Sun, William Brock Wellons withdrew from the
American Christian Convention over the issue of slavery. By
1862, with the Civil War pressing on Suffolk, North Carolina, he
had moved the editorial offices of the *Christian Sun* to Pe-
tersburg, Virginia. Shortly thereafter publication of the *Sun* was

suspended, and Wellons became editor of the *Army and Navy Messenger* and served as a chaplain.[28]

The most influential editor of Christian Church periodicals was Alva Martin Kerr, who edited the *Herald of Gospel Liberty* from 1919 to 1928. His editorials sparkled with his zeal for racial justice. He sought to substitute "human relations" for "industrial relations" and called for better immigration laws. Kerr was at his most eloquent, however, when he was writing about the search for peace and the need for a new international order. He appealed to his readers to support President Wilson's plan for a League of Nations. Opposition to the League was based on a theory that "God wants America to be superior, safer, and stronger than any other nation, instead of a little kinder so that others may love her and not fear her. If you start with the God of Christ," he wrote in an editorial, "you can predict nothing less than some kind of League of Nations." In one Christmas editorial he reminded his readers that Christ could never be the prince of peace to the nations until the spirit of national self-righteousness and self-seeking was destroyed. He believed that Christ could save society, and would enable the nations to practice a Christian internationalism.[29]

After 1934 the pages of *Advance*, building on Christian and Congregational traditions, frequently discussed race relations and an emerging concern for the institutionalization of social action. Under the editorship of Andrew Vance McCracken, *Advance*, and later *United Church Herald*, published articles by Herman Reissig, the international affairs specialist of the Council for Social Action. Many of the articles dealt with the role of the United Nations. During the years of the civil rights movement and the Vietnam war the pages of the *Herald*, and later *A.D.*, carried articles and editorials, along with letters to the editor, showing the commitment of the UCC to the "struggle for justice and peace." *A.D.* kept its UCC readers informed about the incarceration and ultimate release of Benjamin Chavis, a staff member of the Commission for Racial Justice who was falsely convicted on charges related to racial violence in Wilmington, North Carolina. *A.D.* highlighted the needs of women in society and helped the United Church see itself as more than the continuation of four Anglo-Saxon denominational traditions. Through its pages the UCC emerges as an inclusive church in which the heirs of African slaves and Native Americans, Hispanics and Asians, can take their place alongside the descendants of Europeans.

Social commitment continues to shine through the columns of the *United Church News*. UCC readers are pushed to understand "What might it mean to be a 'Just Peace Church'?"[30] or how church efforts to end apartheid in South Africa relate to investments.

THE LEGACY

In his booklet describing the founder of the *Herald of Gospel Liberty*, J. F. Burnett put a high value on the journals of the church.

> The religious newspaper ranks with churches, colleges, and philanthropies as an indispensable institution to Christian progress. None of these could live without the church paper. . . . The church paper brings the entire brotherhood into fellowship; and without it, such fellowship could not exist. . . . It is the unifying force of the whole church, and as such directs the energy of the church toward one common purpose.[31]

Although patterns of denominational life have changed in recent decades, there can be little doubt that church journals have contributed greatly to the style and identity of what is now the United Church of Christ. From our Christian beginnings we have a rich legacy.

PART TWO

Diversity

PHILIP WILLIAM OTTERBEIN AND THE UNITED BRETHREN

Thomas E. Dipko

DISCIPLESHIP REQUIRES MORE than "book" knowledge of the Christian faith. Although Christians in all times have agreed, in mid-eighteenth-century America people were especially agitated about the relationship of "experience" to their salvation. When a respected, scholarly pastor in the German Reformed community, Philip William Otterbein, announced that cognitive Christianity was deficient, he caused a stir. Otterbein declared:

> The question is not whether one has heard or learned something about Christ and his death, or whether one can talk about it, but whether one has experienced the death of Jesus Christ in the putting to death and riddance of the old man [woman]. . . . Consequently, if these things are yet strange to you, then your Christianity is merely appearance, imagination, shadow tricks.[1]

The candor and conviction of this graduate of Herborn Seminary, Nassau, Germany, who was devoted to the teachings of the

Thomas E. Dipko is Conference Minister and Executive of the Ohio Conference of the United Church of Christ.

Heidelberg Catechism, led his pious mother to say of his ministry, "My William will have to be a missionary; he is so frank, so open, so natural, so prophet-like."[2]

NURTURED IN GERMAN PIETISM

William and his twin sister, Anna Margaret, were born on June 3, 1726, in the town of Dillenberg, Germany. They were the fourth and fifth children of the seven sons and three daughters born to John Daniel and Wilhelmina Henrietta (Hoerlen) Otterbein. William's twin and one other sister died in infancy. One brother died at age twelve. William's grandfather, uncle, father, and five surviving brothers were all ordained ministers of the German Reformed Church. His surviving sister married a pastor, and four of his oldest brother's sons also entered the ordained ministry of the German Reformed Church.[3]

When John Daniel Otterbein died in 1742, Wilhelmina was concerned for her children's education and moved the family to Herborn. A theology school had been established there in 1584 by Count Johann VI of Nassau-Dillenberg. Its founding faculty included Caspar Olevianus, who, with Zacharias Ursinus of Heidelberg University, was a coauthor of the *Heidelberg Catechism*. In recognition of Wilhelmina's commitment to the education of her children, the Herborn faculty issued an official commendation in her honor.[4]

When the Otterbein brothers attended Herborn Seminary, it stood firmly within the Cocceian pietistic tradition that had been introduced in the 1670s.[5] According to this "Federal Theology," and in contrast to the predestinarian theology of John Calvin, human beings can make faith decisions in a manner that emphasizes freedom of will. "What God offers and what Christians need is an interiorly experienced faith relation which permits God to release his power in the continuing transformation of the believer's life."[6] Professors Arnoldi and Schramm, two of Philip William Otterbein's teachers, upheld federal theology. At Herborn Seminary their pietism was so congenial and ecumenical that the school's press published the popular Mennonite tract *Geistliches Lustgartlein* in 1787.[7]

Otterbein graduated from Herborn Seminary in 1748. He served as a private tutor until he received a call to serve as vicar of Ockersdorf in 1749. He was ordained June 13, 1749, and quickly introduced in his first parish some of the pietistic devotional practices taught at Herborn.

THE CALL TO AMERICA

Soon thereafter Otterbein responded to the appeal of Michael Schlatter, on behalf of the Synods of North and South Holland, for missionaries among German-speaking settlers in America. After satisfactorily completing the customary examinations at the Hague, Otterbein and five others set sail on April 15, 1752, reaching New York on July 27, 1752. The next day, in a gesture that demonstrates the ecumenical spirit of the time, Schlatter and the six missionaries met with Henry Melchior Muhlenberg, "the eminent pioneer missionary of the Lutheran Church." He greeted them with the words of Jesus: "Behold I send you forth as sheep in the midst of wolves; be ye therefore wise as serpents and harmless as doves."[8]

These ominous words of welcome reflect the spiritual situation of the time. Although the religious enthusiasm of the Great Awakening reached its full flower in the 1730s and 1740s, its influence had begun to wane by midcentury. Otterbein and his missionary colleagues faced a period of decline in the religious commitment of the diverse population. During the struggle for American independence and the Revolutionary War, "only about five percent (one in twenty) of the colonial population openly professed religious faith or admitted church relationship."[9]

As Otterbein began his ministry in Pennsylvania, the Coetus, under whose direction he labored and in whose ranks he held membership, was responsible to the Classis of Amsterdam and the Synods of North and South Holland. This arrangement continued until 1794, when the German Reformed Coetus of Pennsylvania became an independent synod. During this period of subordination to the Reformed Church in Holland, there were occasional disagreements between church authorities in Europe and the Coetus of Pennsylvania. The contention usually involved the proper authorization of ordination because the needs of the church in the colonial setting did not always correspond to established practices. On one occasion, in

117

1773, the Coetus apologized for proceeding with the ordination of several "preachers" before approval had arrived from Holland. The Coetus confessed: "All this was done before we received your fatherly warnings. From these we now learn that we acted hastily, and hereby ask, hoping for a favorable answer, your pardon of this hasty action by Coetus."[10]

The internal spiritual life of the Reformed Church reflected the general religious malaise of the time. A century after Otterbein's arrival in Pennsylvania, John Williamson Nevin looked back at the last half of the eighteenth century and lamented Otterbein's role in the founding of a new sect. However, Nevin added, "he was a good man who seems to have been driven into a false position by the cold, dead temper that he found generally prevalent in the regular church."[11]

LANCASTER AND THE RULES OF ORDER

Otterbein began his American ministry at Lancaster (1752–57). There he responded to the nominal Christianity of the day by insisting that "Rules of Order" be adopted by the congregation. This was deemed necessary to correct irregularities in the life of the parish and to ascertain "who they are that acknowledge themselves to be members of our church."[12] The Rules of Order introduced into the Lancaster Church pietistic practices similar to those that Otterbein had instituted at Ockersdorf. One of these practices was the expectation that each member have a private interview with the pastor before receiving the sacrament of Holy Communion. This practice was not alien to the German Reformed Church. In retrospect, church historians valued it highly: "Pity that the good custom has been suffered to sink out of sight. Its abandonment brought no blessing to the church at Lancaster."[13]

During his pastorate at Lancaster, Otterbein also underwent an experience akin to John Wesley's "special warming of the heart." Many years later when Francis Asbury, a well-known Methodist leader, asked, "By what means were you brought to the gospel of our God and Savior?" Otterbein responded, "By degrees was I brought to the knowledge of the truth, while I was at Lancaster."[14] This led Asbury to remember Otterbein as one who "had been sixty years a minister, fifty years a converted one."[15]

FRIENDSHIP WITH MARTIN BOEHM

Otterbein left the Lancaster Church in 1758, apparently disillusioned that the congregation did not achieve the spiritual growth he had envisioned. He intended to return to Germany that year but was prevented by the turmoil of the French and Indian War in America and the Seven Years' War in Europe. He agreed to supply the church at Tulpehocken, where he continued his emphasis on the personal experience of salvation.

In 1760 Otterbein accepted a call to the church at Frederick, Maryland. It was here that his pietistic zeal led to what has been called a "lock out." Otterbein was barred from preaching in the church and began to conduct the service from the cemetery. The morning ended happily, however, when the majority relented and the key-holder opened the door.[16]

While at Frederick, on April 19, 1762, Otterbein married Susan LeRoy, a woman of French Huguenot background. The marriage was short, however, owing to her death in 1768 at the age of thirty-two. They had no children and Otterbein never remarried.

Otterbein accepted a call to the church in York in 1765. Soon thereafter, probably on Pentecost Sunday in 1767, he attended a preaching assembly or "great meeting" at Isaac Long's barn northeast of Lancaster. After hearing a sermon by the Mennonite preacher Martin Boehm, Otterbein embraced him, greeting him with the words "We are brethren."[17] The close association between these two ministers led to the movement eventually called the United Brethren.

In April of 1770 Otterbein returned to Germany for a visit with his family. In Germany he told others about his experience at Lancaster and his renewed ministry. Georg Gottfried Otterbein, known in Germany for his pietistic interpretation of the *Heidelberg Catechism*, responded, "My dear William, we are now, blessed by the same Lord, not only brothers after the flesh, but also after the spirit. I also have experienced the same blessing."[18] Otterbein returned to York on October 1, 1771, continuing his ministry there until 1774.

BALTIMORE

In 1774 Otterbein received a call to the German Reformed Church in Baltimore, a church deeply troubled with division. Although the Coetus made every attempt to reconcile the parties in the congregation, all efforts failed. A minority faction had built a separate house of worship on Conway Street. They were served for a time by a Pastor Swope, who had recently come from Germany. Otterbein was originally invited to succeed him in 1772, but the Coetus disapproved. However, the new congregation persisted. Francis Asbury also urged Otterbein to accept the call. Finally, in 1774, Otterbein became pastor of the Conway Street church. Later he wrote to the church in Holland: "Finally, I consented because of their many solicitations, yet with the condition that the Coetus would give its approval."[19] In 1775 the Coetus reluctantly blessed the call with the words, "Coetus after mature deliberation deems it advisable for Dom. Otterbein to continue his ministry in the congregation at Baltimore. It appears from the report that his labours are blessed and the opposing party is becoming quiet."[20]

Although the spirit of the new congregation from the outset was independent, it strains the evidence to claim, as a United Brethren historian does, that "in the year 1774, . . . we find William Otterbein in the city of Baltimore, organizing a Church, separate and apart, in doctrine and disciplinary rules from the German Reformed Church."[21] Nevertheless, rebellion was evident. The manner in which the new church held its property, its reluctance to send delegates to the Coetus, its participation in the emerging pattern of "class" meetings in which the United Brethren and others shared, its strong insistence on the personal experience of salvation, and its provision for "preachers" to share in a ministry to other churches under the "superintendency" of William Otterbein were indicative of a local church that in some measure began to take on the features of a seminal local denomination.[22] After examining "The Constitution and Ordinances of the Evangelical Church of Baltimore," it has been argued that "the articles are not only complete in themselves, but they present, in discipline, doctrine, methods, and spirit the antithesis of features belonging to the Reformed Church."[23]

Otterbein, however, tried to remain faithful to the church of his heritage while at the same time responding in innovative ways to the spiritual needs of the people. In 1784 the Coetus belatedly recognized both congregations in Baltimore as separate churches with standing in the German Reformed Church.

In the same year that Otterbein went to Baltimore, the Pipe Creek meetings of the various classes in the United Brethren movement began to meet regularly and keep minutes. However, the rural and small classes of the Pipe Creek region looked on the classes in Otterbein's Baltimore church with some suspicion, indicating on one occasion that "those at Baltimore are at peace; but it is to be feared and guarded against, that with their good order and regular meetings they do not take the appearance for the reality."[24]

LIVING BETWEEN CHURCH AND MOVEMENT

From 1774 until his death in 1813, Otterbein attended many meetings of the Coetus and participated fully in gatherings of the United Brethren. During this time he also became a friend of Francis Asbury, sharing in his consecration as bishop of the Methodist Church in 1784. Otterbein, however, resisted overtures to introduce Methodist polity into the United Brethren movement, even after it was meeting in official Annual Conferences after 1800. Asbury praised him for his learning and piety but expressed disappointment that the United Brethren did not organize along Methodist lines. Asbury remarked one year before Otterbein's death:

> I pause here to indulge in reflections upon the past. Why was the German Reformation in the middle States, that sprang up with [Martin] Boehm, Otterbein and their helpers, not more perfect? . . . There was no master-spirit to rise up and organize and lead them. Some of the ministers located, and only added to their charge partial traveling labors; and all were independent. It remains to be proved whether a reformation, in any country, or under any circumstances, can be perpetuated without a well-directed itinerancy.[25]

It is important to remember that the very time when Asbury and the United Brethren were pressing for a new denomination, the Coetus of Pennsylvania was negotiating its independence from Holland. Autonomy was granted in 1794. The new status raised hopes in the German Reformed Church for a new chapter in its life, and Otterbein stood between two groups anticipating that new day. He provided leadership in the United Brethren movement with the understanding that it was an "unsectarian" endeavor.[26]

In fact, it was not long before the United Brethren began sounding in their gatherings very much like the Coetus with respect to matters of order and discipline. In 1789 the Coetus had reported to Holland that absenteeism was a problem. Otterbein was among the absent that year. The Coetus minutes read: "Since only a minority of the absent ministers had sent in excuses, it was resolved to require from these gentlemen, at next Coetus, a strict account of their conduct. Especially the excuse about serving other congregations at the time of Coetus, was declared invalid."[27] The minutes of the Annual Conference of the United Brethren in 1801 discuss the same problem. Action was taken to require that for the next Annual Conference, "whoever of the preachers cannot come shall write to the conference."[28]

As Otterbein and Boehm aged, new leadership arose among the United Brethren. Christian Newcomer, a Mennonite in his youth, became one of the early second-generation superintendents or bishops of the United Brethren. Unlike Otterbein, who never left the Reformed Church, and Boehm, who was expelled from the Mennonite Church, Newcomer left the Mennonite Church by choice. His *Journal* is a rich source of material concerning the organization and practices of the United Brethren. As Otterbein neared the end of his life, he was urged by some of the United Brethren to ordain Christian Newcomer as an elder. When Newcomer visited him for the last time in October of 1813, Otterbein agreed to the request but added, "I have always considered myself too unworthy to perform this solemn injunction of the Apostle, but now I perceive the necessity of doing so, before I shall be removed."[29]

Newcomer did not object to ordination but asked that two of his colleagues be ordained with him. And so it came to pass that on October 2, 1813, with the consent and participation of the vestry of Otterbein's church, and the assistance of William

Ryland, a minister of the Methodist Episcopal Church, Otterbein ordained elders for the United Brethren.

In this act some see Otterbein making a clean break with the German Reformed Church. Others believe that he was simply regularizing a ministry in a movement that now had an identity of its own. The fact remains that he is claimed with esteem by both the German Reformed Church and its successor, the United Church of Christ, and by the United Brethren, those continuing as a separate denomination and those who, as part of the Evangelical United Brethren Church, came into the United Methodist Church.

> In the typical language of the American church of his day Otterbein would probably have been known as a "New Light" in New England, similar in spirit to Jonathan Edwards, who just a few years before had been discharged from his pulpit in Northampton for his evangelical views. In Presbyterian circles, Otterbein would have been a "New Side" pastor stressing with the Tennents the necessity of both education and religious experience.[30]

At Otterbein's memorial service, held in his Baltimore church, Asbury said: "Forty years have I known the retiring modesty of this man of God: towering majestic above his fellows in his learning, wisdom and grace, yet seeking to be known only of God and the people of God."[31]

THE LEGACY OF OTTERBEIN AND THE UNITED BRETHREN

The United Church of Christ, at significant points, stands in the tradition of Otterbein and the United Brethren. His understanding of the church was covenantal without making a fetish of the term. His Rules of Order in Lancaster and the Constitution of his church in Baltimore are covenant documents that remind every baptized person in the community of faith that "membership" is more than ink on a church register. The importance of "classes" supports the participatory covenant community by providing weekly opportunities for Christians to assemble for prayer, personal sharing of faith journeys, and Bible study. Membership in the full congregation was a privilege prepared for by the nurture and discipline of the small church within the larger one, in the manner of the *collegia pietatis* of German pietism.

Otterbein's concern for vital Christianity within the local church did not cause Otterbein to ignore the larger bond of unity among Christians. Even his early Rules of Order at Lancaster were presented to the Coetus and approved in 1757.[32] When he prepared the Constitution for the church at Baltimore, he was deliberate in including in it the following reference:

> Persons wishing to commune with us at the Lord's Table, although they have not been members of our church, shall be admitted by consent of the Vestry, provided that nothing can be alleged against their walk of life; and more especially, when it is known that they are seeking their salvation.
>
> Forasmuch as the difference of people and denominations end in Christ,—(Romans 10:12, Colossians 3:11)— and availeth nothing in Him but a new creature—(Galatians 6:13–16)—it becomes our duty, according to the gospel, to commune with, and admit to the Lord's table, professors, to whatever order, or sort, of the Christian church they belong.[33]

These words do not represent an indifferentism to matters of polity, but a subordination of diversity in polity to the higher value of common life in Jesus Christ. They are consistent with Otterbein's view of classes in the local church and denominations in the larger church, as *ecclesiolae in ecclesia*, or little churches within the ecumenical church. In his preaching at the great meetings he often said, "I ask you not to leave your church; I only ask you to forsake your sins."[34]

This regard for oneness in Christ that takes precedence over ecclesiastical structures is evident in the language used by the United Brethren to describe themselves. They called themselves, with Otterbein in their midst, "the unsectarian [*unpartheiische*] preachers," dedicated to "preach untrammeled by sect to the honor of God and [the good of all]."[35] For Otterbein, faithfulness across denominational lines was urgent in an age when many within the churches were unregenerate. Otterbein's commitment to ecumenism "led him to participate in the 'unsectarian' meetings of the United Brethren in the hope that, the more pietism grew, the more the church would become one."[36]

Otterbein's relationship with the Coetus, the United Brethren, and the other denominations located in Pennsylvania and Maryland shows that "the Reformed Church has contributed its full share of effective ecumenists."[37] This is reflected in Otterbein's last days. On his deathbed he was ministered to by a Lutheran pastor, who joined with a Methodist minister to conduct his funeral two days later. His commital service was led by an Episcopal minister. Francis Asbury, a Methodist, preached his memorial service. Christian Newcomer remembered, "Here were ministers of different persuasions assembled to pay the last tribute of respect to this servant of the Most High,—Methodists, Brethren, Lutherans, Presbyterians, and Episcopalians— all mingled together to pay homage to [his] departed worth."[38]

Otterbein always held the *Heidelberg Catechism* in high regard. His rules in the Constitution of the Baltimore church specifically required that the pastor "catechize" the children and youth once a week. Although the *Heidelberg Catechism* was not specifically named, it informed Otterbein's teaching and preaching. At the end of his life he arranged to have most of his papers burned. However, the one sermon that remains is organized on the basis of the three-part outline of the *Heidelberg Catechism*. Concerning human sin, he stated: "For by nature we are in a desperate condition. We are without God and are children of wrath."[39] Concerning redemption, he wrote: "But just as fear arises from our sin, so also it ceases with the blotting out of the same. And that happens through Jesus Christ."[40] With respect to part three, human gratitude and obedience, he asked: "Has Jesus delivered you from sin? . . . Have you sat—and how long have you sat—weeping with Mary at the feet of Jesus? Which sin in you has been put to death by Jesus? Does Christ and his Spirit live and dwell in you? What good thing has grace wrought in you?"[41]

Otterbein's use of the *Heidelberg Catechism* demonstrated an irenic spirit that affirmed the place of human confessions and yet subordinated them to scripture and the informed conscience. In the language of the United Church of Christ, he saw the *Heidelberg Catechism* more as a "testimony" than as a "test." In the Constitution of the Baltimore church one finds that "no doctrinal standard outside the Bible, is . . . referred to. The Heidelberg Catechism while prized by Mr. Otterbein, was yet, doubtless, at this time, accepted by him as Wesley accepted the Thirty-Nine Articles—with the reserved liberty to modify and construe. He catechised rather than taught a catechism."[42]

Under the influence of the *Heidelberg Catechism*, Otterbein gave considerable attention to Christian education for persons of all ages. His brother Georg Otterbein was a champion of a sound psychology of education that sought to counter the rationalism of the age with concern for the affective nature of persons.[43] In all of Otterbein's ministry the parish parochial school and the Bible study that characterized the classes extended the privilege of church education to adults as well.[44] The United Brethren, with some initial dissent on the part of an anti-intellectual minority, recognized Otterbein's high regard for education by naming their first institution of higher learning Otterbein University.

The importance of the local congregation in Otterbein's thought also shows a special affinity with the United Church of Christ. Although he respected the Coetus, he shared fully in the decision of the Baltimore church to hold the title to its property separate from the Coetus. This eventually led to litigation between the Coetus and the Baltimore church in which a civil court decided in favor of the congregation.[45]

Otterbein's regard for the local church is also seen in his refusal to imitate the itinerancy system of the Methodists as a means to settle clergy. However, and despite Otterbein's personal views, the United Brethren later opted for the Methodist pattern. For Otterbein, itinerancy was a "voluntary" matter. There was a presbyterate among the "preachers" in the Pipe Creek meetings and the Annual Conferences, "but the primary governing power lies, according to Otterbein, in the local church."[46] Local churches could not agree on the scriptural warrant for membership lists; therefore, the decision was left to each local church. Preachers should "love one another" in spite of differing views on this issue.[47]

Otterbein was a moderate in doctrinal disputes. When confronted with those who wished to develop a schematic blueprint of the millennium, he would say: "Some of them believe that Christ will personally reign in his Church on earth a thousand years; but the best and most judicious divines do not believe that. And in this I agree with them."[48] To those who wished to make him an advocate of instantaneous conversion in opposition to growth in faith, he refuted the charge that he "ever preached that a person must be converted in a moment."[49] "God acts according to his free and unlimited power and wisdom, calling one directly, another indirectly; pulling some at once fully from destruction as a brand from the burning, while with others the work proceeds more slowly."[50]

Even his disagreement with Calvin on predestination was expressed with humility and sensitivity. He explained to synodal authorities in Holland,

> to tell the truth I cannot side with Calvin in this case. I believe that God is love and that he desires the welfare of all his creatures. I may be permitted to explain myself more clearly. I believe in election, but cannot persuade myself that God has absolutely and without condition predestined some to perdition.[51]

Otterbein pressed the issue of human responsibility in answer to what God has done in Christ for our salvation. He distinguished between the power of the cross to reconcile "God to us" and Christ's yet-to-be-"concluded" work of reconciling us to God. With an impassioned emphasis on the place of suffering in the Christian life, he admonished the hearer to bear Christ's cross so that the "mystery, Christ in us," may become the means whereby Christ concludes his saving work in each believer.[52] Although he spoke eloquently about the possibility of "sanctification," and the "assurance" that one "can know whether Christ has killed sin in him [her]," he also cautioned: "If anything does cost, then certainly this does, in terms of determination and effort. That is why we only seldom meet such [people] in Christ in our time."[53] Ottterbein had an optimism about human nature that did not adequately take into account the Reformation teaching of simul justus et peccator, but he also had a spiritual realism.[54]

Finally, Otterbein's view of the relation of the gospel to social issues was liberal for his time. When asked whether it was wise for a preacher to address political matters from the pulpit, he replied, "He that goes upon the sea will be tossed about by the waves, and whether he will get to shore, time must determine."[55] On other matters he was more direct. Although he smoked and used alcoholic beverages, he was firm in condemning excess and in calling an alcoholic friend to total abstinence.[56] He was opposed to the theater and once reasoned that the death of two relatives in a theater fire was a warning from God to others in the family and to the city of Baltimore that such entertainment was inappropriate for Christians.[57]

On the question of slavery, there is little evidence of Otterbein's views. However, in 1815, two years after his death, the United Brethren established a constitutional rule that read: "All slavery, in every sense of the word, is totally prohibited, and shall in no wise be tolerated in our Church."[58] Observers note that these early leaders of the United Brethren, "living in Maryland, a slave state—showed it no favor, neither did they make war with it, but guarded the Church against this sin of sins."[59]

On the question of gambling, Otterbein and his Baltimore church took the road of expediency. In 1789, when a new bell was needed for the steeple, funds were raised by a special lottery authorized by the Maryland legislature.[60]

Otterbein decided not to occupy the large manse built for him while he was in Baltimore. He chose to remain in the old four-room house and asked that the income from the manse be distributed to the poor.[61] Otterbein, like Asbury, did not aggressively address social problems in a manner we might value today. However, personal faith was judged meaningless if it did not bear the fruits of righteousness in daily life. "Together, they held that both irreligion and conventional religion imperiled true religion."[62]

Philip William Otterbein, although he was a charismatic leader of an evangelical movement that became a separate denomination, remained a minister of the German Reformed Church until his death. In the debate between United Brethren historians and German Reformed historians, both sides sometimes lose sight of the fact that this "scholarly pietist" wished to maintain "a double relation."[63] "Fault" is easily assigned to the person of conscience who wishes, in the Pauline sense, to be all things to all persons.

Looking back one asks: How comprehensive can any one denomination be? Was it really necessary for the United

Brethren movement to find a home outside the German Reformed Church? In their defensive response to "sectarianism," a term readily applied to any group that stretches the norms of the majority, denominations behave like sects and exclude those within their ranks who express the Christian faith with peculiar fervor. The wonder is not that Philip William Otterbein chose a "double relation," but that his choice so troubled others. History will bear him out that in the midst of the polemical debate, he was more an ecumenist than a schismatic.

In 1929 the United Brethren and the German Reformed Church, known as the Reformed Church in the United States, sought reconciliation in a united church, which would have included the Evangelical Synod of North America. Discussions proceeded to the extent of preparing a "Plan of Union" for the new denomination, "The United Church in America."[64] The "Plan of Union" was never adopted. However, it is evidence that the relationship between the United Brethren Church and the German Reformed Church had experienced God's healing grace.

The United Church of Christ, like the German Reformed Church of Otterbein's day, faces the question of how inclusive, how comprehensive, how catholic it can be. A review of Otterbein's "double relation" could help the UCC support those contemporary saints who, like Otterbein, wish to call the church to renewal and reform.

CHAPTER
8

JOHN WINEBRENNER: FROM GERMAN REFORMED ROOTS TO THE CHURCHES OF GOD

J. Harvey Gossard

JOHN WINEBRENNER WAS a German Reformed minister who founded a religious movement known as the Church of God.[1] In the 1820s, as pastor of the Salem German Reformed Church in Harrisburg, Pennsylvania, he came into conflict with the vestry over his use of New Measures revivalism and other issues. Eventually this dispute led to his dismissal by the vestry and his removal from the rolls of the Synod of the German Reformed Church. He developed new theological views about the Bible, the church, free will, baptism, the Lord's Supper, and foot washing that were in opposition to the beliefs of the German Reformed Church. In 1830 his followers officially organized, forming a denomination known as the Churches of God, General Conference.

J. Harvey Gossard is Associate Professor of Church History at Winebrenner Theological Seminary, Findlay, Ohio. He is an ordained minister in The Churches of God, General Conference. His wife, Barbara Chong, is part of a well-known Hawaiian UCC family.

In the 1840s he became an antagonist of John Williamson Nevin, a professor at the German Reformed seminary in Mercersburg, Pennsylvania. Winebrenner's activities, letters, and publications were among the precipitating factors that led Nevin to write *The Anxious Bench* and "The Sect System," two important early expressions of what became known as the Mercersburg Theology.

A study of Winebrenner's life reveals that, in addition to being a religious leader, he was an advocate of moral and social reform, a publisher, and a businessperson. His reform activities included antislavery, temperance, and peace.

EARLY LIFE AND MINISTRY

John Winebrenner was born March 25, 1797, in Frederick County, Maryland. He was baptized and confirmed in the Glades Valley Church, part of the Frederick County German Reformed circuit. His father, Philip, a second-generation German-American, wanted him to prepare for a career in business, law, or medicine. But John decided to follow the advice of his mother, Eve, a pious woman of Scotch and German ancestry, who encouraged him to pursue his interest in the ministry.

The German Reformed Church did not develop its own seminary until 1825, so John followed the common practice of persons wishing to enter its ministry and served an apprenticeship under a well-known pastor. After preparatory study at Dickinson College in Carlisle, Pennsylvania, he spent three years under the tutelage of Dr. Samuel Helffenstein Sr. of Philadelphia, a pastor who trained twenty-seven persons for the ministry. Helffenstein came from a prominent ministerial family. His father, three brothers, and three sons were all German Reformed pastors. Helffenstein was held in such respect by his peers that he was invited to become the professor of the proposed German Reformed seminary. He declined the invitation.

From Helffenstein, Winebrenner learned Latin, Greek, Hebrew, theology, and the practice of ministry. Like most German Reformed leaders in America in the early nineteenth century, Helffenstein held to a form of Reformed theology that was influenced more by Melanchthon and Zwingli than by strict Calvinism. The *Heidelberg Catechism*, not the Westminster

Confession, was the foundation of his faith. He also appreciated German pietism, which had widely affected all Pennsylvania religious groups with roots in the Palatinate, and encouraged his members to lead moral and pious lives.[2]

Winebrenner was influenced by Samuel Helffenstein's theological ideas and a form of ministry that stressed a warm, personal relationship with Christ. On Easter Sunday 1817 he underwent what he later described as a conversion experience, when "the 'Sun of Righteousness' arose, and shone upon my soul, 'with healing in his wings.'"

During his apprenticeship in Philadelphia a controversy over the use of the English language in worship came to a head in Helffenstein's Race Street Church (today known as Old First Reformed Church, United Church of Christ). A German party, who controlled the board, dismissed the pastor because he had promised those favoring English to conduct some services in that language. The board locked the doors of the church against him, forcing Helffenstein and those loyal to him to worship in the nearby parochial school. In a short time the court ordered the board to open the doors and recognize Helffenstein as their pastor. Six years later, when Winebrenner was locked out of his church in Harrisburg, he continued to hold services with those loyal to him at a nearby location. Winebrenner appealed his being locked out to church judicatories rather than to the court, but his refusal to compromise may well have been influenced by Helffenstein's example. Like his mentor, Winebrenner felt that, in the end, he would be vindicated and return in triumph to his church.[3]

Upon completing his studies in 1820 Winebrenner accepted the call to Harrisburg. This charge included the German Reformed church in the capital city of Pennsylvania, and three churches in nearby villages. His ministry went well during the first several years, and he proved to be a popular preacher in his congregations and in community interdenominational meetings. During his pastorate a new church building was erected for the Harrisburg congregation and a Sunday school established. (The building erected during Winebrenner's pastorate at the corner of Fourth and Chestnut Streets is still in use by Salem United Church of Christ.) Winebrenner also published a book, an abridged English translation of the *Heidelberg Cate-*

chism, which he used in instructing the young people of his congregations.

This happy relationship was shattered in the fall of 1822 when the vestry of the Harrisburg parish presented the synod with a document listing ten grievances against the pastor. It contained a list of complaints that Winebrenner had been using a number of practices, later called "New Measures," and associated with the Second Great Awakening revivals of Charles G. Finney. Specifically, Winebrenner was accused of holding

> prayer-meetings, denominated anxious meetings, where he divided the members into two classes—first, those that say they have experienced a change, and believe themselves to be Christians; and, secondly, the sinners, those who believe themselves to be mourning sinners. And during all prayer meetings he encourages groaning, thereby disturbing others who might, if the groaning were omitted, receive some benefit. Allows during prayer certain persons to respond "Amen! Amen!" thereby drawing the attention of the gazing crowd which usually collect on the outside.[4]

The most sensational allegation was that he kept an "experience meeting" going until four o'clock in the morning, at the conclusion of which he remarked: "This is the way to fan the chaff from the wheat." The document also charged that Winebrenner invited Methodists and ministers of other denominations to occupy the pulpit, that he worked independently and failed to consult the vestry, and that he was given to intemperate outbursts and derelictions of duty.

Winebrenner answered the charges during a seven-hour meeting with the vestry. He later published his account of that session in a pamphlet entitled *The Truth Made Known.* Winebrenner admitted that most of the actions he was accused of were true, but he denied that there was anything reprehensible about them. He saw nothing wrong with participating in the services of other denominations and holding experience meetings in his own congregation. In his view, the low state of spiritual life in the church and community justified extraordinary measures. However, he denied most of the inflammatory statements attributed to him, or claimed that they were taken out of context.

Much of the friction between vestry and pastor lay in different understandings of their roles. The vestry charged that Winebrenner usurped its responsibilities by admitting members or scheduling guest ministers without its approval. Members of the vestry were particularly upset when he invited the congregation to examine them as to their fitness for office before their installation. They believed that the election itself was all that was necessary for establishing their right to serve. The examination and installation constituted interference by the minister. Winebrenner, in turn, was dismayed that funds collected to pay his salary had been used by the vestry to pay other church debts, even though his pay was already significantly in arrears.

At the end of the meeting each side pledged to be more temperate in their treatment of each other and to seek harmonious solutions to their disagreements. The vestry asked Winebrenner to stop holding prayer meetings in local homes. He declined to do so, saying that many members desired the meetings, but he promised to maintain better order and decorum in all future experience meetings. The agreement was soon shattered, however, when Winebrenner invited a United Brethren minister to speak in his absence and one of the elders refused to allow the sexton to ring the bell or unlock the door. The church split over Winebrenner's use of extreme revivalistic techniques and the right of the vestry to control the actions and countermand the decisions of the pastor.[5]

CHURCH DISPUTE

Attempts at reconciling the dissident members and the pastor failed. In April of 1823 Winebrenner arrived at Salem German Reformed Church in Harrisburg and found the doors locked. Undaunted, he led the waiting crowd to the shore of the Susquehanna River and held a worship service. By 1824 the synod ordered the four churches on the circuit to hold elections to determine whether they wanted Winebrenner as their pastor. He won all four elections. Whereas he continued serving the three rural congregations, at the Harrisburg church his opponents refused to attend the election or recognize its results. They had called Albert Helffenstein, son of Samuel Helffenstein Sr., to be their pastor six months earlier.

Winebrenner continued to meet with members who were loyal to him at various locations in Harrisburg. Both sides appealed to denominational judicatories. This process was complicated by the fact that the Harrisburg church had been transferred to the newly formed Lebanon Classis, while Winebrenner still had ministerial standing in the Susquehanna Classis. The Lebanon Classis sided with the vestry, and the Susquehanna Classis with Winebrenner. The synod was called on to arbitrate the dispute. In 1825 the synod sustained the vestry's actions.

Soon thereafter, in 1826 and 1827, the three rural churches also dismissed Winebrenner as their pastor. Winebrenner became an itinerant minister, preaching in many small towns in central Pennsylvania. He also promoted and spoke at a number of camp meetings in the area. His activities continued to upset several German Reformed pastors and churches. Finally, in 1827, the Lebanon Classis requested the synod to expel Winebrenner, since he "rejects infant baptism, holds camp meetings and forces himself into other congregations."

In 1828, when Winebrenner failed to appear to defend himself before a committee appointed to investigate the charges, the synod accepted the recommendation that his name be dropped from the rolls.[6]

After the synod sided with the actions of the vestry and dismissed Winebrenner, his supporters decided to build a permanent house of worship of their own in Harrisburg. A modest building was erected on Mulberry Street in 1826, just two blocks from the German Reformed Church. During this period Winebrenner carried on a correspondence with members of Zion German Reformed Church in Hagerstown, Maryland. They were seeking a new pastor. Winebrenner was elected in January 1826 over two other candidates and continued to negotiate with the church as late as April. The salary offered and his reluctance to leave Harrisburg led him to decline the call.[7]

THEOLOGICAL CHANGE

By 1827 Winebrenner had begun a theological transformation that would have prevented him from staying with the German Reformed Church, even if other differences could have been resolved. Two points became central in his new theological position: first, the Bible is the "only authoritative rule for faith and practice"; and second, every Christian needs to have a personal conversion experience, or "new birth."

In American religious history these two emphases were held by a number of small Protestant groups that came into existence after the Revolution. The most widely known were those movements that became the Disciples of Christ and the Free Will Baptists. Many smaller groups also shared a desire to reinstitute principles of "primitive Christianity," as they discerned them in the scriptures, and a belief in the importance of being "born again." The stress on the individual in this theology was very much in keeping with the emphasis on individualism in American society and politics. The Disciples of Christ, the Free Will Baptists, the United Brethren, and the Evangelical Association expressed a common dissatisfaction with the traditions and spiritual life of churches rooted in Europe. These new groups wanted churches to be informal in worship, less strict in doctrine, and free of ecclesiastical control. They encouraged spontaneity and emotion in worship and stressed human responsibility and personal morality. They aggressively sought the conversion of the unchurched and held to a basic belief system that was simply stated but rigorously practiced. Thus Winebrenner stands among those people who sought to "Americanize" the church by returning to first principles and emphasizing the person over the institution.[8]

Generally speaking, most members of the German Reformed Church would have agreed with the two cardinal principles of John Winebrenner. They had been taught the Reformation principle that the scriptures were the "authoritative rule for faith and practice." They believed in the necessity of regeneration, and many of those who favored revivalism stressed the need for a definitive conversion experience. But in practice, Winebrenner interpreted these principles too narrowly for most German Reformed people. When he proclaimed the superiority of divine scriptures as the basis for faith and practice, he condemned the use of all "human creeds." As a result, he rejected the beloved doctrinal formulations of the German Reformed Church, including the *Heidelberg Catechism*. When he insisted on a conversion experience as the gateway to discipleship, he

136

rejected confirmation as the primary route to church membership.

Winebrenner also repudiated the doctrine of predestination. Most German Reformed in America were mild Calvinists. They maintained belief in God's election of persons for salvation. Winebrenner argued that God had given each person a free will, the capacity to accept or spurn God's offer of redemption. He readily accepted the label "Arminian" but was angered when his enemies called him "Pelagian," being quick to point out that regeneration was made possible by God's mercy, not by human ability.

The charges of the Lebanon Classis noted that Winebrenner questioned the doctrine of infant baptism. Winebrenner came to the conclusion that a personal conversion experience must precede this important act. Later he decided that immersion, not sprinkling or pouring, was the only proper mode. In 1830 he was rebaptized by that manner in the Susquehanna River by Jacob Erb, a minister in the United Brethren in Christ and coparticipant in area camp meetings. Through association with the United Brethren, Mennonites, and Dunkards in interdenominational revivals and camp meetings, Winebrenner reshaped his theology. He upheld believer's baptism and saw the Lord's Supper as a memorial meal, preferring to call both of these acts "Ordinances," not "Sacraments." Foot washing, which was also practiced by these groups at camp meetings, became a third ordinance. Winebrenner said that because baptism, the Lord's Supper, and foot washing were instituted and commanded by Christ, it was mandatory to observe them. However, they imparted no special grace in and of themselves.

In 1829 he summarized his new theology in *A Brief View of the Formation, Government and Discipline of the Church of God*. In this book he declared that the term "Church of God" was the only true scriptural name for both a local church and for the invisible church that was made up of all truly regenerated Christians. "New birth" was the sole requirement for initial membership in the church, and a godly life was the essential requirement for continued membership.

He condemned the practice of forming churches into "sectarian" denominations; however, his solution to the problem of denominationalism was vague. He did not urge all Christians to join his movement, or to combine into one large ecumenical group, as Count Zinzendorf did earlier with his "Congregation of God in the Spirit." Rather, he implied that every Christian body should reform itself by dropping human names and polity and restoring the use of biblical forms of church government.

By 1830 a number of congregations associated themselves with Winebrenner's views and felt the need to form some kind of formal association. After studying the Bible, Winebrenner asserted that the correct form of polity was neither the congregational pattern of the Mennonites and Dunkards, nor the episcopal system of the Methodists and United Brethren, but the presbyterian organization of the German Reformed Church. Each local church should have a "teaching elder" (the pastor) and one or more "ruling elders" (elected laypersons). Each year the teaching elders and the ruling elders ought to meet to conduct the affairs of the church at large. Therefore, in 1830, six elders met in Harrisburg for the purpose of establishing the first "General Eldership" of the Church of God. In time this organization became known as the East Pennsylvania Eldership. As Church of God pastors followed the population west, they established many new churches among the settlers. By Winebrenner's death in 1860, Church of God Elderships were found in Western Pennsylvania, Ohio, Indiana, Illinois, Michigan, Iowa, and Texas.[9]

REVIVALISM AND NEW MEASURES

Attitudes about the proper conduct of revivals of religion played an important part in German Reformed dissatisfaction with Winebrenner. Some German Reformed leaders were antagonistic toward Methodists and United Brethren, which in past years had taken away a number of their members. German Reformed people maintained a settled ministry and were especially wary of itinerant preachers, who came uninvited to local communities and caused disruption in established churches. Winebrenner's association with these groups was undesirable. His activities as an itinerant evangelist after 1826 were unacceptable.

But it was his methods that ultimately upset the vestry, the classis, and the synod, not the issue of revivalism. In fact, most

German Reformed pastors in Pennsylvania favored and held revivals. What upset Winebrenner's critics were the methods he used, techniques considered disruptive and excessive.

In the late eighteenth century a "German Revival" swept through German religious groups in the Middle Atlantic states. Rooted in German pietism and influenced by English-speaking groups, like the Methodists, the German Revival featured spirited preaching and an "experiential knowledge" of Christ. One feature of the German Revival was the practice of holding "big meetings" in which ministers from many denominations attracted large numbers of unchurched persons. These meetings stressed pious living and a personal relationship with Christ. They were conducted with a high degree of decorum. Preaching and prayer were emphasized, but no special techniques were used to identify or excite sinners to repentance.

German Reformed ministers and members participated in these revivals, along with Mennonites, Dunkards, Moravians, Lutherans, and Methodists. Two new religious bodies arose among German-Americans: the United Brethren in Christ and the Evangelical Association. Another German Reformed minister, Philip Otterbein, was closely associated with the founders of the United Brethren but never officially joined the denomination. Jacob Albright, a Lutheran layperson, spiritually awakened by the preaching of several German Reformed ministers, founded the Evangelical Association.[10]

By the 1820s many German Reformed people felt antipathy toward the "big meeting." They were ambivalent about association with Methodists, United Brethren, and other divisive groups. Stories about falling, jumping, and other disruptive behavior at frontier revivals, such as one at Cane Ridge, Kentucky, disturbed them. Nevertheless, they continued to promote revivals in their local churches, feeling that the state of religion was at a low ebb and that sinners needed to be converted.

The Helffenstein family leaders in the German Reformed Church of the early nineteenth century, had a favorable attitude toward revivals. J. C. Albertus Helffenstein, father of Samuel Sr., died while conducting a revival service. Jonathan Helffenstein, brother of Samuel Sr., held successful revivals while he was pastor of the Frederick, Maryland, circuit from 1811 to 1829. Samuel Jr., Albert, and Jacob Helffenstein, sons of Samuel Sr., all conducted revivals in their churches. The fact that the Harrisburg vestry replaced Winebrenner with Albert Helffenstein, a person known to favor revivals, indicates that their dissatisfaction with Winebrenner stemmed more from personal dislike than from an aversion to revivals.[11]

If revivals were so widely accepted, why were so many people upset with Winebrenner's promotion of them? Generally, they were not upset by his stress on the need for spiritual rebirth, but by his controversial methods. He used techniques that departed from the decorum of previous revivals—techniques later known as "New Measures." New Measures involved using protracted meetings to stimulate greater religious response, praying for sinners by name, allowing women to pray and speak in public, promoting "inquiry meetings" for persons under conviction of sin, and using exceptionally emotional preaching. The most controversial practice was the "anxious bench," designating a place in the church or camp meeting where those seeking a conversion experience went for special prayer and assistance.

New Measures are often associated with the revivals of Charles G. Finney, which began in the late 1820s. Reports of New Measures used in his campaigns in Upstate New York shocked traditional revivalists like Lyman Beecher and Asahel Nettleton. In 1827 they called a meeting at New Lebanon, New York, to question Finney about his methods and motives.[12] Finney always insisted that New Measures existed before his ministry, and that people attending his meetings instigated their use without his encouragement. The complaints against Winebrenner are examples of the use of New Measures before they were popularized by Finney.

Winebrenner's ministry in Harrisburg marked one of the first reported uses of New Measures in the German Reformed Church. In the 1820s the denomination was not ready to accept these innovations. However, by 1840 a large percentage of the ministers in the synod favored the use of such methods. A review of the pages of the German Reformed newspaper, The Weekly Messenger, in the late 1830s contains appreciative comments about revivals in which New Measures were used. Not all segments of the church looked with favor on these trends. Areas with large percentages of German-speaking members were generally unwilling to endorse them.[13]

An interesting illustration of the acceptance of New Measures revivalism by the German Reformed Church was a story about Samuel Helffenstein Sr. and Charles G. Finney. When Finney was invited to conduct a campaign in Philadelphia, he was offered the use of the German Reformed Church on Race Street, where Helffenstein was pastor. The congregation was so taken by Finney and the results of his methods that they forced Helffenstein to resign, so that they might secure the great evangelist as their pastor. Finney declined the offer, but a pastor with New Measures leanings was called.[14]

It is ironic that the denomination that had so severely criticized Winebrenner a few years earlier for his use of New Measures later moved to accept those same methods. Eventually, however, new forces gathered to call the German Reformed Church and Winebrenner to task for these practices.

JOHN WINEBRENNER AND JOHN NEVIN

John Winebrenner was a chief spokesperson for revivalism and the Americanization of the German Reformed Church. John Williamson Nevin became the chief critic of revivalism and an advocate for a return to traditional Reformed theology and practice. The encounter between Winebrenner and Nevin is an important chapter in the history of the Churches of God, General Conference, and the United Church of Christ.

Nevin was born near Shippensburg, Pennsylvania, in 1803. He was raised a Presbyterian, educated at Union College and Princeton Seminary, and served for a decade as a professor at Western Theological Seminary in Allegheny, Pennsylvania. In 1840 he was called to teach at the German Reformed seminary at Mercersburg, Pennsylvania. In concert with Frederick Rauch and Philip Schaff he developed the Mercersburg Theology.

On a philosophical level, this new theology tried to introduce the insights of German idealism to American Protestantism. On a practical level, it tried to replace the emphasis in American churches on individualism and revivalism with a view of the church and the sacraments that represented a return to the traditional confessional standards of the Reformed faith. German idealism is best illustrated by Nevin's The Mystical Presence (1846), which condemned spiritualistic, subjective, and memorial views of the Lord's Supper and urged an appreciation of the "spiritual real presence" in the Eucharist. A more practical contribution to Reformed theology is seen in Nevin's essays on The History and Genius of the Heidelberg Catechism, which he describes as the "crown and glory of the whole Protestant Reformation." Mercersburg theologians stressed the significance of the incarnation, the corporate nature of the church, and a high view of the sacraments. They stimulated liturgical renewal, leading in 1866 to a new Order of Worship for the German Reformed Church.[15]

In the August 10, 1842 issue of the Weekly Messenger, as part of an article on the Heidelberg Catechism, Nevin spoke out against Winebrenner and the Church of God, saying: "This latter sect especially glory in being the patrons of ignorance, rail at hireling ministers, encourage all sorts of fanatical unscriptural disorder in their worship, institute their own fancies and feelings in religion, for the calm deep power of faith. In doctrine they are of course pelagianistic." This statement, which probably described Nevin's view of all persons who stressed revivals, resulted in a series of ten letters between the two men. The first was written in August 1842 and the last in July 1843. Both Winebrenner's Gospel Publisher and Mercersburg's Weekly Messenger reprinted the correspondence.

Winebrenner quite naturally took offense at Nevin's characterization of his movement. He admitted the correctness of the charges that "groaning, crying, shouting, clapping of hands, jumping, falling down, etc." did take place in his meetings, and that women did pray in services in which men were present, but he denied that these things deserved to be called "fanatical." These were all secondary issues to Winebrenner; it was the "true conversion of soul" that was of primary importance.

Nevin was not satisfied with Winebrenner's defense and announced that he was going to "take up the subject of 'New Measures' in a separate publication, without direct reference to Mr. Winebrenner, or 'THE CHURCH,' commonly distinguished by his name. . . . I have prepared a tract according to this intimation which may be expected to appear under the title the ANXIOUS BENCH, in a few days."[16]

Nevin's pamphlet *The Anxious Bench* was one of the most renowned condemnations of New Measures revivalism ever published. It first appeared in 1843 but was followed the next year by a revised and enlarged edition. Nevin declined to specify which activities he was against but used the anxious bench as a symbol of the entire New Measures system. He contrasted the weaknesses of the "system of the bench" with the strengths of the "system of the catechism." He said the anxious bench promoted a vulgar, irreverent style of religion that was unfavorable to earnest piety and even discouraged the serious seeker of religion. Despite his promise not to mention Winebrenner and his movement, he specifically referred to the "spurious conversions" at Winebrennerian camp meetings. Nevin's consistent use of the term Winebrennerians must have especially irritated Winebrenner. Winebrenner spoke out against the use of human names for religious bodies and insisted that "Church of God" was the only bibical name for churches. Perhaps that was Nevin's intention.[17]

A lively debate followed the publication of the pamphlet. Many denominations, especially those of Pennsylvania German background, agreed or disagreed with the position taken by Nevin. Years passed before most of the German Reformed Church accepted Nevin's position. Revivals were still popular with clergy and laypersons in the German Reformed Church.

Winebrenner was indirectly the stimulus for another important statement by Nevin in 1849. In 1848 Winebrenner published a revised collection of essays on American denominations, first issued by I. D. Rupp in 1844. This widely distributed 600-page *History of All the Religious Denominations in the United States* was an impressive reference work. The advertisements spoke of its articles on fifty-three denominations and twenty-four engravings of "distinguished men in different denominations." Nevin made a two-part review of the book entitled "The Sect System," in which he lamented the number of "sects" that had arisen in the United States.[18]

Nevin was scandalized by the number of small religious groups that had splintered off larger denominations and held to narrow theological viewpoints. He satirically noted that most of these small groups claimed to have "no creed but the Bible." How could so many "sects" believe so firmly in the authority of the Bible and yet have so many differing opinions on what it said? The problem, stated Nevin, was the overemphasis that American Christianity placed on private judgment. The "unhistorical" approach of most sects, which gave little credence to the historical judgments of the church over the centuries, made them irrational, tyrannical, and inconsistent.

In the review Winebrenner received numerous jabs from Nevin's caustic pen. Nevin commented:

> Mr. Winebrenner's portrait may be said to go beyond all the rest, in a certain self-consciousness of its own historical significance and interest. It has an attitude, studied for dramatic effect; an air of independence; an open Bible in the hands; in token, we presume, that Winebrennerism makes more of this blessed volume than any other sect, and that it was never much understood till Mr. Winebrenner was raised up at Harrisburg, in these last days, to set all right, and give the "Church of God" a fresh start, by means of it, out of his own mind.[19]

Both Nevin and Winebrenner lamented the low level of piety in mid-nineteenth-century America, but they had different solutions for its remedy. Winebrenner stressed the importance of individual regeneration through new birth. Nevin stressed a deeper knowledge of what it meant to be a Christian through the traditional system of catechism and confirmation. Winebrenner emphasized the "unity, visibility, sanctity, universality and perpetuity of the Church of God," believing that the true church derived these attributes from the fact that it was made up only of regenerate people. Nevin stressed the view that the church was established by God through Christ and that its members received Christ only through the church.

A MANY-FACETED PERSON

The story of Winebrenner's relationship with the German Reformed Church, the conflict over New Measures, his role as antagonist to John Nevin, and his founding of the Church of

God fails to note that John Winebrenner was also a reformer, a publisher, and a businessperson.

Like many other religious leaders of American history during "the Second Great Awakening," Winebrenner considered moral and social reform a natural concern of the church. He believed that the best way to effect a better society was through moral suasion of persons, not through political action. Among the reform movements he supported were antislavery, temperance, and peace.

His first antislavery activity was supporting the colonization movement, an effort to establish African colonies for freed slaves. Like many other nineteenth-century reformers, he eventually became dissatisfied with this effort and joined the abolitionist movement. He became the manager of the newly formed Harrisburg Anti-Slavery Society in 1836 and later was elected corresponding secretary. Speaking for the Church of God in 1844, he said that it "believes the system or institution of slavery to be impolitic and unchristian."

Temperance reform was also an enduring concern of Winebrenner. He wrote many articles for church publications that condemned the use of "ardent spirits" and tobacco. Although he preached abstinence from hard liquor, like whiskey and rum, he saw nothing wrong with limited use of wine, beer, and cider. Church of God congregations used wine in communion services until the late 1800s, and church periodicals advertised patent medicines that contained considerable amounts of alcohol. He opposed the use of tobacco in all forms, recognizing that it was a potential hazard to one's health.

Winebrenner also associated himself with the aims of the peace movement. His editorials kept readers informed of the activities of the American Peace Society and various international peace congresses. He thought that the war with Mexico (1846–48) was an irrational and immoral venture. One of the principles of the Church of God was a belief that "all civil wars are unholy and sinful, and in which the saints of the Most High ought never to participate."

In his espousal of reform views on slavery, temperance, and peace, Winebrenner often ran counter to the popular opinion of the nation and even the Church of God. It took time before the members of the denomination accepted his reform positions as their own. For example, in 1857, when Winebrenner urged a more tolerant attitude toward slaveholders, with the hope of persuading them of the evils of slavery and preventing a civil war, he was loudly condemned for his views by church leaders.[20]

A significant amount of Winebrenner's time was spent as a publisher. In 1835 he established *The Gospel Publisher and Journal of Useful Knowledge* as the official church paper. He served as both editor and printer, being responsible for both the production and the debts of the newspaper. He turned editorial duties over to others in 1840, only to see the paper go bankrupt. In 1846 he founded the *Church Advocate*, which is still the denomination's official periodical. A number of books were published by Winebrenner. The most successful was his *Prayer Meeting and Revival Hymnbook*. First published in 1825, it went through twenty-three editions. The *History of All the Religious Denominations in the United States* was a modest financial success. He operated a printing establishment in Harrisburg until 1857, as well as a bookstore that carried Bibles, religious works, hymnals, and schoolbooks.

After 1830 Winebrenner spent only four years as pastor of a local church, usually being appointed as "preacher at large" or "general missionary" of the church. Because he did not have the regular income of a pastor and church periodicals usually operate at a loss, he became involved in a number of business ventures to provide a livelihood for himself and his family. When his first wife died he inherited part-interest in an apothecary shop, which he moved into the printshop next to the Mulberry Street church. During his travels as an evangelist, he often sold books and patent remedies. The pages of the *Gospel Publisher* and *Church Advocate* contain advertisements for his books and drug products, fruit trees, seed wheat, and new varieties of corn. Late in his life he sold farm machinery and even won a medal for his harrow at the 1856 Pennsylvania State Agricultural Society Exhibition.

His most infamous business enterprise was the silkworm episode. Convinced that the production of silk would be one of America's next boom industries, he set up the Harrisburg Silk Agency in the late 1830s. There one could purchase *Morus multicaulis* (mulberry trees) and silkworm eggs, as well as obtain information on how to enter "this valuable branch of home industry." Winebrenner grew silkworms for a while, assigning to his children the task of keeping the cocooneries warm. This ill-fated venture became a standing joke among friends and enemies alike.[21]

WINEBRENNER IN PERSPECTIVE

Winebrenner's main contribution to the German Reformed Church was the lesson his disaffection taught that body. His New Measures activities and his theological inclinations helped to establish the boundaries of what was acceptable and unacceptable ministerial practice for the German Reformed Church during the 1820s. Although his banishment from the German Reformed Church did not prevent others from adopting New Measures, it did make people more aware of the importance of maintaining doctrinal purity. In time, persons like Winebrenner made German Reformed leaders more appreciative of the historic creeds and confessions of the church. They could see in him the dangers of departing too far from their traditions. Winebrenner's theology was a living illustration of what could happen when the *Heidelberg Catechism* was ignored and the formulation of doctrine was left to individual interpretation of the Bible. As one of the antagonists that caused John Nevin to speak out against the excesses of revivalism and individualism, Winebrenner deserves to be recognized as a significant footnote in German Reformed history.

Although Winebrenner wandered far from the traditions and theology of the German Reformed Church, the Churches of God still proudly traces its roots to that religious body. After Winebrenner's death the Churches of God and the German Reformed Church became less antagonistic toward each other. One former Churches of God pastor played an important part in the history of the German Reformed Church and the United Church of Christ. Dr. James E. Wagner grew up in the Altoona Fourth Street Church of God, served as pastor of St. Peter's German Reformed Church in Lancaster, Pennsylvania, as president of the Evangelical and Reformed Church, and as one of the two copresidents of the newly formed United Church of Christ.[22]

United Church of Christ members may find themselves a little uncomfortable with the approaches of Winebrenner the evangelist and theologian. But they need to remember that there was another side to this many-faceted person. He was an advocate of social reform. He was not afraid to speak out against the evils of racial inequality and the immorality of war. He was concerned over social issues like alcoholism and smoking. His business ventures remind us that even founders of denominations are human. John Winebrenner was at times idealistic and unbending, but he was also practical. Perhaps our greatest affinity with him can be that amid all the controversies and problems surrounding his life, he took time to speak out for peace and justice.

CHAPTER
9

THE CONGREGATIONAL TRAINING SCHOOL FOR WOMEN

Dorothy C. Bass

"WHAT SHALL I DO WITH MY LIFE?" a recruiting pamphlet from the Congregational Education Society early in the twentieth century urged its readers to ask themselves. Careers of service in the church, the pamphlet answered, offered exciting opportunities to make a difference in the world and to develop one's own life to the full. "The need is great. Christian leaders are called for at home and abroad. The strongest and best of our young men and women are wanted. No others can fully meet the need. Where and how will you invest your life?"[1]

Congregational women who sought to invest their lives in Christian leadership during the early decades of this century responded to this challenge. They were supported by the Congregational Training School for Women, established by Congregationalists in Chicago in 1909. The school aimed to be "a school for women where a high grade of instruction is offered along the lines of modern thought in religious life and modern

Dorothy C. Bass is Assistant Professor of Church History at the Chicago Theological Seminary.

methods in social work."[2] According to the school's founders, the churches sorely needed trained laywomen to take on staff positions in congregations and agencies. However, the Congregationalists' dominant image of paid leadership was that of the clergyman. Could the churches be convinced to hire professional women? Those who supported and attended the school hoped to develop new forms of employment for laywomen that would both enrich the churches and provide women with an opportunity to answer the call to Christian service.

WOMEN AND SERVICE

Although women who devoted their lives to Christian service can be found in every era, women have often been excluded from paid leadership and service in the churches. Around the turn of the century, however, a mass movement of American Protestant laywomen developed new models for women's participation in ecclesiastical life. Like the woman suffrage movement of the same period, with which it was closely connected, this movement of churchwomen raised women's expectations about their own ability to make public contributions.

Early in the nineteenth century, women had discovered the rewards and effectiveness of unified moral action in support of missions, education, and social reform. By 1900 they had developed large organizations to further these ends, and hundreds of women held paying positions as Christian workers in bodies such as the Women's Christian Temperance Union (WCTU) and the Young Women's Christian Association (YWCA). The foreign mission field also provided opportunities. In 1900 more than half of all American Protestant missionaries overseas were women, most of them single women supported by denominational women's missions organizations. In addition, more and more institutions of higher education were opening their doors to women. For middle-class women, the period was one in which the excitement of emerging opportunities and the genuine necessity of many women to support themselves financially created a quest for new careers, inside and outside of the church.

Progressive church leaders were open to receiving the public contributions of this generation of women. It was an era of growth and excitement about the mission of the churches. Advocates of the Social Gospel, which had a strong following among Congregationalists, were aware of the pressing need for a Christian response to the turmoil and injustice that accompanied rapid social change. Christian workers were needed to respond to human crises in rapidly growing cities transformed by industry and immigration. Many city congregations explored new forms of social outreach to their communities. Overseas, the foreign missions movement was at its peak, as confident American Protestants sought to minister to the spiritual and physical needs of a vast but shrinking world. For millions of liberal Protestants, at the turn of the "Christian" Century, the tasks of ministry at home and abroad were exceptionally urgent, alongside the hope that the current ferment would soon usher in the kingdom of God. In these circumstances, women's desire to participate in the work of the churches was hard to rebuff.

As the career expectations of women and the mission of the churches rapidly expanded, the idea of training dedicated laywomen to assist churches in meeting the challenges of the day was appealing. Located in a city transformed by immigration and industry, the Congregational Training School for Women fostered an activist view of the church in the world. Continuing the Congregational commitment to education, it sought to maintain high academic standards and raise the status of women employed by the churches. In the two decades of its existence about 200 women attended, most of them going on into employment in the churches.

The school was never large, but its story contains in microcosm a larger story of women's search for positions of usefulness and respect as professional workers in the churches. It is a story of accomplishment and limitation. It is a story that sheds light on many of the dilemmas faced by church-employed women in all times.

DEACONESS MOVEMENT

The Congregational Training School for Women was incorporated as an independent institution in 1909. Its origins, however, must be traced from earlier sources. Two separate initiatives on the part of women seeking opportunities for employment and education formed the wellspring of the institution.

The first initiative came from a group of now-forgotten women who claimed the ancient church title of "deaconess" as they sought to develop new opportunities for ministry for themselves and other women. In the late nineteenth century a movement to restore the office of deaconess swept through many Protestant denominations. The idea originated in Germany around 1836, and German Lutheran deaconesses arrived in the United States in 1884. American Lutherans, Episcopalians, and Methodists authorized orders of deaconesses within the next few years.

In the Evangelical Synod, a forerunner of the United Church of Christ, an order of deaconesses was founded in 1889 in St. Louis, where hundreds of women eventually trained and lived in consecrated service, usually as nurses. Their historian has called them "pioneer professional women" for the United Church of Christ.[3] These late-nineteenth-century deaconesses and their advocates were proud that deaconesses were *trained* for their duties; a pious heart, though essential, was not enough for a world in need of service. And so schools to train deaconesses—early institutions of theological education for women—were founded in a number of denominations.[4]

In 1896 a Miss Dockery, a Congregationalist who had graduated from the Methodists' Chicago Training School for City, Home, and Foreign Missions, called herself a deaconess and went to a small town in Illinois that was in the throes of a miners' strike. Another deaconess soon joined her, and together they opened a home for the sick, poor, and homeless. Once the strike was over, their work expanded to include a Sunday school, weekly prayer meetings, and a Christian Endeavor program. It was a Christian settlement house, providing the kind of service offered by Jane Addams' Hull House in Chicago.[5]

The work of these pioneer deaconesses and others doing similar work in a church on the South Side of Chicago soon attracted the interest and support of other Illinois Congregationalists. Support came from the Illinois Home Missionary Society for Miss Dockery's Deaconess Home. A resolution was made in the General Association of Illinois to charter the American Congregational Deaconess Association. When these actions were reported to the triennial meeting of the National Council of Congregational Churches in 1901, the council expressed "profound sympathy with a movement which looks toward the special training of forces long unused, but which are essential to the speedy and fuller development of the Kingdom of God."[6]

Arrangements for training Congregational deaconesses provided the first initiative for what later became the Congregational Training School for Women. In 1901 the American Congregational Deaconess Association obtained housing in the west side neighborhood where the Chicago Theological Seminary was located and persuaded the seminary to offer some courses for prospective deaconesses. A few part-time instructors were also hired. Few records remain of this institution, which was called the Deaconess Training School and then the Chicago Christian Training School for Women, but by 1904 thirty-six women had attended it.[7]

As time passed, however, it became clear that Congregational women did not find the office of deaconess attractive. "Perhaps the atmosphere in the United States is unfavorable to such a movement," suggested the disappointed advocates of the deaconess movement at the National Council meeting in 1907. American women—and particularly independent-minded Congregationalists—may have felt "prejudice against the costume as savoring too much of Romanism."[8] Although the deaconess movement in Congregationalism failed, it provided a crucial step toward theological education for women. It was the first root from which the Congregational Training School for Women would grow.

FLORENCE AMANDA FENSHAM

The second initiative providing a point of origin for the Congregational Training School took place in 1900, when a woman sought admission to the regular Bachelor of Divinity program at Chicago Theological Seminary. Florence Amanda Fensham, a missionary on furlough from her position as dean of religious work in the American College for Girls in Constantinople (now Istanbul), was already an accomplished scholar, knowledgeable in the biblical languages and experienced in graduate study after previous furloughs spent at Cornell and Oxford Universities. Thirty-eight years old, she had lost her father in the Civil War and her mother a few years later; women's need to support themselves financially was something she understood firsthand. After attending a normal school in New York state she taught for a few years. Her academic aspirations were high, and she continued to study, hoping to go to Radcliffe College. A conversion experience and a minister's challenge that she dedicate herself to foreign missions led her to change her plans. She sailed for Turkey in 1883. There she advanced from teacher to associate principal to professor of Old Testament to dean. Intelligent and learned, she asked for admission to Chicago Theological Seminary with no desire to seek ordination. But she did want graduate theological study to satisfy her intellectual appetite.[9]

Florence Fensham's application caused considerable consternation when it was presented to the seminary's board of directors. Was there any legal obstacle to admitting a woman to an institution whose chartered purpose was to train "men" for the Christian ministry? The directors stewed over this question, refusing to seek a legal change in the charter on account of pending litigation about the seminary's tax exemption. They granted Fensham a sizable scholarship and welcomed her to classes, but they avoided the question, would a degree be awarded? Finally, they answered her affirmatively, although without changing either the charter or the institution's de facto policy of neglect on the issue of women in ministry. Fensham was granted the Bachelor of Divinity degree in January 1902 and returned to Constantinople to resume her work.[10] She had made an impression in Chicago. Later one of her professors reported that while at the seminary, she had "raised the tone of the student body distinctly."[11] In autumn of 1904 she was back.

From that time until her death in 1912, Florence Fensham was the key figure in the Chicago Congregationalists' efforts to provide theological education for women. Her first position was as instructor of Bible in the Christian Institute, a school for both men and women that had been founded in 1903 to consolidate the seminary's undergraduate instruction and provide for deaconesses. Three years later she became the assistant dean of the institute. Moreover, she maintained an active presence within the all-male seminary itself: she served as librarian, as secretary of correspondence work, and, when a professor of Old Testament died suddenly, as an instructor.[12] A woman teaching an all-male seminary class on the Bible was uncommon, perhaps even unique. Although it is likely that none of these positions gave her the recognition she deserved, she was a busy and valuable member of the seminary community.

As an activist Protestant laywomen she was ambitious to find new ways of expanding educational and vocational opportunities for women in missions, education, and parish work. The coeducational Christian Institute made only limited contributions toward these goals. Women who enrolled alongside men in the two-year course did find church-related employment on graduation. If they were college graduates, they could cross-register into the seminary's regular courses. Many did so, although no woman again took the B.D. degree at CTS until 1926.[13] Most courses, although taught in seminary buildings by seminary professors, were shared with the institute's undergraduate male students. These men planned to enter ordained ministry in many of the Congregational churches that were too small to afford seminary graduates. In this setting the contrast between men's and women's aspirations and opportunities was striking.

A supportive environment to deal with women's special concerns was needed. Consequently, when the Christian Institute closed in 1909—the victim of financial difficulty and professorial exhaustion—Florence Fensham determined to found an institution dedicated to the theological education of women.

The Congregational Training School for Women was the result of her vision and the culmination of her life's work. She designed it in 1909 and served as its dean until February 15, 1912, when her heart stopped as she ran to catch a train back to the school after a missions meeting with her students. "To it she gave all she was and all she had," declared Graham Taylor, the seminary's prominent professor of sociology and economics; "she herself was its inspiration and initiative, its principal instructor and only administrator, its home-maker and outside representative."[14] Rather than pursuing a Ph.D. degree or ordination—difficult but possible courses of action for a Congregational woman in 1909—this exceptionally accomplished churchwoman worked to further opportunities for laywomen's service. She hoped to make available to Congregational women of the twentieth century a scope of action, a field of learning, and a means of support similar to what she had enjoyed as a teacher and missionary.

THE SCHOOL

Incorporated as an independent institution, although still able to draw on the instructional resources of the Chicago Theological Seminary, the Congregational Training School for Women received from a wealthy physician a fine old mansion that served as its residence and base of operations. Congregational churches, especially their women's organizations, contributed money, food, furnishings, and other necessities. Twenty young women, along with one or two leaders including the dean, lived together while enrolled in the school, sharing meals, conducting vespers every evening, and receiving edifying visits from denominational officials and missionaries on furlough. One young teacher from Kansas, considering enrollment, wrote to a friend that although it might be wise to attend the less expensive Moody Bible Institute, she wanted to go to CTSW because it seemed "more like a home."[15]

Although eminently proper and quite domestic, the school was hardly a quiet enclave. All students were required to do "practical work" in the city. They worked in settlement houses such as Graham Taylor's Chicago Commons, urban congregations, or charitable agencies struggling to respond to the needs of immigrants. Jane Addams and her associates at Hull House, thoroughly immersed in the city's problems, offered an elective course during the first year. In addition, students were required to exercise regularly to enhance their own health and to learn children's games for later use in teaching. Many women held part-time jobs as secretaries or Sunday school teachers to help meet expenses.

Chicago Theological Seminary contributed office and classroom space, as well as numerous educational, religious, and social opportunities. CTSW students with college degrees could enroll in the seminary's regular courses, and seminary professors also taught special courses for CTSW. The women took active part in the extracurricular life of CTS, including worship and many conferences.

Bible study in English formed the core of the CTSW curriculum. A few "supplementary" courses in the traditional theological disciplines of ethics, church history, and apologetics were required, along with the newer disciplines of economics and psychology. Then came a host of practical courses, often taught by part-time instructors who were practitioners in these skills: teaching, story telling, music, physical education, public speaking, business skills, domestic arts, crafts, nursing, and foreign languages (Italian and Polish, for use among immigrants). During the two-year program about two thirds of a student's courses were required, so that a woman could take time to develop the skills she particularly wished to develop.[16]

The city, the women's residential life, and the seminary combined to shape an atmosphere of activism and newness that retained elements of piety and domestic warmth. The initial catalog stated that the school was needed because "changing conditions" necessitated "a new program of work and new activities for the church." Later catalogs justified the "modern" forms of thought and social work being taught, and numerous visiting lecturers at the school, because they kept everyone up-to-date.

> It is the aim of the school to foster a type of religious life which expresses itself in a broad human sympathy and efficiency; which is vigorous and wholesome; which has many interests and is open to new points of view and methods so that the women who go from the school may understand something of the world's need, and what are the approved ways today of meeting that need; in short, to nurture an intelligent, consecrated, practical spiritual life in the service of Jesus.[17]

Who attended the school? Students had to be at least twenty-five years old, single, and of high moral and religious character. Once a twice-divorced, thoroughly dishonest woman slipped in, creating quite a pastoral challenge for the compassionate but straight-laced administration. Most of the women were from the Midwest. Many had been teachers, which was seen as good background for church work. They were largely middle-class women, but they seldom had any money and had to work their way through the school. Part-time positions and interest-free loans enabled them to meet the annual expense of $244 a year.[18] Ideally, they were college graduates, but frequently this ideal was not attained. After 1913 a one-year program especially for college graduates became available.

The women at CTSW were eager to do something important with their lives. As a small-town algebra and chemistry teacher wrote, her present career was interesting, but "it just doesn't quite satisfy me for a life work. . . . Maybe I am foolish, and I am probably not fitted for the work, but I have been interested in the Immigration question ever since we studied it in 'Endeavor,' and I wanted to find out if I could not work among those people."[19]

AFTER GRADUATION

The Congregational Training School's publicity always claimed, apparently with justification, that there were far more jobs available than there were graduates to fill them. "UNABLE TO MEET THE DEMAND OF THE CHURCHES," a recruiting advertisement in the denominational magazine blared; "unlimited opportunities await young women of education and pleasing personality who are interested in Christian Service as a life work, and who are willing to prepare themselves for specialized fields of service."[20]

The possible fields of service were many. Among the first five graduates, one became the minister of a home missions parish in North Dakota, two served as church assistants for religious education in large Midwestern congregations, one worked at a settlement house in Appalachia, and the other joined the staff of the Chicago office of the Congregational Education Society. In the fairly typical class of 1920, there were two church assistants, one director of religious education, one church visitor, and one who stayed on as an administrative secretary at CTSW. That autumn five recent graduates departed for the foreign mission fields, joining four who were already overseas. (Sending graduates overseas had been one of Florence Fensham's dreams, although fewer were sent than she would have hoped, as the missions movement diminished during and after World War I.) Other positions held by graduates were in the YWCA, denominational agencies, weekday schools of religion, city church federations, and girls' work.[21]

Marriage to a minister also counted among CTSW alumnae as a distinctive church career. Virtually all graduates took it for granted that they would resign their paying positions on marriage—a convention followed by most educated, middle-class women in the early twentieth century. Although some alumnae records simply indicate that a woman "married," others are listed as if they had a job, "wife of minister," with the church named. School publicity mentioned "minister's wife" as one of the forms of church service in which graduates were active.[22] One amusing testimony to how well the school prepared women for church work came from a graduate's minister husband. He waxed eloquent about how useful his wife's knowledge of scripture and church life was to him. "My personal appreciation of what the Training School did for Mrs. P., who was then Miss M., is far beyond my power to express," he concluded. It is difficult to know whether to lament the absorption of these trained women into their husbands' careers, or to rejoice that they could un-self-consciously celebrate the contributions of ministers' wives.

The most frequent position taken by CTSW graduates was that of "church assistant." Church assistants could carry any number of duties (educational, secretarial, social) and any number of titles (including "pastor's assistant," which the CTSW women found obnoxious). Sometimes the women were well rewarded—in money, respect, and personal satisfaction—but often they were not. Churches characteristically did not prize female leadership. Moreover, as laity in institutions that associated paid leadership with ordination, church assistants confronted many obstacles.

Perhaps the biggest obstacle was the pastor, a figure one of the graduates called "a stone wall in the shape of a man." Some pastors were overbearing, glad to have another pair of hands around the church, but reluctant to share authority. Other pastors were lazy; "I do not think I can truthfully say they need an assistant here but I wish they had a live minister," one woman reported. Sometimes they were old fogies, like the pastor who blocked an assistant's contributions because he did not understand "modern religious education." When a survey asked ministers what qualities they sought in a church assistant, ministers said they wanted a woman who was "good-looking, refined, attractive in appearance, resourceful, tactful, adaptable, wholesome, sympathetic, healthy, patient," and possessed "initiative" and "strong Christian purpose." One Training School student summed it up: "She should be a combination of all the cardinal virtues plus every minor virtue known to the mind of man."[23] All in all, the survey boded ill for the full professional acceptance of women church assistants.

Another major obstacle was the laity; would church members accept the leadership of these women? Some church assistants clearly thrived in their work. When they expressed disgruntlement about the laity, they did so with humor and love. One woman, ebullient about her work in religious education in Wichita, reported shyly but proudly that "it really scares a person when you see them turning to you to know what to do." Others celebrated successful Camp Fire or Christian Endeavor programs, or joked about how hard it was to delegate work to volunteers when it was easier to do it oneself. Many of these women found their work personally rewarding. But that was not the whole story; as one woman put it, "I was terribly lonely in the work and yet I was supremely happy in it."

"The church people evidently expected her to be largely a church secretary and office girl, and used her as such," reported a sympathetic pastor about a CTSW graduate. Fighting this image was a constant struggle, especially since the school anticipated that a little secretarial work would be included in positions and offered electives in typing, stenography, and filing. At the same time the dean insisted in 1916 that "the work of a Church Assistant is almost never limited to secretarial or clerical work."

Graduates found that congregations did diminish the status and effectiveness of church assistants because of prejudice against women. "Women as Church Assistants just at present are still greatly handicapped unless they are fifty years old and although the time is slowly coming when the church will look at it differently, it isn't here yet," one woman reported in 1918. "It is my opinion that at present as far as the relationship with the Church outside of the office is concerned, a good tactful man can do it better, but that is not saying it will always be so—it will not."[24]

Careers of church assistants were also hampered by the absence of avenues for promotion and advancement and by low pay. Salary was an ambivalent issue for Christian women who had been trained to diffidence about their financial needs. One of the most forthright women put it this way:

> I am interested in an increase of salary; I feel that I am situated so that it is my duty to look to that side and it helps the cause to demand a reasonable salary. . . . I feel that women assistants ought to be willing to sacrifice in salary for struggling churches but when the pastor is paid a magnificent amount, I feel that the assistant who has had five years of training and also experience ought to be paid an amount that would correspond with the man's salary. But I hope always to be above mere salary.[25]

OTHER OPPORTUNITIES FOR WOMEN

The Congregational Training School for Women is just one institution among many that were built by women, for women in the late nineteenth and early twentieth centuries. Women's colleges, all-female labor unions, and organizations like the YWCA and the Women's International League for Peace and Freedom were major achievements of this era. They not only reflected the fact that women were excluded from male-dominated institutions; they also expressed women's own self-esteem and passion for justice. Within major Protestant denominations, including Congregationalism, women created semi-independent organizations. There, women executives controlled substantial funds raised by laywomen to support missions—usually missions conducted by women on behalf of women and children.[26] For middle-class American women in 1900, training in an all-female school for a predominantly female profession was a positive statement of women's vision for themselves and their society.

CTSW was not the only Congregational institution in this period to train laywomen for church professions. Alternative models were provided by the Schauffler College of Religious and Social Work in Cleveland and the Hartford School of Religious Pedagogy.

Schauffler was established in 1886 by a former missionary and his wife as a small training program to prepare Slavic immigrant women to do religious work among their own people. It gradually grew into a two-year training school, not unlike CTSW. It started at a lower academic level and later developed into a small four-year college. In 1954, unaccredited and underenrolled, the college deeded its resources to the Graduate School of Theology at Oberlin College, which established the Schauffler Division of Christian Education.[27] Still later it became part of Vanderbilt University Divinity School when Oberlin closed its graduate school.

At Hartford it was possible for women to obtain theological education at a higher academic level. In 1889 the trustees of the Hartford Theological Seminary—a three-year graduate institution granting the Bachelor of Divinity degree—voted to admit women to all courses of study. Yet some limitations applied: women could not live in the dormitory or draw on regular financial aid funds. They were expected to have as a goal "religious work other than the pastorate." Few women enrolled in this program, never more than three each year. Larger numbers of women were recruited after a training school, the Bible Normal School (formerly the School for Christian Workers), made a cooperative arrangement with the seminary and moved to its campus in 1902. Rechristened the Hartford School of Religious Pedagogy, it trained a few men and many women, most of whom were not college graduates, for the same sorts of positions CTSW graduates held.[28]

All these schools exemplify the flexibility of Congregational institutions of theological education in the early twentieth century. Less concerned about graduate professional degrees than today's institutions, these schools found ways to serve disadvantaged constituencies and to respond to the needs of their time. Women were not the only beneficiaries of this flexibility. In Chicago, the seminary produced leaders for immigrant communities through foreign institutes. After the 1880s, theological instruction was offered in German, Swedish, Danish, and Norwegian. Even instruction for English-speaking undergraduate men was made flexible through a variety of arrangements, first at the seminary and then, from 1915 to 1934, at the Union Theological College. "We are training workers to meet the conditions, not adjusting men to courses of study that have been inherited from the past," declared CTS president Ozora Stearns Davis in 1919.[29] Although this flexibility in theological education fell short of the Congregational ideal of a learned clergy, it disclosed another ideal of Congregationalists in the age of the Social Gospel: pragmatism.

ESTABLISHING PROFESSIONAL IDENTITY

To overcome the obstacles they confronted, women took organizational steps to enhance their status. In 1910, Florence Fensham founded the Congregational Woman's League of Church Assistants; in 1915, with support from denominational headquarters, the organization became a national body. Its object was "the promotion of the interests of the Congregational churches, especially in matters relating to the service rendered by salaried women workers," including their recruitment and placement. In 1915 official Congregational statistics counted 125 such workers, and in 1919 about 300. National Councils passed ringing resolutions about the importance of these workers in 1915 and 1921. However, no nationwide policies to enhance their status were adopted, owing to the denomination's decentralized structure.[30]

The leaders of this new church profession for women—including the strong and well-educated women who succeeded Fensham as CTSW dean, Agnes M. Taylor and Margaret M. Taylor—were well aware of the churches' reluctance to treat trained women workers as they deserved. These deans kept up a warm and frank correspondence with CTSW alumnae. They traveled widely in denominational circles in quest of recruits, funds, and recognition. The secondary status of women church workers was evident in denominational policy. Denominational scholarship funds were reserved for Bachelor of Divinity students, although Dean Margaret Taylor unsuccessfully protested this policy in 1920.[31]

Despite the limitations of the role of church assistant, these women honestly believed that it provided the most direct path for women toward greater participation in church leadership.

Although ordination was closed to women in almost all denominations, it was *possible* for Congregational women; Antoinette Brown had blazed this trail in 1853. The ordination of women, however, did not seem to be *likely* on any large scale.

Biases against women clergy were well known, and few women had followed this path to church service. In 1900 Congregationalism included about forty ordained women in its ministry; in 1919 there were 67 women among 5,695 men. Eighteen women were pastors of "very small" churches, 14 were copastors with their husbands, 14 were religious educators or church assistants, and 21 were employed outside the churches. A 1921 Commission of the National Council reported that "so far as your Commission has knowledge, no scandal or seriously unpleasant incident has grown out of the ordination of women in our denomination." The commission "rejoice[d] in the freedom of our churches in recognizing the prophetic gift in women as well as in men." Even so, this freedom had not led to the entrance of sizable numbers of women into the ministry. The commission thought that this would continue to be the case.[32]

Dean Margaret Taylor agreed in 1926: "It does not seem likely that women would enter the ministry in large numbers even should all theological seminaries remove their restrictions, but they are finding new and interesting use for their talents and energies in the field of religious education." Another leading advocate of women's leadership in the church, Georgia Harkness, a Methodist, concurred in this assessment. These views were also supported by the statistics: in 1926 Congregational women included 74 ministers, 23 licentiates, and 367 church assistants.[33]

A few Training School alumnae were eventually ordained, and the school took pride in their accomplishments. Only one of these has left a record of her difficulties as a woman minister. "The preaching is yet, as has been, so hard for me," Orpha Greep wrote in 1913. "I can hardly describe the feeling I have had in preparing the sermon a good deal of the time. There has been an inner tightening something like the feeling one has when it is hard to get one's breath." This woman left her isolated little parish and became a nurse.[34]

In choosing to de-emphasize ordination and develop a

female-identified job as a special path for women into church careers, these women underestimated their denomination's discrimination against women and its bias in favor of the clergy. On the one hand, their strategy represented an accommodation to reality: churches were known to be reluctant to hire women as pastors, and few women were academically qualified for graduate Bachelor of Divinity programs. On the other hand, they were motivated by understandable ideals: their feeling of solidarity with the activist movement of Protestant laywomen, their sense that the times demanded short training programs rather than lengthy academic ones, and their endeavor to create a new professional role.

ABSORPTION OF THE SCHOOL

Professionalism became a strong force in twentieth-century America, both inside and outside the church. In this context, advocates of laywomen in church professions argued for higher educational standards, while ministers increasingly insisted that church assistants needed both collegiate and graduate education. Increasingly, national standards of accreditation for all degree-granting institutions were established. CTSW, which had a policy of preference for education at the college-graduate level, responded to these pressures by devising a Bachelor of Religious Education program in 1922. Soon thereafter it found a way to secure graduate-level training for all its future students.[35]

In February 1926 the board of directors voted the Congregational Training School for Women out of existence, having arranged for "the setting up of a program for the training of women workers of college-graduate grade" at the Chicago Theological Seminary. Both seminary and CTSW leaders were happy about the merger. Although CTSW alumnae expressed some misgivings.[36]

Two factors brought the seminary and CTSW together. First, both institutions relocated to Chicago's South Side, where the University of Chicago stood at the hub of an interdenominational complex of graduate theological schools. Second, there was increasing interest at both these institutions and at CTS in religious education, which might be called the theological growth industry of the 1920s. Drawing on the intellectual work of leaders such as John Dewey and George A. Coe, religious education grew into an impressive and exciting field of study, not only for prospective church assistants, but also for ministerial and doctoral students. The Master's Degree in Religious Education became the goal for most of the seminary's new women students.

At first, excitement about the merger moved women's issues to the fore at the seminary. In 1929 the president announced that a search had begun for a woman faculty member. In 1930 Clara E. Powell, who held a University of Chicago Ph.D. in religious education, was hired. In the same year the seminary trustees and alumni resolved that "in view of the co-educational character of the Seminary, it was time to have both men and women on the Board of Directors." Two laywomen were promptly elected. Special statements in the catalog announced the seminary's commitment to "The Education of Women for Christian Service." Women would work as "church assistants, directors of religious education, instructors in week-day religious schools, missionaries, and ministers." Male students celebrated the ways in which the presence of women improved seminary social life. At about the same time, a few women enrolled in the Bachelor of Divinity program. The first two women, since Florence Fensham, graduated with the B.D. degree in 1926.[37]

However, this promising beginning did not prepare a smooth path for women into church careers. Through the next several decades attention to women's issues was at low tide in churches and seminaries, as well as in American society at large. Congregational women who sought ordination encountered obstacles of many kinds, while religious education professionals saw opportunities shrink as the Depression bit into church budgets. Few theologicial seminaries, including Chicago, consistently had women on their boards or as regular members of their faculties. Although women students were admitted to more and more theological seminaries, there is little evidence that the issues that created the Congregational Training School for Women in 1909 had been completely resolved.

The Congregational Training School for Women, founded

during the first wave of American feminism, represented a creative response within its own time to the issue of women's preparation for church leadership. During the second wave of American feminism, the issue is once again being addressed. In this new context it is not likely that CTSW will provide a model for how women's theological education should be structured. It can, however, provide a model of hope, innovation, and mission that is part of the heritage of women in the United Church of Christ.

CHAPTER
10

CHINESE CONGREGATIONALISM

Barbara Brown Zikmund
(with the assistance of
Dorothy Wong, Rose Lee, and Matthew Fong)

CHINA IS ONE of the great civilizations in the history of the world. For more than 5,000 years Chinese people have nurtured greatness in the arts, culture, and society. When the peoples of Europe were little more than barbarians, Chinese science and literature thrived in a politically and economically stable environment. It is not surprising, therefore, that from the time of Marco Polo, trade with the Chinese has been eagerly sought by Europeans.

Furthermore, because China is densely populated, during times of drought, floods, and war the Chinese people have emigrated to find a better life. This is especially true of peasants and merchants from the southern coast, where the land is

Barbara Brown Zikmund is Dean and Professor of Church History at Pacific School of Religion, Berkeley, California. Dorothy Wong and Rose Lee are active members in the Berkeley Chinese Community Church (UCC). Matthew Fong has served as senior pastor of the Chinese Congregational Church (UCC), San Francisco, since 1978.

extremely poor. Today Chinese people may be found throughout Southeast Asia.[1]

Trade between Europe and China dates from 1757, when the port of Guangzhou (Canton) was opened for trade. The British and the Portuguese dominated the situation and initially built a lively commerce around opium. When the Chinese government tried to stop the drug traffic, the British became furious at their loss of profits. Soon the so-called Opium War (1839–42) broke out. China, however, was no match for the sea power of the British empire. In defeat, the Chinese were forced to open more trading ports and deed the island of Hong Kong to Britain.

In south China the combination of war, drought, and floods led to famine. The land could not support the people and taxes increased. Soon Chinese contract laborers (coolies) were working in many parts of the world. Although Chinese law prohibited emigration, it became acceptable for young Chinese men to go overseas to work and send money home to their needy families. The abolition of slavery by the British in 1833 had created a great demand for cheap labor.[2]

In 1848, when news came that gold had been discovered in California, the Chinese had still another reason to come to the United States. By 1852 20,000 Chinese had arrived in San Francisco to prospect for gold. American resentment against foreign miners caused the California state legislature to pass a foreign miners tax, making it especially difficult for Mexicans and Chinese to continue prospecting. The Chinese refused to give up. They grouped together for protection, bought up old claims, and worked abandoned tailings. Through team effort they were able to make a living where individual American miners could not. The Chinese also worked in the quicksilver and borax mines. By 1870 one third of the miners in California were Chinese.[3]

As the first wave of Chinese workers spread throughout the American West, British relations with China deteriorated again and the Second Opium War broke out (1856–60). In defeat, China allowed foreigners to recruit Chinese labor and deeded more land to Britain.[4]

At first, Californians welcomed Chinese workers. The Chinese endured difficult conditions to build the railroads.[5] They drained the swamps of the river deltas and enhanced California agriculture.[6] They cooked and did laundry for American men who considered such things "women's work."[7] Chinese society in America, however, was never stable. For one thing, it was composed almost entirely of men who wanted to earn their fortune and return home as quickly as possible.[8]

THE AMERICAN MISSIONARY ASSOCIATION

The American Missionary Association (AMA) had been founded in 1846 by East Coast Congregationalists incensed at the racism of many missionary boards. Before and after the Civil War the AMA functioned as an effective evangelical/abolitionist educational agency for blacks in the South. It also became interested in the needs of American Indians and Chinese and Japanese immigrants.[9]

Work among the Chinese began in 1853, when the Rev. Samuel V. Blakeslee was sent by the AMA to San Francisco. He devised an English phonetic system to teach English to Chinese pupils, but it was not successful. Before long the Presbyterian Chinese Mission, led by William Speer, took over this work with the Chinese.[10]

Fifteen years later, concern for the Chinese surfaced again among Congregationalists. In the fall of 1868 the First Congregational Church of Oakland (founded in 1860) started a Chinese sabbath school. Not long afterward, three men from the school asked to be baptized and became the first Chinese members of a Congregational church on the Pacific Coast (1870).[11] At almost the same time (1869), the AMA renewed its commitment to Chinese mission work and appointed the Rev. John Kimball AMA superintendent.[12]

Typically, the AMA did not organize churches; it founded schools. Also, because the Methodists and others were already at work in San Francisco, the AMA made a conscious effort to serve populations in other parts of the state. In 1871 the AMA started a school in Stockton, followed by other schools in Oakland, Sacramento, Santa Cruz, and Los Angeles. A Chinese convert, Jee Gam, was hired as a missionary worker for the AMA.[13]

San Francisco's First Congregational Church and Third Congregational Church began sponsoring Chinese Sunday schools.

The Third Church school was especially large because of its location near several factories where Chinese worked. Soon AMA superintendent John Kimball approached the Rev. William C. Pond, pastor of Third Congregational Church, and suggested that the church start an evening school. This was the beginning of Pond's half-century ministry among the Chinese.[14]

WILLIAM C. POND

Pond did not start off optimistic about work with the Chinese:

> I had no expectation of immediate results. I had heard for so many years of the very slow progress and the very little fruit in the work in China that I supposed that it would take two or three years before Chinese conservatism could be overcome and conversions reward our labor. My surprise therefore was great when after not more, I am sure, than three months, our teacher came to me and said that eight of her pupils seemed to have given themselves to Christ, and that they desired to be baptized and received into the church.[15]

Pond decided to meet with the converts to assess their understanding of the gospel. His first interview with a "convert" was disappointing, and the man left to return to China soon thereafter. With the assistance of AMA worker Jee Gam, however, Pond found discussions with the remaining seven encouraging. Yet he was not sure. He asked the head of the Presbyterian mission, who knew Chinese, to determine whether the men were sincere and invite them to join the Presbyterian church, if it was appropriate.

When this was done, the Chinese converts told the Presbyterian missionary: "Your church is nearly three miles away; we were converted in this church, we love our teachers, we would like to be baptized and received here." With this news, Pond was convinced that "our Saviour was committing these souls to our care, and that we ought not to refuse the responsibility."[16]

By 1873, however, anti-Chinese sentiment in California was on the increase. Although the Standing Committee of the Third Congregational Church recommended the seven Chinese for membership and the majority of the congregation agreed, a minority group asked that the matter be postponed for two months so that "they could enquire for themselves as to the fitness of these candidates." According to Pond, they never even tried to meet the men. When the probation was extended six months longer, a major church quarrel ensued. In the fray, support for the Chinese increased and Pond noted that there was "such an uprising of public sentiment against those who would forbid men of a particular race, as such, to be at home in a church of Christ, that at the end of six months, the church had become far more anxious to receive them than they were to be received." Pond, however, was disgusted. He determined to "withdraw from the battle-field" and submitted his resignation. But he refused to depart until he could baptize the Chinese converts and receive them into the membership of Third Church.[17]

The Chinese wanted Pond to be their pastor. They were not alone. On February 23, 1873, about thirty leaders left Third Church and started a new Sunday school and church about a mile and a quarter from their old congregation. They asked Pond to be their pastor. Although Pond had already committed himself to raise money for Pacific Theological Seminary and could not assume pastoral duties for a year, he consented. At his suggestion they named the new venture Bethany Congregational Church.[18]

During the ensuing year Pond worried about the Chinese. On a trip to New York he called at the AMA offices and learned that the association leadership wanted Pond to be superintendent of Chinese work in California. Pond was reluctant to usurp Kimball's role. But before Pond left New York, Kimball resigned and Pond was commissioned to work for the AMA. He returned to California and Bethany Congregational Church to develop plans for a permanent AMA headquarters in San Francisco's Chinatown.[19] In accepting the commission, Pond wrote:

> I received the commission with accompanying instruction. I enter on the work with much good cheer. The idea is this: to form the Chinese who seem to have become Christians in any locality a class duly organized. It remains to be seen whether we can carry this idea out: but something of this sort, I believe would be useful. Give us your prayer.[20]

Pond's work among California Chinese is impressive. Although he did not anticipate that he would be asked to raise money, as needs increased and money from New York was exhausted, he took it upon himself to raise needed funds locally. He visited schools and over the years was involved in forty-nine missions to Chinese.

> Not even one-half of these became permanent. We never had at one time more than twenty-three missions. But those that were planted and lived only a year or two, were not fruitless. Of but one do I think as a failure. One was discontinued because the mob drove all the Chinese from the town; some because the business which gathered Chinese in that locality was discontinued; some because through lack of funds we were compelled to let them die in order that those with brighter prospects might continue. It is impossible for us to know how many souls were led out of darkness into light.[21]

ANTI-CHINESE SENTIMENT

From the late 1850s through the mid-1870s Chinese immigration steadily increased, reaching an all-time high of 60,000 between 1871 and 1875.[22] From the beginning, Americans debated the question of Chinese immigration. Most Americans expected the Chinese to go back to China when the railroads were built and the swamplands reclaimed. But conditions in China kept them coming. Soon American workers found competition with Chinese labor bitter, and they organized against the "Yellow Peril" and the "Chinese Menace." In 1873 the San Francisco Chronicle asked: "Who have built a filthy nest of iniquity and rottenness in our midst? The Chinese. Who filled our workshops to the exclusion of white labor? The Chinese. Who drives away white labor by their stealthy but successful competition? The Chinese."[23] In the 1870s and 1880s San Francisco passed city ordinances prohibiting people to use poles for carrying merchandise on the sidewalks, requiring prisoners in city jails to get hair cuts if their hair was more than one inch long, and demanding high license fees for transporting laundry without using wagons drawn by horses. These blatant anti-Chinese laws were challenged in the courts and eventually declared unconstitutional, but not before they made life miserable for the Chinese.[24]

Although many Protestant clergy supported Chinese immigration, some did so with qualifications. While calling for evangelistic work, they argued that Chinese immigration was dangerous to America. Conversion was the only solution, but because success was improbable, even people like Blakeslee, the first AMA agent in San Francisco, initially argued for immigration restrictions.[25] In 1877 the General Association of Congregational Churches of California called for modification of the 1868 Burlingame Treaty, advocating open immigration, to provide for some restrictions. It wanted to stop the influx of prostitutes and ease the pressure on American and Christian institutions.

Back East, however, Congregational purists like Lyman Abbott rejected all restrictions. He asked, "By what right do the children of the immigrants of 1620 say to the immigrants of 1880, 'You shall not set foot upon this soil?' By what right do the sons of the Pilgrim Fathers say to the pilgrims of this generation, 'You shall keep off?' "[26] At the thirty-third annual meeting of the AMA, in 1879, the Chinese Missions committee reported:

> We would utter, therefore, our solemn protest as an Association against the discriminating legislation of State or nation, and the insults and wrongs of individuals, by which the lives of the Chinese among us have been vexed and the name of the Christian religion has been dishonored. And we would urge this Association to lead the van in arousing public sentiment against the wrongs already inflicted as now threatened, and to prosecute its work of evangelization among them, until the Chinese shall be as undisturbed in America as immigrants from other lands. The cry that the Chinamen must go is unworthy of our nation and our religion.[27]

Eventually nativist pressures on Congress led to the Oriental Exclusion Act of 1882. It stopped the immigration of Chinese laborers for ten years, permitting only teachers, students, merchants, and tourists to enter the United States. It also prevented the Chinese from becoming naturalized American citizens.

This was the first immigration law in U.S. history to single out a specific ethnic group.[28]

As anti-Chinese sentiment increased through the 1880s the Scott Act was passed in 1888, preventing any Chinese worker who left the country to visit family in China from returning to America. In 1892, when the ten-year Exclusion Act was up, labor pressures on Congress resulted in the passage of the Geary Act. The act not only continued prohibitions on Chinese immigration, but also required all Chinese in America to register and to carry a "photo passport" that could be shown to authorities on demand. Laws in 1894, 1902, 1904, and 1924 further tightened exclusion policies by preventing Chinese laborers from coming into the United States unless they were sponsored by family members already in the country. Women who were not the wives of merchants, teachers, and students were barred. Because the Chinese could not bring their wives from China, or marry American women, second-generation Chinese communities remained small.[29]

FROM MISSIONS TO CHURCHES

Although the AMA pioneered in using English instruction as a means of evangelizing the Chinese in America, by 1892 there were at least 271 schools or missions sponsored by numerous denominations. An 1876 Congregational report argued: "For bringing the Chinese within our reach, no other plan compares with this of proffering to them instruction in the English language. These thus attracted are, in general, and by a process of natural selection, the choice spirits, most eager for knowledge, and thus most open to impression."[30] Congregationalists often said that they were "baiting the Gospel hook with the English alphabet."[31]

By 1875 California Congregationalists moved to set up a local organization to coordinate the work of the AMA and independent Chinese Sunday schools. The new society, named the California Chinese Mission (CCM), came into being on March 9, 1876, with William C. Pond as secretary. Headquarters were established at 5 Brenham Place, in the heart of San Francisco's Chinatown. From that time on AMA activity in California was carried out through the CCM.[32]

In its first annual report the CCM boasted that it had 1,500 students enrolled in thirteen mission schools throughout California. There were three schools in San Francisco and ten more schools, one each, in Antioch, Eureka, Los Angeles, Oakland, Oroville, Petaluma, Sacramento, San Leandro, Santa Barbara, and Stockton. Later schools were founded in Marysville, Suisun, Visalia, Woodland, Tucson, San Diego, Fresno, Ventura, Pasadena, Riverside, Santa Cruz, Berkeley, and Bakersfield.[33]

Congregational missions never required their teachers to learn Chinese because, argued Pond, the object of the schools was not to train the intellect, but to save the soul. The Chinese were eager to learn English and even risked becoming Christian. The CCM relied on Chinese helpers and "close hand-to-hand teaching," making less use of books and tracts than did other missions. Even if the missionaries could speak Chinese, Congregationalists believed that it was better to let recent Chinese converts speak from their own experience.[34]

For the Chinese it was not always easy. Lee San Hong, a Chinese mission worker in San Diego, recalled how his friends ridiculed him when he became a Christian. "The Chinese made fun of me, calling me a Jesus Boy. After I was baptized by immersion they asked me if the water was wet. I thought my father in China would not like it, so I did not tell him for a long time. When they [in China] saw my photograph with my queue off they called me a monk."[35]

Besides educating the Chinese and defending them against unjust laws, some of the most dramatic missionary work was on behalf of Chinese women. As pointed out earlier, American Chinese society was dominated by men. Although more than 8,000 women had come to the United States before the Exclusion Act, by 1890 there were only 3,868 Chinese women left in the country, as compared with 102,620 men. Missionaries were especially concerned about Chinese prostitution, encouraging church women to raise money to support programs to rescue young girls. They believed that there was little hope of redeeming the Chinese until the women were converted.[36]

Congregational women, unlike other Protestant groups, did not establish any organized work with Chinese prostitutes. In the late 1880s a single woman, Minnie G. Worley, told Pond that she felt called to work with the Chinese in San Francisco. She said that she was concerned about married women. "The poor slaves in the brothels are encouraged to escape and when they escape are housed and protected and taught and led to Christ in the Presbyterian and Methodist homes, but the wives living in womanly wedlock, have next to no care." Soon the Congregationalists hired a woman worker to do visitation among Chinese mothers and children. This visitor offered aid, sang gospel songs, told Bible stories, taught reading, and advised Chinese women on family problems. Yet the number of female converts remained few. In 1887 William Pond reported that he baptized his second Chinese woman. This was a small proportion of the 120 persons he had baptized to that date. Evangelism among Chinese women continued to be hindered by Chinese customs that prevented women from going out to church on their own.[37]

From the late 1880s, nativist harassment and declining Chinese population made missionary efforts more difficult. In the face of growing discrimination, Chinese laborers wondered whether it was worth the effort to learn English. Fewer students enrolled in the mission schools. The Congregationalists in 1887 reported that they needed to go out into the streets and lanes and "compel them to come in." They began promoting churches, visitation, and street preaching. But street preaching went against the Confucian traditions of schoolroom teaching. Chinese Christian leaders who at first were reluctant eventually were convinced. In 1895 Loo Quong, a Congregational leader in Fresno, argued that street preaching was the most important part of missionary work.[38]

Congregationalists also developed a new philosophy about church growth. At first, Congregationalists encouraged Chinese converts to join the American church to which their mission school was attached. New Christians needed to be under the watch and care of those who were maturer. Yet most Chinese church members had no real part in the work of the American churches in which they were members, and the churches cultivated no genuine understanding of the Chinese. Pond began to promote the idea of a "branch church."

> The branch of a tree is itself a tree, with trunk and bark and branches and leaves and flowers and fruit like any other tree,—but it is rooted not directly in the soil but in the trunk of the mother tree. It is in vital connection with that

mother tree, receives sustenance from it and is in an important sense, ordered in its growth by it.[39]

Pond used the branch concept as a way of encouraging the development of separate churches and the maintenance of ties between American churches and their Chinese members or missions. Not until 1911 did the Congregationalists state that it was their policy to develop each mission as rapidly as possible into a self-supporting church. Other Protestant denominations tended to start separate Chinese churches with no ties to American congregations from the very beginning.[40]

In 1900 a Berkeley record book listed fourteen missions: two in San Francisco and one each in Los Angeles, Fresno, Marysville, Riverside, Pasadena, San Diego, Ventura, Berkeley, Oakland, Sacramento, Santa Barbara, and Santa Cruz.[41] The Los Angeles mission was taken over by the Presbyterians and the Santa Barbara mission involved cooperation with the Methodists and the Presbyterians.[42] A survey conducted by the Home Missions Council and the Council of Women for Home Missions in 1921 reported that the Congregationalists had nine Chinese missions.[43]

As the years went by, many of the schools folded, populations shifted, and missionary zeal faded. In the end only three of the missions sponsored by the CCM developed into freestanding churches that still relate to the Congregational tradition through the United Church of Christ: the Chinese Congregational Church of San Francisco, the Chinese Community Church of San Diego, and the Chinese Community Church of Berkeley.

THE SAN FRANCISCO CHINESE CONGREGATIONAL CHURCH (UCC)

The San Francisco Chinese Congregational Church marks its beginning from 1873, when Pond and seventeen friends left Third Congregational Church to found Bethany Congregational Church. When Pond became AMA superintendent for Chinese work in California, he leased a building near Portsmouth Square and saw to it that English classes for Chinese were offered at night. The number of people attending these classes steadily increased.

178

By 1902 the program had expanded and money was sought from the East to purchase a building at 21 Brenham Place, in San Francisco's Chinatown. The upstairs became residential apartments and the first floor was reserved for church services and English classes. In 1904 the Rev. Gum Gee was called to serve as pastor to the Chinese congregation, and 199 Chinese members of Bethany Congregational Church were transferred to the Chinese church roll. It was found that many of these were no longer active, so that the Chinese church ended up with about 96 members.[44]

When the San Francisco earthquake and fire struck on April 18, 1906, the church building was destroyed. A longtime church member who as a child had lived on the fourth floor described the scene:

> Our Church withstood the impack [sic] of the first quake, but the doors and windows could not be opened. Portsmouth Square was filled with people, some in their night clothes. The children of our building were herded to the park for fear that the building might crumble. My parents returned to the Church to clean up, but another quake brought them hurrying down again. . . . Soon a fire broke out. . . . People began to run back to their homes to gather what they could of their belongings, and the migration commenced. . . . Our Church group kept together and together we walked all the way towards the west to the West School. . . . My father clutched tightly in his hand the small suit-case which contained the most valuable and treasured things—the records of our Church.[45]

A partially damaged school building that was adjacent to the old church was used by the Chinese congregation until a new building could be constructed. Again Pond helped the church get financial help from Eastern sources. When that money was combined with local funds, the church had $30,000 to erect a new building at 21 Brenham Place. It was not until 1921, however, that the Chinese church became an independent organization, with the provision that the building could not be sold for commercial purposes. From that date on, the finances, ministry, and associated activities were handled by the officers of the church.

Although many ministers have served the Chinese Congregational Church over its 100 years, one pastor is especially important. From 1913 to 1920 the Rev. B. Y. Leong worked at the church as an assistant and was ordained. In 1920 he left San Francisco to serve churches in Bakersfield and Chicago. After a few years he returned to the San Francisco church to be its pastor (1927–53). His total length of service to the church remains unequaled (thirty-three years).

As California Congregationalists became part of the United Church of Christ in the 1960s, the Chinese Congregational Church joined the UCC. In 1965–66 its building was renovated, and in 1971 the church was able to "burn its mortgage." It continues to serve the Chinese community in San Francisco.[46]

THE SAN DIEGO CHINESE COMMUNITY CHURCH (UCC)

In June 1885 William C. Pond noted that two Christian Chinese had moved to San Diego. Soon thereafter the CCM started a Chinese Mission School at the First Presbyterian Church in that city. Late the next year the *San Diego Union* ran a short announcement that twenty students were enrolled in classes.

> They learn reading and writing and are taught religious precepts from the Bible in their own language. . . . Several "boys" have recently "graduated" and gone back to the Flowery Kingdom, to disseminate the Gospel among their benighted countrymen, providing they themselves don't back-slide.[47]

During the early years the mission moved several times, seeking to be closer to the Chinese community and to have more space to provide sleeping rooms for the "Christianized Chinese." It was believed that association with unconverted friends was "not conducive to morality and steadfastness in the faith." One of the early Chinese mission workers described the difficulties faced by new converts: "We Chinese Christians are very much hated by our relatives, they say that the Christians are a people of no use—ungrateful, because we do not worship ancestors. It is common thing in China that Christians are severely beaten by parents for accepting the Christian doctrine."[48]

Several teachers served the mission during the early years. In 1903 excessive harassment of Chinese under the Oriental Exclusion Act made life extremely difficult for all Chinese in San Diego. (Because the city was situated on the Mexican border, it was used by the Chinese for illegal entry from Mexico.) During his annual visit in 1905, Pond found the mission "near death." The situation was aggravated because four Protestant mission stations were competing for the attention of the 400 Chinese persons living in the area. The Congregational mission was the oldest and best situated; therefore, it survived.

In 1911, when the fifty-year charter of the CCM ended, the local Congregational Association took over supervision of the mission. An Oriental Committee comprising representatives from all Congregational churches in San Diego County supervised the work. In 1925 the mission called its first minister, the Rev. C. C. Hung, and in 1927 dedicated a new brick structure containing sixteen dormitory rooms at 645 First Avenue. It was not until 1946 that the mission became a self-sustaining Chinese Congregational Church with its own constitution. In 1950 the church changed its name to the Chinese Community Church, to reflect its mission to the community. Finally, in 1960, the church sold its First Avenue property and began construction of a facility at 1750 47th Street.

Over the years the church sponsored youth organizations and special programs to keep second-generation Chinese in touch with their cultural roots. During World War II the laws against the Chinese were repealed, and the Chinese were allowed to enter the United States on a quota basis. As the number of Chinese living in the United States increased, the church began to divide philosophically, theologically, and culturally. In 1978 the pastor resigned and with about half the members left the church to found a more conservative Chinese Evangelical Church. The remaining members regrouped, called a new pastor, and rebuilt the congregation as part of the United Church of Christ. In 1985 the church celebrated its centennial.[49]

THE BERKELEY CHINESE COMMUNITY CHURCH (UCC)

The beginnings of the Berkeley Congregational Chinese Mission go back to the early 1890s, when the Women's Missionary Society of the First Congregational Church of Berkeley raised concerns about Chinese mission work in the area.[50] By 1900 a Sunday school for Chinese students opened in the basement of the First Congregational Church. A year or so later it officially came under the supervision of the CCM and moved to a "cottage" on Shattuck Avenue that provided living quarters and various meeting rooms. The mission was especially dedicated to serve the needs of students from China who were studying at the University of California.

About 1905 the lot on Shattuck Avenue was sold. The building, however, was moved to a new location (1917 Addison Street) and raised up for a second floor. The new first floor had a large meeting room with kitchen, dining room, and bath at the back of the building. English classes and Christian education programs flourished. So much so, in fact, that by 1909, a decision was made to organize a branch church. Because several of the mission teachers came from the North Berkeley Congregational Church, the Chinese asked the North Berkeley Church to be its "mother church." They reflected, "We were not in a position to organize an independent church." However, they appreciated the fact that a church ought to "supply the educational, social, as well as the spiritual need of its members." They hoped that with the blessing of God the branch church would become independent.[51]

In May 1910 the branch church was organized. The Mission House, as it was called, held Sunday services, launched a Christian education program, and started a Chinese Literary Club. The Literary Club helped older members learn Chinese and held programs on social reforms, such as queue-cutting, the American system of marriage, and the eating of Chinese food at the table with individual bowls and chopsticks. In 1912, when the Manchu government was overthrown and the Republic of China established, the church went through turmoil as some members returned to China or worried about relatives back home. Shortly thereafter new leadership embarked on a program to make the church independent of the mother church. This goal was realized on December 15, 1914, when the Berkeley Chinese Congregational church became a self-sustaining independent congregation.

In the years that followed the church flourished, becoming the center of social and cultural life for Chinese residents of

Berkeley and for Chinese students at the university. When families with children were drawn into the church, a Chinese language school was started. Ironically this mission, which started out to teach English to Chinese students, soon found itself called to teach Chinese to second-generation Chinese-Americans.

By 1940 more space was needed. Although plans were formulated to build a modern building, changes in pastoral leadership and wartime obligations kept things at the planning stage for another decade. Property finally was purchased at 2117 Acton Street, and in 1955 a new building was dedicated. The Berkeley Chinese Community Church continued to grow, adding a parsonage and a Christian education building, and became an important force in the development of the United Church of Christ.[52]

MISSION AND OUTREACH

The story of Chinese Congregationalism is not simply the story of mission schools evolving into churches. From the beginning, concerns about Chinese immigrants were linked to the evangelization of China. Pond and other missionaries viewed the conversion of the Chinese in the United States as the first step in bringing all of China to Christianity. As early as 1878 Pond expressed the need for a mission in Hong Kong that would be closely related to his work in California. This mission could meet returning converts, assist them in relocation, and keep track of them. Many Chinese converts agreed with Pond. In 1880 the CCM recommended that a mission be established in China to connect its foreign and home work.[53]

The American Board of Commissioners for Foreign Missions had some history in south China. However, its mission in Canton, the oldest of the board, was suspended in 1866. Twenty years later the board responded to the argument that the churches needed to keep in touch with converts returning to their native land. C. R. Hager, experienced with the Chinese in San Francisco, was sent to Hong Kong in 1883. He itinerated from that city and established outstations on the mainland.[54]

Back in San Francisco, Chinese Christians also became more concerned about China. In 1886, when a Mr. G. L. Fong delivered a series of lectures on the hard times in China, the need for missionaries to build churches to help the people, and the duty of the Chinese people in the United States to assist their homeland, a Chinese Congregational Missionary Society was started. The idea spread to other Chinese missions and all contributions were sent to the San Francisco church. In 1887 the missionary society supported the efforts of the Rev. Chui Get to lead worship and start a library of Chinese and English books in Canton. In the years that followed, contributions from the Chinese Congregational Missionary Society helped to start new churches in Sun Ning (1889), Hoy Ping (1901), Yun Ping (1901), and Sun Woy (1904).[55]

The Chinese-Americans also took responsibility for mission and outreach in California. Methodists and Presbyterians had special programs to rescue young girls from prostitution. The Baptists supported a home for boys. In San Francisco the Congregationalists and the Presbyterians started Hip Wo School. Beginning in 1924 the school grew into a quality secondary school for second- and third-generation Chinese young people. It was argued that the purpose of the school was "to introduce Chinese culture to the Americanized Chinese students, to develop a Christ-like spirit in the students, most of whom come from Godless homes."[56]

One final word about Chinese mission work needs to be added. Although the (German) Reformed Church in the United States did not have any direct work with Chinese immigrants, it was not unaffected by mounting Christian concerns for China. In 1895 William Hoy, a Reformed missionary home on furlough from work in Japan, was challenged to think about launching a mission to China. Four years later Hoy left his friends in Sendai, Japan, and established a new Reformed China Mission at Yochow City, Hunan. His careful report of that work shows another way in which the efforts of those denominations that shaped the United Church of Christ have longstanding commitments to the well-being of the Chinese people.[57]

HAWAII

Although much has been written about the development of Congregationalism in Hawaii, we cannot complete this story of Chinese Congregationalism without a brief description of what happened in Hawaii. The history is different, but the concerns are the same.[58]

The history of Chinese Christians in Hawaii begins with the work of Lutheran missionaries from the Basel, Berlin, and Rhenish missionary societies in south China. These Lutheran societies worked with the Hakkas, a nomadic group that settled north of Guangzhou many generations earlier. Perhaps because the Hakkas spoke a different dialect and were considered "outsiders" to the "Cantonese," they were especially receptive to the Christian message. Furthermore, in the 1850s and 1860s, when Hawaiian sugar plantations started recruiting Chinese labor, the Hakka people emigrated in large numbers.

It was not long before the Hawaiian Evangelical Association (the continuing Congregational mission organization) found a young man named S. P. Aheong to work with the Chinese. Aheong came to Hawaii as a Chinese laborer and married a Hawaiian. He spoke many Chinese dialects and learned English quickly. Although many of the Hakka Chinese immigrants were already Christian, in 1868 Aheong was appointed to "Christianize the 1500 Chinese then in Hawaii."

At about the same time, the Bethel Church (a chapel for seamen) in Honolulu also reached out to the Chinese. Its minister, the Rev. Samuel C. Damon, set up a Sunday school for Chinese and began providing English instruction. By 1870 the Young Men's Christian Association (YMCA) purchased Chinese Bibles and organized programs. A Chinese YMCA, later known as the Chinese Christian Association, was organized in 1877. Chinese-language services at Bethel Church served a growing community until, in 1879, a group of young Chinese converts petitioned the Hawaiian Evangelical Association to organize a Chinese church. They purchased a lot on Fort Street and obtained a charter from King Kalakaua. The Fort Street Chinese Church was dedicated in 1881.

For forty-five years the church, supported by mission funds, served the Chinese community of Honolulu. After becoming self-supporting in 1919, the church decided to move to a more suburban area to follow the Chinese population. In 1926 a site was chosen at 1054 South King Street and a building was erected. The church renamed itself the First Chinese Church of Christ in Hawaii. In 1979 it celebrated its centennial.[59]

During the early years the Fort Street Church served Hakka Chinese, many of whom were converted to Christianity by German missionaries before coming to the islands. By the end of the century, however, most Chinese entering Hawaii spoke the more common Cantonese or Punti dialect. Furthermore, many of them had no knowledge of Christianity. It was time to organize a church to serve their needs.[60]

A small mission was begun in 1906 by Elijah and Jessie MacKenzie. It attracted older Cantonese-speaking Chinese and many young people. By 1915 the "Chinese Second Congregational Church," or, in Chinese, the "Yee Jee Wui," was organized. Because the church erected a building at 74 North Beretania Street, it was also known as the Beretania Mission or the Beretania Church of Christ.[61]

The congregation was made up of persons from the mission school, a group from the old Fort Street Chinese Church, and students from nearby Mills School, later known as the Mid-Pacific Institute. By the late 1920s the Beretania Church was Honolulu's largest Chinese church. Its youth programs were especially strong.

Before long, however, conflicts arose between the young members of the church and a non-English-speaking pastor who was called to the church in 1928. Finally, in 1934, twenty members of the Beretania Church Young People's Board withdrew from the parent church to establish a new English-speaking church. Although the Beretania Church suffered a setback, it eventually initiated bilingual services and responded to more progressive leadership after 1938. In 1948 the church relocated, constructing a building on Judd Street near Liliha and changing its name to the United Church of Christ. During 1975 and 1985 the church celebrated its sixtieth and seventieth anniversaries with great vigor and enthusiasm.

A third congregation serving the Chinese community in Honolulu got its start from those young people who left the Beretania Church in 1934. At first, because they met in an old building on Keeaumoku Street, the church was known as the Keeaumoku Church of Christ. It held services in English and voted to allow membership without requiring baptism. Steady attendance and earnestness in embracing the new faith were considered more important than the rite of baptism in determining membership. This was important to many parents who were afraid to risk having their children show disrespect and ignorance of the deities that were part of Chinese culture.

In 1938 the young church changed its name to The Community Church of Honolulu. Its new church creed read in part:

> We purport to be democratically Christian, believing that the democratic process is the most educative in the development of the personality. . . . We purport to be a community church in fact—a community church is supra-racial and supra-national, open to all, regardless of race, class or caste, and seeks to render a real service to the community in the light of its needs.[62]

By 1944 the young church became self-supporting, and in 1949 it was formally incorporated. During 1984 it celebrated its fiftieth anniversary.

In the late nineteenth century Chinese workers settled on all the Hawaiian islands. Francis W. Damon was chosen to be superintendent of Chinese work for the Hawaiian Evangelical Association in 1882. Before long, Chinese schools and churches existed on Maui (Kula, Wailuku, and Paia), Kauai (Waimea, Hanapepe, and Hanalei), and Hawaii (Hilo, Kau, and Kohala). The new immigrants were receptive to Christianity, often bringing their own ministers and Christian traditions from the Lutheran missions. They also brought their wives and children with them.[63] But the Chinese for the most part did not stay on the plantation. They gradually moved to the city, and so 100 years later only one UCC church, which started as a Chinese church, is still in existence on the outer islands. It is in Hilo, until recent years the second largest city in Hawaii. The Hilo Chinese Christian Church, in 1956, changed its name to The United Community Church in order to express its openness to persons other than Chinese.[64]

CHINESE CHURCHES AND THE UNITED CHURCH OF CHRIST

The situation of Chinese-Americans has dramatically changed during the latter half of the twentieth century. While the old Chinese communities in major cities have matured, new waves of immigrants have arrived from Taiwan and the cities of Southeast Asia. New Chinese UCC churches founded in the 1970s carry labels like the Formosan United Church of Christ (Seattle, 1977), Chinese Community Church (Detroit, 1977), and Brookline Chinese Christian Church (Boston area, 1979).[65]

In the early 1970s church leaders from Chinese, Japanese, and Pacific Island churches began to discover common concerns in the life of the United Church of Christ. The Pacific and Asian American Ministries of the United Church of Christ (PAAM) was formed in 1974 to give expression to the growing pluralism of the UCC. Members from the historic Chinese Congregational churches have joined with representatives from the younger Chinese UCC churches and other UCC churches that have large Asian or Pacific islander memberships for fellowship and to influence the wider church.

Finally, Chinese UCC churches developed deep ecumenical loyalties. In San Francisco the Chinese Congregational Church (UCC) works closely with the Chinese Christian Union of San Francisco. This organization, which celebrated its sixty-fifth anniversary in 1981, brings together eight Chinese church bodies in the city of San Francisco: Baptist, Methodist, Presbyterian, Christian Reformed, Church of the Nazarene, Episcopal, Salvation Army, and Congregational (UCC).[66] In Honolulu four Chinese churches are affiliated with the Chinese Christian Association (two Episcopal and two UCC).[67] Every three years most of the Chinese UCC churches participate in CONFAB, an ecumenical gathering of the National Conference of Chinese Churches in America.

The Chinese churches have tried to affirm their identity as Chinese and to preserve the values that come from their history and culture. At the same time they have been full participants in the life of the denomination. In so doing they have brought richness to the whole United Church of Christ. Rooted in their Congregational and United Church heritage, they live out the ecumenical spirit of the gospel. The Chinese Congregational story is a sign that it is possible to be particular and universal, denominational and ecumenical.

Notes

Chapter 1: The Union Church: A Case of Lutheran and Reformed Cooperation

1. *The COCU Consensus: In Quest of a Church of Christ Uniting.* (Princeton, NJ: COCU, 1985), p. 7.
2. Philip Schaff, *The Creeds of Christendom* (New York: Harper & Brothers, 1877), vol. 1, p. 212.
3. Ibid., pp. 533ff.
4. Max Gobel, *Beschichte des Christlichen Lebens*, vol. 1, pp. 36ff.
5. James I. Good, *History of the Reformed Church in the United States, 1725–1792* (Reading, PA: Daniel Miller Pub., 1899), p. 32.
6. Ibid., p. 50.
7. Theodore E. Schmauk, *The Lutheran Church in Pennsylvania, (1638–1800): An Address, Pennsylvania German Society Proceedings And Addresses*, at Easton, PA, Oct. 26, 1900, vol. 11, p. 3.
8. Martin L. Montgomery, *School History of Berks County* (Philadelphia: J. B. Rodgers Printing, 1889), p. 63.
9. *A History of the Commission on the Welfare of the Union Church*, 1961, p. 4.

Chapter 2: The German Evangelical Protestants

1. Early Pittsburgh history is found in Stefan Lorant, *Pittsburgh: The Story of an American City* (Garden City, NY: Doubleday, 1964).
2. A history of the German Evangelical Protestant Church in Pitts-

burgh (Smithfield) was written by Pastor Friedrich Ruoff in 1882. The German text and an English translation are in the archives of Smithfield United Church, Pittsburgh, PA.

3. Quotations from Weber's journal are found in Ruoff (see n. 2).
4. The Penns also gave land to the First Presbyterian Church and Trinity Episcopal Church, now Trinity Cathedral.
5. The Voegtly Church did not become part of the Evangelical Protestant Church of North America. It joined the Reformed Synod (later the Evangelical and Reformed Church). It no longer exists.
6. The names (locations) and dates of these churches, except for St. John's in Wheeling, are listed as the Evangelical Protestant Conference in the *Congregational Year Book*, 1926, 1927, 1928 and 1929. Information on St. John's, Wheeling, was obtained from Carl Hermann Voss, whose grandfather, Eduard Voss, was its pastor. The church did not join the Congregational fellowship and probably no longer exists.
7. Information on the founding of St. Peter and St. Paul is taken from a brochure published by the church.
8. *Congregational Year Book*, 1926–29.
9. From a brochure published by the church.
10. I am indebted to Hermine Munter of Smithfield United Church, Pittsburgh. The quotation is taken from a letter from her.
11. Sketches of Eisenlohr and Schmidt are drawn from Charles William Hanko, *The Evangelical Protestant Movement* (Brooklyn, NY: Educators Publishing Co., 1955), pp. 30–31.
12. Ibid., pp. 32–33, plus information given by Ruoff's daughter-in-law, Cecile Ruoff of Smithfield United Church, Pittsburgh.
13. Hanko, op. cit., pp. 56–57. Copies of the publications mentioned are in the archives of the Congregational Library, Boston.
14. *Catechism of the Religion of Jesus Christ, with Supplement* (Cincinnati: The Evangelical Protestant Church of North America, n.d.), pp. 84–85. In the archives of Smithfield United Church, Pittsburgh.
15. This summary of the problems of Evangelical Protestant churches is based on an address given by Carl August Voss published in *Volkskalender*, the yearbook of the Evangelical Protestant Conference, 1926, pp. 57–64.
16. *Who's Who in America*, 1944; and from Carl Hermann Voss, the son of Carl August Voss.
17. Information on the merger is found in Hanko, op. cit., pp. 77–79; from conversations with Carl Hermann Voss; and from the *Congregational Year Book*, 1926, p. 118.
18. Voss, address in *Volkskalender*, 1926, pp. 57–64.

19. Statistics on the Evangelical Protestant Conference are found in the *Congregational Year Book*, 1926 to 1947, and in the minutes of the Annual Meeting of the Evangelical Protestant Conference, May 16–18, 1947. Evangelical Protestant churches that joined the Congregational fellowship in 1925–27 were as follows: Pittsburgh: Smithfield, Birmingham, West End, Duquesne Heights, Spring Hill, Manchester, Mt. Washington, Baum's (Bloomfield), Homestead; Pittsburgh vicinity: McKeesport, Etna, Tarentum, Beaver Falls, Saxonburg; Cincinnati: St. Peter's, St. Paul's, St. John's on Neeb Road, St. Mark's, St. John's of Mt. Auburn; Cincinnati vicinity: Bridgetown, Barnesburg (Mt. Healthy); Kentucky: Newport, St. John's; Johns Hill, St. John's; West Covington, St. John's; Indiana: Madison, United; Osgood, St. Peter's; Missouri: St. Louis, Independent. Later two new churches were founded and joined the Evangelical Protestant Conference: St. John's in Harrison, Ohio (1943), and St. Peter's in Brooksville, Indiana (1945).
20. Information on St. Peter and St. Paul UCC is found in a brochure published by the church.
21. From a letter from Carl Hermann Voss.
22. I am indebted to Harold F. Worthley of the Congregational Library in Boston for his help; to the ministers who have answered letters and sent information about their churches; and especially to Carl Hermann Voss, Hermine Munter, and Cecile Ruoff, who shared their knowledge of the Evangelical Protestant movement and read the manuscript of this chapter, offering suggestions for its improvement.

Chapter 3: Origins of the Christian Denomination in New England

1. Austin Craig, "Ourselves: Our Principles; Our Present Controversy; Our Immediate Duties" (Feltville, NJ, 1850). Craig, a prominent Christian pastor, biblical scholar, and educator in the mid-1800s, is today best known for the United Church of Christ conference center on Cape Cod that bears his name.
2. Louis H. Gunnemann, *The Shaping of the United Church of Christ: An Essay in the History of American Christianity* (New York: United Church Press, 1977), pp. 161–63.
3. "Doctor Channing's Letter," *The Christian Palladium*, February 14, 1837, pp. 305–11.
4. Milo True Morrill, *A History of the Christian Denomination in America, 1794–1911 A.D.* (Dayton: Christian Publishing Association, 1912), pp. 184–85.
5. "Channing's Letter," p. 306.

6. Stephen A. Marini, *Radical Sects of Revolutionary New England* (Cambridge, MA: Harvard University Press, 1982). This is an excellent source and the only major study of its type.

7. All material on Jones is from A. D. Jones, *Memoir of Elder Abner Jones* (Boston: William Crosby & Co., 1842).

8. Elias Smith, *The Life, Conversion, Preaching, Travels, and Sufferings of Elias Smith* (Portsmouth, 1816); *The Christian's Magazine*, June 1, 1805, pp. 11–12.

9. No church statistics exist before the publication of the *Herald of Gospel Liberty* (hereafter *HGL*). This assessment is based on the earliest published list of agents for the paper, representing 26 towns—eight each in Maine, Massachusetts, and New Hampshire and one each in Rhode Island and Vermont. *HGL*, September 15, 1808, p. 8.

10. *HGL*, August 17, 1810, p. 206.

11. *HGL*, December 11, 1812, pp. 447–48.

12. *HGL*, April 10, 1812, p. 380; August 17, 1810, p. 206.

13. *HGL*, October 25, 1811, p. 331.

14. *HGL*, December 20, 1811, pp. 4–9.

15. *HGL*, October 15, 1812, pp. 430–31.

16. Nathan O. Hatch, "The Christian Movement and the Demand for a Theology of the People," *Journal of American History*, December 1980, pp. 545–67.

17. *HGL*, October 30, 1812, p. 434.

18. *HGL*, October 1816, pp. 65–66.

19. *HGL*, April 29, 1814, p. 599.

20. The Free Will Baptists were perhaps the first group in New England to support women in traditionally male roles. As early as 1787 Abigail Amerzeen appears to have been in a position of authority at the church in New Castle, New Hampshire, and in 1791 Mary Savage of Woolwich, Maine, became the first in the denomination to "take the position of a gospel laborer." *The Centennial Record of Freewill Baptists, 1780–1880* (Dover, NH, 1881), pp. 45–47.

21. J. F. Burnett, *Early Women of the Christian Church Heroines All* (Dayton: Christian Publishing Association, n.d.), pp. 9–13; the Rev. E. W. Humphreys, *Memoirs of Deceased Christian Ministers; or, Brief Sketches of the Lives and Labors of 975 Ministers, Who Died Between 1793 and 1880* (Dayton: Christian Publishing Association, 1880), pp. 96–97.

22. *HGL*, August 1817, p. 224.

23. *Christian Herald*, July 1818, p. 47; ibid., September 1818, p. 70.

24. Humphreys, op. cit., pp. 92, 267.

25. *HGL*, February 1817, pp. 132–33.
26. *Christian Herald*, September 1818, p. 70.
27. *Christian Herald*, November 1818, pp. 86–89.
28. *HGL*, March 4, 1814, p. 575; *Christian Herald*, April 13, 1821, pp. 157–58. Anne Rixford (sic), Sara Hidges (sic), and Abigail Roberts are listed as "Unordained Preachers in the East Conference" of New York in the latter periodical.
29. *HGL*, February 19, 1813, p. 467.
30. *HGL*, July 17, 1815, p. 61; ibid., December 1816, pp. 73–77. See also *Christian Herald*, January 1819, p. 95.
31. *HGL*, September 1, 1808, p. 1; *Christian Herald*, May 1818, p. 1.
32. *Christian Herald*, March 1819; pp. 126–27.
33. *Christian Herald*, November 1819, pp. 72–73; December 8, 1820, pp. 79–88.
34. *Christian Herald*, August 1820, p. 12.
35. Ibid., p. 15.
36. *Christian Herald*, March 1820, p. 135.
37. *Gospel Luminary*, June 1826, pp. 125–32.
38. *Christian Palladium*, October 1, 1836, pp. 161–64.
39. Minutes of the Convention of 1834, reprinted in *The Christians' Annual 1899* (Dayton: Christian Publishing Association), p. 5.
40. If confusion existed over the antitrinitarianism of some Christians, especially in New York state, it was the Adventism of William Miller in the late 1830s and early 1840s that was most troublesome to New Englanders. Miller, a deist-turned-Baptist from Massachusetts, was convinced that the second advent was to take place on October 22, 1844; gathering thousands of followers throughout the northeast, he found the Christians, with their open pulpits and wide-ranging theologies, to be easy converts. Morrill estimates that "several thousand communicants" were eventually lost to the Millerites, with the most significant losses in Vermont. *History of the Christian Denomination*, pp. 175–76.
41. Ibid., p. 189.
42. The *Palladium*, published out of Union Mills, New York, was one of many religious journals sponsored by the Christians. For a complete account of the movement's voluminous output of print, see J. Pressley Barrett, ed., *The Centennial of Religious Journalism* (Dayton: Christian Publishing Association, 1908).
43. *Christian Palladium*, December 15, 1841, p. 251.
44. Quoted in Craig, op. cit., pp. 8–9.
45. *Christian Palladium*, August 2, 1843, p. 50.

Chapter 4: Evangelical Pietism and Biblical Criticism: The Story of Karl Emil Otto

1. For Evangelical Synod history, see Carl E. Schneider, *The German Church on the American Frontier* (St. Louis: Eden Publishing House, 1939), and David Dunn, ed., *A History of the Evangelical and Reformed Church* (Philadelphia: The Christian Education Press, 1961).
2. Carl E. Schneider, *History of the Theological Seminary of the Evangelical Church* (St. Louis: Eden Publishing House, 1925), and Walter A. Brueggemann, *Ethos and Ecumenism, An Ecumenical Blend: A History of Eden Theological Seminary, 1925–1975* (St. Louis: Eden Publishing House, 1975).
3. For Otto, see Schneider, *German Church*, p. 368, and Dunn, op. cit., pp. 223–29.
4. For Schaff, James Hastings Nichols, *Romanticism in American Theology: Nevin and Schaff at Mercersburg* (Chicago: University of Chicago Press, 1961), and *The Mercersburg Theology* (New York: Oxford University Press, 1966), and John B. Payne, "Philip Schaff: Christian Scholar, Historian and Ecumenist," *Historical Intelligencer* 2 (1982):17–23.
5. Winthrop S. Hudson, *Religion in America* (2d ed.; New York: Charles Scribner's Sons, 1981), p. 286, and William R. Hutchison, *The Modernist Impulse in American Protestantism* (New York: Oxford University Press, 1976), pp. 31–40.
6. Kenneth K. Bailey, *Southern White Protestantism in the Twentieth Century* (New York: Harper & Row, 1964), p. 12, and Pope A. Duncan, "Crawford Howell Toy: Heresy at Louisville," *American Religious Heretics: Formal and Informal Trials*, ed. George H. Shriver (Nashville: Abingdon Press, 1966), pp. 56–88.
7. Egbert C. Smyth, *Progressive Orthodoxy* (Boston: Houghton, Mifflin, 1885); Newman Smyth, *Dorner on the Future State* (New York: Charles Scribner's Sons, 1883). See Daniel Day Williams, *The Andover Liberals* (New York: Octagon Books, 1970).
8. On Briggs, see Lefferts A. Loetscher, *The Broadening Church: A Study of Theological Issues in the Presbyterian Church Since 1869* (Philadelphia: University of Pennsylvania Press, 1958), ch. 4, and H. Shelton Smith, Robert C. Handy, and Lefferts A. Loetscher, *American Christianity, 1820–1960* (New York: Charles Scribner's Sons, 1963), pp. 275–79.
9. Noted in Hudson, op. cit., p. 280. The Disciples of Christ expelled their first modernist minister, Robert C. Cave, in 1889. See Lester G. McAllister and William E. Tucker, *Journey into Faith: A History*

of the Christian Church (Disciples of Christ) (St. Louis: Bethany Press, 1975), pp. 363–64.

10. E. Otto obituary, Evangelical Herald (August 17, 1916), pp. 4–5, for a brief summary of his life.

11. For the influence of German Mediating theology on Amerian theology and philosophy, see Bruce Kuklick, Churchmen and Philosophers: From Jonathan Edwards to John Dewey (New Haven, CT: Yale University Press, 1985), pp. 126–27; Ragnar Holte, Die Vermittlungstheologie (Uppsala: Almquist & Wiksells, 1965).

12. For Heppe, see Lowell H. Zuck, "Heinrich Heppe: A Melanchthonian Liberal in the Nineteenth-Century German Reformed Church," Church History 51(1982):419–33.

13. Sketches of Ragué and Nollau in Lowell H. Zuck, New-Church Starts: American Backgrounds of the United Church of Christ (St. Louis: United Church Board for Homeland Ministries, 1982), pp. 12–14.

14. For Andreas Irion, see John W. Flucke, Evangelical Pioneers (St. Louis: Eden Publishing House, 1931), pp. 127–40, and Schneider, German Church, pp. 314–18, 416–17.

15. Walter Merzdorf translated Otto's 1873 Dogmatics (1967) in 149 typewritten pages from student notes. Copy in Eden Archives, Webster Groves, MO.

16. H. Kamphausen, Geschichte des Religioesen Lebens in der Deutschen Evangelischen Synode von Nord-Amerika (St. Louis: Eden Publishing House, 1924), p. 160.

17. Quoted in ibid., p. 165.

18. Protokoll der General-Conferenz (St. Louis, September 1880), p. 21.

19. Walter Merzdorf translated Otto's Romans in 1964–65. Copy available in Eden Archives, typewritten, 414 pages.

20. From Samuel D. Press, typewritten Autobiographical Reflections, in Eden Archives. See William G. Chrystal, "Samuel D. Press: Teacher of the Niebuhrs," Church History 53 (1984):504–21.

21. Der Gestohlene Knabe: Eine Geschichte aus der Revolutionszeit (St. Louis: Eden Publishing House, 1898).

22. Die Braut von Damaskus (St. Louis: Eden Publishing House, 1895).

23. Das Leben George Washingtons (St. Louis: Eden Publishing House, 1897).

24. Magazin fuer Evang. Theologie und Kirche 18 (1916):321–29, 329–39; 251–63, 287–97.

25. Carl E. Schneider, The Place of the Evangelical Synod in American Protestantism (St. Louis: Eden Publishing House, 1933), p. 25.

26. Otto, *Romans*, Merzdorf MSS, p. 4.
27. Ibid., pp. 100–101.
28. Ibid., pp. 114–15.
29. Ibid., pp. 395, 397–98.
30. Ibid., p. 402.
31. Ibid., p. 414.
32. Ibid., p. 411.
33. Schneider, *German Church*, p. 409.
34. Quoted in Schneider, *Place of the Evangelical Synod*, p. 25.
35. Ibid.
36. Samuel D. Press, Otto obituary, *The Keryx*, October 1916, pp. 26–27.

Chapter 5 : Women's Mission Structures and the American Board

1. Congregational, Methodist, American Baptist, Presbyterian, and Reformed Church in America.
2. The Hawaiian board (WBMPI), although organized at the same time as the other three boards, remained independent of the organizations on the mainland.
3. Grace T. Davis, *Neighbors in Christ: Fifty-eight Years of World Service by the Woman's Board of Missions of the Interior* (Chicago: Woman's Board of Missions of the Interior, 1926), p. 9. A document written in 1877 to clarify the relationship between the women's boards and the American Board indicates that male denominational leaders continued to think of the women's boards as a type of auxiliary. See "A Few Thoughts on Woman's Boards," *Missionary Herald* 73 (December 1877):392–94, reprinted in Priscilla Stuckey-Kauffman, "For the Sake of Unity: The Absorption of Congregational Woman's Boards of Foreign Missions by the American Board, 1927, with Special Attention to the Woman's Board of Missions for the Pacific" (M.A. thesis, Pacific School of Religion, Berkeley, California, 1985), pp. 141–43. Further documents clarifying the relationship between the women's boards and the American Board were written in 1906 and 1923. The former appears in Fred Field Goodsell, *You Shall Be My Witnesses* (Boston: ABCFM, 1959), p. 166, and the latter in *Missionary Herald* 119 (January 1923):3–4. Both are reprinted in Stuckey-Kauffman, op. cit., pp. 144–46.
4. *Minutes of the National Council of the Congregational Churches of the United States, 1921*, p. 118.
5. "A Few Thoughts," op. cit., p. 394; *Minutes of the National Council, 1923*, p. 88; Goodsell, op. cit., pp. 165–67. The women's contri-

butions represented net figures, since they always subtracted their own administrative and promotional expenses first.

6. Prudential Committee report, *Missionary Herald* 116 (November 1920):534–35.
7. Davis, op. cit., pp. 6, 15–16; R. Pierce Beaver, *American Protestant Women in World Mission: A History of the First Feminist Movement in North America* (2d ed.; Grand Rapids, MI: Eerdmans, 1980), pp. 106–7.
8. For instance, the Woman's Foreign Missionary Society of the Methodist Protestant Church, organized in Pittsburgh, Pennsylvania, in 1879, was in 1884 confiscated by a vote of the General Conference, a body comprised only of men. See Beaver, op. cit., pp. 105–6.
9. Helen Barrett Montgomery, *Western Women in Eastern Lands* (New York: Macmillan, 1914), p. 38.
10. Ibid., pp. 264–73.
11. Beaver, op. cit., pp. 184–91.
12. For lists of committee members see "Preliminary Report of the Committee of Twelve on Missionary Organization, Presented to the Commission on Missions, Chicago, January 21, 1925," Woman's Board of Missions for the Pacific Papers, Badé Institute, Pacific School of Religion, Berkeley, California. For attitudes toward ordained women see "Report of the Commission on Ordained Women, Church Assistants, and Lay Workers," *Minutes of the National Council, 1921*, pp. 37–46.
13. For a thorough study of the bureaucratic changes taking place in American religion between 1876 and 1929, see Ben Primer, *Protestants and American Business Methods* (Ann Arbor, MI: UMI Research Press, 1979).
14. "Constitution of the National Council of the Congregational Churches in the United States," quoted in Gaius Glenn Atkins and Frederick L. Fagley, *History of American Congregationalism* (Boston: The Pilgrim Press, 1942), p. 213.
15. *Minutes of the National Council, 1871*, pp. 46–47.
16. *Minutes of the National Council, 1907*, cited in Atkins and Fagley, op. cit., pp. 313f.
17. Summarized in Atkins and Fagley, op. cit., pp. 309–11.
18. Henrietta F. Brewer, "The Apportionment Plan and the Board of the Pacific," Woman's Board of Missions for the Pacific, *Thirty-eighth Annual Report, 1911*, p. 11.
19. W. E. Strong to Elisabeth S. Benton, September 8, 1920, WBMP Papers, Badé Institute, Pacific School of Religion, Berkeley, California.
20. Ibid.

21. James L. Barton to Henrietta F. Brewer, August 14, 1920; proposal for cooperative council inserted between letters dated June–July 1920; L. T. Evans to Mrs. Kirkwood, November 23, 1920, all found in WBMP Papers.

22. *History of Fifty Years: Woman's Board of Missions for the Pacific and Program of Jubilee Meetings* (San Francisco, 1923), pp. 32–36; Council of Congregational Woman's Foreign Mission Boards, Minutes, February 2, 1923, WBMP Papers; Elisabeth Benton, "Annual Report of the Assistant Recording Secretary," WBMP *Forty-seventh Annual Report, 1920*, p. 8.

23. Evans to Mrs. R. C. Kirkwood, October 16, 1921, WBMP Papers.

24. Woman's Boards' Council minutes, January 8, 1923, WBMP Papers.

25. In 1913 this had meant that the COM roster consisted of twenty-one men and two women, whose names appeared at the bottom of the list (*Minutes of the National Council 1913*, p. 394). By 1921 the women were no longer listed in last place, but the proportion of women had decreased to three out of forty-nine members (*Minutes of the National Council, 1921*, pp. 5–6).

26. Evans to Helen Street Ranney, December 6, 1921, WBMP Papers.

27. WBMP minutes, April 4, 1923, WBMP Papers.

28. "Hark to the New 'Herald'!" *Missionary Herald* 119 (January 1923):3.

29. Woman's Boards' Council minutes, February 13, 1923, WBMP Papers.

30. WBMP minutes, "Main Points," February 6, 1924, WBMP Papers.

31. "Preliminary Report of the Committee of Twelve on Missionary Organization," WBMP Papers. It is not clear how the proportion of one third women was agreed on. The fourfold structure of benevolent and mission groups was probably borrowed from Presbyterians, who in 1923 had effected sweeping consolidations (including the women's missionary boards) along these lines. See the Presbyterian Church (U.S.A.), *General Assembly Minutes, 1923*, I:58–88, cited in Lois A. Boyd and R. Douglas Brackenridge, *Presbyterian Women in America: Two Centuries of a Quest for Status* (Westport, CT: Greenwood Press, 1983), p. 61.

32. "Plan of Proposed Merger of the American Board and the Three Woman's Boards, March 10, 1925," WBMP Papers. Reprinted in Stuckey-Kauffman, op. cit., pp. 147–54.

33. See Stuckey-Kauffman, op. cit., pp. 97–101, for details of the women's agreements and differences with the "Tentative Plan."

34. "Report to the Committee on Missionary Organization," WBMP Papers. Reprinted in Stuckey-Kauffman, op. cit., pp. 157–59.

35. Calder to women's boards, April 28, 1925, WBMP Papers.

36. Helen Calder, "Report of Meeting of Committee of Twelve in New York City," May 19, 1925, WBMP Papers.
37. Letitia Evans to Helen Calder, May 27, 1925, American Board of Commissioners for Foreign Missions Papers, Houghton Library, Harvard University, Cambridge, MA.
38. WBMP minutes, August 31, 1925, WBMP Papers.
39. Ibid.
40. Minutes of the National Council, 1925, pp. 59–62.
41. Ibid., pp. 58, 67.
42. Atkins and Fagley, op. cit., p. 330.
43. The Pacific Board spent the ensuing nine months discussing the merger proposal and negotiating terms with the appropriate men's committees. For a full review of their negotiations, see Stuckey-Kauffman, op. cit., pp. 116–18.
44. Rosa B. Ferrier, "After the Merger, Whither?" WBMP Fifty-third Annual Report, 1926, p. 2.
45. Pacific 76 (October 1926):2.
46. WBMP minutes, April 6, 1927 and December 7, 1927, WBMP Papers.
47. Minutes of the National Council, 1929, p. 96, quoted in Atkins and Fagley, op. cit., p. 333.
48. Minutes of the National Council, 1929, p. 18, quoted in Atkins and Fagley, op. cit., p. 333.
49. Goodsell, op. cit., pp. 148–49.
50. Mrs. W. C. Blasdale to Harold Belcher, August 31, 1939, WBMP Papers.
51. Receipts of the Woman's Boards in 1925 equaled 34 percent of the American Board's. See the Congregational Yearbook, 1925 (Boston: Executive Committee of the National Council of Congregational Churches, 1925), pp. 19, 26.
52. Grace T. Davis of the WBMI wrote: "We have endeavored to show a great and inescapable sense of the value of working together. The very vocabulary of the annual reports [shows that] words [such as] cooperation, interdenominationalism, internationalism, unification, occur with increasing frequency" (Neighbors in Christ), p. 200. See also Stuckey-Kauffman, op. cit., pp. 81–83.

Chapter 6: Religious Journalism: A Legacy from the Christian Church

1. J. F. Burnett, "Elias Smith, Reformer, Preacher, Journalist, Doctor," one of a series of undated booklets issued sometime before 1931 by the Department of Publishing of the American Christian Con-

vention, "that members of our churches and Sunday-schools may be well informed as to the history and distinctive principles of The Christian Church," pp. 18ff.

2. Ibid., pp. 20–24. Dates for periodicals mentioned or related to those mentioned in this essay are:

The Christian Magazine, June 1805–August (?) 1808
   succeeded by *Herald of Gospel Liberty* in September 1808.

Herald of Gospel Liberty, September 1, 1808–1934
   absorbed *Christian Messenger and Palladium*, in December 1862;
   absorbed *Gospel Herald*, on January 4, 1868;
   absorbed *Christian Messenger* of New Bedford, MA, in January 1907;
   was merged with *The Congregationalist* to form *Advance* in 1934.

Christian Herald, May 1818–April 2, 1835 (absorbed *Watchman*, in May 1829)

Christian Journal (formerly *Christian Herald*), April 2, 1835–April 1841
   absorbed *The Christian* on June 28, 1838;
   name changed back to *Christian Herald*.

Christian Sun, February 17, 1844–December 31, 1965

Christian Messenger, c. 1848–January 1861
   absorbed *Christian Herald* on March 27, 1850;
   was merged with *Christian Palladium* in January 1861 to form *Christian Messenger and Palladium*.

Christian Palladium, c. 1831–January 1861

Christian Messenger and Palladium, January 1861–December 1862

Christian Banner, ?–1861 (consolidated with *Gospel Herald*)

Gospel Herald, October 2, 1843–January 4, 1868
   (consolidated with *Herald of Gospel Liberty*).

Christian Messenger (of New Bedford, MA), February 1900–January 1907

Advance, April 1934–September 1958

United Church Herald, October 9, 1958–July/August 1972

A.D., September 1972–June/July 1983

United Church News, May 1985–

3. Daniel Benoni Atkinson, "The Herald of Gospel Liberty: The Pioneer Religious Journal—A History," in *The Centennial of Religious Journalism*, ed. J. Pressley Barrett (Dayton: Christian Publishing Association, 1908), pp. 37–75.

4. Ibid.

5. In a unpublished manuscript by Dr. Denison in the files of Mary Denison Fiebiger.

6. William B. Lipphard, *Fifty Years an Editor* (Valley Forge, PA: Judson Press, 1963), pp. 16, 218–19.

7. J. F. Burnett, "The Origin and Principles of the Christians," the first booklet in an undated series, p. 56.
8. Elias Smith, in an "Address to the Public," published September 1, 1808, in the first issue of the Herald of Gospel Liberty and reprinted in The Centennial of Religious Journalism, pp. 29–34.
9. Quoted by Atkinson, op. cit., p. 49.
10. Douglas Horton, The United Church of Christ (New York: Thomas Nelson & Sons, 1962), p. 180.
11. Burnett, "Elias Smith," pp. 21–23.
12. Atkinson, op. cit., pp. 55–58.
13. P. J. Kernodle, Lives of Christian Ministers (Richmond, VA: Central Publishing Company, 1909), pp. 114, 127, 205, 219, 256.
14. Alfred Wesley Hurst, in an unpublished monograph on the life and work of Alva Martin Kerr called "The Fun of Being an Editor" (1976), p. 19. Copies are on file in the archives of the Congregational Christian Historical Society.
15. Louis H. Gunnemann, The Shaping of the United Church of Christ (New York: United Church Press, 1977), pp. 59–60.
16. A.D., September 1975, pp. 39–48.
17. A.D., August 1981.
18. A.D., June 1982.
19. Quoted in The Centennial of Religious Journalism, pp. 105–106.
20. Ibid., pp. 76–77. The hymn was written by the Rev. Thomas S. Weeks of Troy, Ohio.
21. Hurst, op. cit., p. 39.
22. Malcolm K. Burton, Disorders in the Kingdom (Rev. ed.; New York: Vantage Press, 1982), p. xii.
23. John Scotford, "The Council Faces Church Union," an editorial in the June 1948 Advance.
24. J. Martin Bailey, "My Hope for Our Church" in A.D., August 1981, p. 6.
25. Dorothy G. Berry, "A Continuing Search for Unity" in A.D., June 1982, p. 25.
26. Atkinson, op. cit., pp. 56–58.
27. Ibid., p. 59.
28. Kernodle, op. cit., pp. 257–58.
29. Hurst, op. cit., pp. 51–52.
30. United Church News, July 1985, p. 3.
31. Burnett, "Elias Smith," pp. 21–22.

Chapter 7: Philip William Otterbein and the United Brethren

1. Philip William Otterbein, "The Salvation-Bringing Incarnation and Glorious Victory of Jesus Christ Over the Devil and Death," in

Philip William Otterbein, ed. Arthur C. Core (Dayton: The Board of Publication, The Evangelical United Brethren Church, 1968), pp. 86–88. Referred to hereafter as "Sermon."

2. A. W. Drury, *The Life of Rev. Philip William Otterbein, Founder of the Church of the United Brethren in Christ* (Dayton: United Brethren Publishing House, 1884), p. 47. As was the custom in Germany, Otterbein used his second name throughout his life.

3. Ibid., p. 23.

4. Ibid.

5. Core, op. cit., pp. 14–15.

6. Ibid., p. 15.

7. John Steven O'Malley, *The Otterbeins: The Postlude of Pietism*. Ph.D. diss., Drew University, 1970, p. 284.

8. Drury, op. cit., p. 56.

9. J. Bruce Behney and Paul Eller, *The History of the Evangelical United Brethren Church*, ed. Kenneth W. Krueger (Nashville: Abingdon Press, 1979), p. 27.

10. *Minutes and Letters of the Coetus of the German Reformed Congregations in Pennsylvania 1747–1792* (Philadelphia: Reformed Church Publication Board, 1903), p. 340. Hereafter *Coetus*.

11. Drury, op. cit., p. 256.

12. Core, op. cit., p. 109. This was not new. It had been done in 1725 by John Philip Boehm in Philadelphia. See O'Malley, op. cit., p. 413.

13. Henry Harbaugh, *The Fathers of the German Reformed Church in Europe and America*, vol. 2 (Lancaster, PA: J. M. Westhaeffer, 1872), p. 52.

14. Drury, op. cit., p. 68.

15. Paul H. Eller, "Philip William Otterbein and Francis Asbury" in Core, op. cit., p. 66.

16. Drury, op. cit., pp. 102–3.

17. Ibid., p. 117.

18. O'Malley, op. cit., p. 429.

19. Core, op. cit., p. 99.

20. *Coetus*, op. cit., p. 300.

21. Henry G. Spayth, *History of the Church of the United Brethren in Christ* (Circleville, OH: Conference Office of the United Brethren in Christ, 1851), p. 43.

22. Core, op. cit., pp. 109–14.

23. Drury, op. cit., p. 183.

24. Core, op. cit., p. 27.

25. Francis Hollingsworth, "Notices of the Life and Labours of Martin Boehm and William Otterbein; and other Ministers of the Gospel

among the United German Brethren," The Methodist Magazine 6 (July 1823):253.

26. Core, op. cit., p. 34.
27. Coetus, op. cit., p. 428.
28. Core, op. cit., p. 122.
29. Christian Newcomer, The Life and Journal of the Rev.'d Christian Newcomer, Late Bishop of the United Brethren in Christ, trans. John Hilst (Hagerstown, MD: F. G. W. Knapp, 1834), p. 219.
30. Raymond W. Albright, "Philip William Otterbein: Reformed Pietist" in Core, op. cit., p. 55.
31. Eller, in Core, op. cit., p. 66.
32. Coetus, op. cit., pp. 154–55.
33. Core, op. cit., p. 111.
34. Harbaugh, op. cit., p. 68.
35. Core, op. cit., p. 120.
36. O'Malley, op. cit., p. 340.
37. Core, op. cit., p. 28.
38. Newcomer, op. cit., p. 223.
39. Otterbein, "Sermon," in Core, op. cit., p. 78.
40. Ibid., p. 82.
41. Ibid., p. 88.
42. Drury, op. cit., p. 177.
43. O'Malley, op. cit, p. 448.
44. Core, op. cit., pp. 20–21.
45. Drury, op. cit., pp. 165–66.
46. Jeffrey P. Mickle, "A Comparison of the Doctrines of Ministry of Francis Asbury and Philip William Otterbein," Methodist History 19 (July 1981):197.
47. Core, op. cit., p. 124.
48. Ibid., p. 102.
49. Ibid., p. 101.
50. Ibid.
51. Ibid., p. 100.
52. Ibid., p. 84.
53. Ibid., pp. 84–86.
54. O'Malley, op. cit., p. 386.
55. Drury, op. cit., p. 331.
56. Core, op. cit., p. 105.
57. Ibid., p. 106.
58. Spayth, op. cit., p. 155.
59. Ibid.
60. Drury, op. cit., p. 333.
61. Core, op. cit., p. 60.

62. Ibid., p. 69.
63. Drury, op. cit., p. 261.
64. *The United Church in America,* A Handbook of Information Published by the Reformed Church in the U.S.A., the United Brethren in Christ, and the Evangelical Synod of North America (n.p., n.d.).

Chapter 8: John Winebrenner: From German Reformed Roots to the Churches of God

1. The standard modern biography of John Winebrenner is Richard Kern, *John Winebrenner Nineteenth Century Reformer* (Harrisburg, PA: Central Publishing House, 1974). For accounts by a person who knew him see C. H. Forney, *History of the Churches of God in the United States of North America* (Harrisburg, PA: Publishing House of the Churches of God, 1914), pp. 3–118, 130–41, and George Ross, *Biography of Elder John Winebrenner—Semi-Centennial Sketch* (Harrisburg, PA: George Ross, 1880).
2. Kern, op. cit., pp. 7–17.
3. John Winebrenner, comp. *The Testimony of a Hundred Witnesses* (Baltimore: J. F. Weishampel, 1858), pp. 29–30; James I. Good, *History of the Reformed Church in the U.S. in the Nineteenth Century* (New York: Board of Publication of the Reformed Church in America, 1911), p. 10.
4. Forney, op. cit., pp. 11–12; John Winebrenner, *The Truth Made Known* (Harrisburg, PA: Michael W. McKinley, 1824), p. 8.
5. Winebrenner, *Truth Made Known,* pp. 4–26.
6. Ross, op. cit., pp. 12–13; Kern, op. cit., pp. 26–33.
7. Daniel Schurbly to John Winebrenner, January 8 and 18, 1825; John Winebrenner to Daniel Schurbly, January 14, 1825; Committee of Correspondence of German Reformed Congregation, Hagerstown, to John Winebrenner, January 10, 1826; John Winebrenner to Consistory of German Reformed Congregation of Hagerstown, April 18, 1825 and April 27, 1826, in Winebrenner Letters, Churches of God Archives, Findlay, Ohio.
8. John Winebrenner, comp., *History of all the Religious Denominations in the United States* (Harrisburg, PA: John Winebrenner, 1848), pp. 78–79, 176–77, 229–30.
9. John Winebrenner, *Doctrinal and Practical Sermons* (Baltimore: John F. Weishampel, 1860), pp. 97–124, 259–402; John Winebrenner, *A Brief View of the Formation, Government and Discipline of the Church of God* (Harrisburg, PA: Montgomery and Dexter, 1829).
10. John B. Frantz, "Revivalism in the German Reformed Church in

America to 1850 With Emphasis on the Eastern Synod." Ph.D. diss., University of Pennsylvania, 1961, pp. 32–58, 63–68.

11. Ibid., p. 118; Kern, op. cit., pp. 15, 36.
12. Charles C. Cole Jr., "The New Lebanon Convention," *New York History* 31 (October 1950):385–97.
13. Frantz, op. cit., pp. 81, 95–109, 111–21, 140–41.
14. Marion L. Bell, *Crusade in the City* (Lewisburg, PA: Bucknell University Press, 1977), pp. 62–67.
15. For a summary of Mercersburg Theology see James Hastings Nichols, *Romanticism in American Theology* (Chicago: University of Chicago Press, 1961).
16. Kern, op. cit., pp. 57–73.
17. The second edition of the *Anxious Bench* has been reprinted in *Catholic and Reformed: Selected Theological Writings of John Williamson Nevin*, ed. Charles Yrigoyen Jr. and George H. Bricker (Pittsburgh, PA: Pickwick Press, 1978), pp. 9–126.
18. *Mercersburg Review* 1 (September and November, 1849): 482–507, 521–39; John Williamson Nevin, *Anti-Christ; Or the Spirit of Sect and Schism* (New York: J. S. Taylor, 1848), passim. The *Mercersburg Review* articles have been reprinted in Yrigoyen and Bricker, op. cit., pp. 128–73.
19. Yrigoyen and Bricker, op. cit., p. 489.
20. Kern, op. cit., pp. 93–176.
21. J. Harvey Gossard, "John Winebrenner: Founder, Reformer and Businessman." Unpublished manuscript of paper presented at Rose Hill Seminar, Chambersburg, PA, July 15, 1985, pp. 15–20.
22. "James E. Wagner Remembers: An Oral History Interview," *Historical Intelligencer* 3 (Fall 1985):2–7.

Chapter 9: The Congregational Training School for Women

1. F. M. Sheldon, "What Shall I Do with My Life? A Message on Christian Leadership" (Boston: Congregational Education Society, n.d.), p. 6.
2. The Congregational Training School for Women, Chicago, *Register for 1911–1912*, p. 6. Hereafter issues of this periodical catalog will be refered to as CTSW *Register.*
3. General histories of the nineteenth-century deaconess movement are "The Deaconess Movement in Modern Times," in The National Council of the Congregational Churches of the United States, *Addresses, Reports, etc. . . . of the Thirteenth Triennial Session* (hereafter National Council *Minutes;* Boston: Office of the Secretary of the National Council, 1907), pp. 292–308; Jackson W. Carroll,

Barbara Hargrove, and Adair T. Lummis, *Women of the Cloth* (San Francisco: Harper & Row, 1981), pp. 20–48; Virginia Lieson Brereton and Christa Ressmeyer Klein, "American Women in Ministry: A History of Protestant Beginning Points," in *Women of Spirit,* ed. Rosemary Radford Ruether and Eleanor C. McLaughlin (New York: Simon and Schuster, 1978), pp. 171–90; and Catherine M. Prelinger and Rosemary S. Keller, "The Function of Female Bonding: The Restored Diaconessate of the Nineteenth Century," in *Women in New Worlds,* ed. Rosemary Skinner Keller, Louise L. Queen, and Hilah F. Thomas (Nashville: Abington Press, 1982), 2:318–37. On deaconesses in the heritage of the United Church of Christ, see Ruth W. Rasche, "The Deaconess Sisters: Pioneer Professional Women," in *Hidden Histories in the United Church of Christ,* ed. Barbara Brown Zikmund (New York: United Church Press, 1984), 1:95–109.

4. Virginia Lieson Brereton, "Preparing Women for the Lord's Work: The Story of Three Methodist Training Schools, 1880–1940," in *Women in New Worlds,* ed. Hilah F. Thomas and Rosemary Skinner Keller (Nashville: Abingdon Press, 1981), 1:178–99, emphasizes the training of deaconesses.

5. National Council, *Minutes of the Twelfth Triennial Session* (1904), pp. 481–83.

6. Ibid., pp. 483–84; National Council, *Minutes of the Eleventh Triennial Session* (1901), p. 24.

7. National Council, *Minutes of the Twelfth Triennial Session* (1904), p. 481. *The Chicago Seminary Quarterly,* Year Book Number, 1:4 (January 1902):79–80.

8. National Council, *Minutes of the Thirteenth Triennial Session* (1907), pp. 293–308. A denominational report in 1921 confirmed that the 1907 report had been the death knell of the Congregational deaconess movement. Although a few denominations had sizable numbers of deaconesses in the early twentieth century, most historians conclude that the movement had a surprisingly small impact on American women. In 1917 the dean of the Congregational Training School for Women noted that deaconess recruitment was flagging in other denominations as well, as other opportunities for salaried work in churches opened to women. Agnes Mabel Taylor, "Standards of Preparation of Women Church Assistants," *Religious Education* 12:6 (December 1917):440.

9. Information is from the Biographical File on Florence A. Fensham in the Hammond Library, Chicago Theological Seminary, Chicago, which includes unidentified clippings, some correspondence about Fensham, and Graham Taylor's "Funeral Address for Florence Amanda Fensham," February 18, 1912.

10. Minutes of the Executive Committee of the Board of Directors, November 2, and 11 and December 7, 1900, January 4, 1901, and January 3, 1902. Manuscript in the Office of the President, Chicago Theological Seminary.

11. Taylor, op. cit.

12. Arthur Cushman McGiffert Jr., *No Ivory Tower: The Story of the Chicago Theological Seminary* (Chicago: Chicago Theological Seminary, 1965), pp. 129, 130, 241, 313, and catalog numbers of the *Chicago Seminary Quarterly*.

13. This fact is disputed; indeed, the best manuscript on the history of the Chicago Theological Seminary (a longer version of McGiffert's *No Ivory Tower*, in the Hammond Library) contains conflicting reports about whether the second woman graduated in 1906 or 1926, V:36–37 and IX:104. My research has led me to conclude that a woman was enrolled soon after Fensham, but that she did not graduate.

14. Taylor, op. cit.

15. CTSW *Register* (1909–10), pp. 7–9; Florence Ripperton to Rose, March 3, 1912, manuscript in the dean's correspondence, Hammond Library. All other correspondence cited later in this article is in the same collection.

16. CTSW *Register*.

17. CTSW *Register* (1911–1912), p. 16.

18. This is the 1909 figure; CTSW *Register*, 1909–1910, p. 14. Expenses rose as years passed, but the effort to keep costs down was unrelenting, and it appears that financial difficulties did not prevent many women from enrolling. The correspondence of the deans with prospective students shows considerable concern for the students' financial problems. A 1920 study showed that the Training School's budget (which consistently ran a deficit) came from these sources: 7.5% student fees, 8.6% endowment, and 50.9% contributions. Minutes of the CTSW Board of Managers, Hammond Library.

19. Florence Ripperton to Rose, March 3, 1912.

20. *The Congregationalist*, June 17, 1926.

21. CTSW *Register* (1924–25), pp. 28–36.

22. Ibid. This is a list of all graduates and the jobs each had held since graduation.

23. The survey results are reported in Taylor, "Standards of Preparation," p. 443. The other quotations are from letters to the deans of CTSW, Hammond Library, CTS.

24. Agnes M. Taylor to Miss Beard, April 1, 1916; Harriet E. Gates to Agnes M. Taylor, December 9, 1918.

25. See Mrs. Henry W. Hunter, "The Work of the Church Assistant,"

Religious Education 12:1 (February 1917):24–30. The quotation is from Ana M. Truax to Agnes M. Taylor, November 9, 1915.

26. There is much historical literature on these organizations. See, for example, Rosemary Skinner Keller, "Lay Women in the Protestant Tradition," in *Women and Religion in America, vol. 1*, ed. Rosemary Radford Ruether and Rosemary Skinner Keller (San Francisco: Harper & Row, 1981), and Barbara Brown Zikmund and Sally A. Dries, "Women's Work and Woman's Boards," in Zikmund, *Hidden Histories, 1:140–53.*

27. Grace L. Schauffler, *Fields of the Lord: The Story of Schauffler College* (Oberlin, OH: Oberlin College, 1957).

28. Curtis Manning Geer, *The Hartford Theological Seminary, 1834–1934* (Hartford, CT: Case, Lockwood, and Brainard, 1934), pp. 174–75, 195–201; Elwood Street, "A Living Vision: A Brief Story of The Hartford Seminary Foundation," *The Bulletin of the Hartford Seminary Foundation* 25 (October 1958):1–61.

29. McGiffert, op. cit., pp. 169–71; Davis in *The Chicago Theological, Seminary Register* 9:3 (September 1919):1.

30. Hunter, op. cit., p. 26; Taylor, "Standards of Preparation," p. 439; National Council, *Minutes of the Nineteenth Session* (1921), pp. 37–46. In the Presbyterian Church, in contrast, the new office of commissioned church worker was created for similar workers, although its status also left much to be desired by advocates of laywomen in church professions. Elizabeth Howell Verdesi, *In But Still Out: Women in the Church* (Philadelphia: Westminster Press, 1976), offers an interesting analysis of this status, with reference to the power of women and men in the Presbyterian Church.

31. Margaret M. Taylor to F. M. Sheldon, September 16, 1920.

32. National Council, *Minutes of the Nineteenth Session* (1921), pp. 40–41; Brereton and Klein, op. cit., p. 183.

33. Margaret M. Taylor, "The Advance of the Women," *The Chicago Theological Seminary Register* 17:1 (January 1927):23–24; Georgia Harkness, in *Women and Religion in America*, vol. 3, ed. Rosemary Radford Ruether and Rosemary Skinner Keller (San Francisco: Harper & Row, 1986), p. 300.

34. Orpha Greep to Rachel R. Rogers, July 28, 1913.

35. Robert W. Lynn et al., *Why the Seminary? An Introduction to the Report of the Auburn History Project* (privately distributed, 1979), p. 73; Brereton, op. cit., pp. 192–93; CTSW *Registers.*

36. CTSW *Register* (1925–26), pp. 7–8; CTSW Alumni Association Minutes and Correspondence, June 1928. These records indicate that the alumnae appointed a committee to "prepare a statement to be sent to the Board of Directors and the Faculty of the Seminary of

the things essential for women in the curriculum," but this document, if ever written, cannot now be located.

37. Report of the President to the Board, June 5, 1929; Report of the President to the 25th Triennial Convention, June 4, 1930; Resolutions Committee of the 25th Triennial Convention; all typescripts in the Office of the President, Chicago Theological Seminary. *The Chicago Theological Seminary Register*, Announcements for 1929–30, p. 22. Gregory Vlastos, "Student Life," *The Chicago Theological Seminary Register* 19:2 (March 1929):28.

Chapter 10: Chinese Congregationalism

1. Ruthanne Lum McCunn, *An Illustrated History of the Chinese in America* (San Francisco: Design Enterprises, 1979), pp. 12–15. This popular history has a good survey of general information about the Chinese in America. Other useful surveys are Jack Chen, *The Chinese of America* (San Francisco: Harper & Row, 1980); Stanford Lyman, *Chinese Americans* (New York: Random House, 1974); William L. Tung, *The Chinese in America: 1820–1973* (New York: Oceana Publications, 1974). I have also relied heavily on a doctoral dissertation by Wesley S. Woo, "Protestant Work Among the Chinese in the San Francisco Bay Area, 1850–1920," Graduate Theological Union, 1983.

2. McCunn, op. cit., pp. 16–18.

3. Ibid., pp. 24–28.

4. Ibid., p. 17.

5. Ibid., pp. 31–35, and Woo, op. cit., pp. 22–24.

6. McCunn, op. cit., pp. 36–37.

7. Ibid., pp. 63–65.

8. Woo, op. cit., pp. 28–29.

9. Ibid., p. 66. Descriptions of the American Missionary Association are found in many places. In *Hidden Histories in the United Church of Christ* (United Church Press, 1984) there is a chapter on "Blacks and the American Missionary Association," 1:81–94. See also the *History of the American Missionary Association: Its Churches and Educational Institutions Among the Freedmen, Indians, and Chinese* (New York: American Missionary Association, 1874).

10. Woo, op. cit., p. 67.

11. *A Century Closes, the Church Continues: A Brief History of the First Congregational Church of Oakland, California, 1860–1960*, a centennial booklet (published by the church, 1960), p. 4.

12. Charles M. Bufford, "A Hundred Years of Congregationalism in San Francisco: 1849–1949" (a typewritten manuscript prepared

for the Centennial Meeting of First Congregational Church, San Francisco, 1949), pp. 10–12; and Woo, op. cit., p. 68.

13. William C. Pond, *Gospel Pioneering: Reminiscences of Early Congregationalism in California 1833–1920* (Oberlin, OH: The News Printing Company, 1921), p. 131; also quoted in Woo, op. cit., p. 68.
14. Pond, op. cit.
15. Ibid.
16. Ibid., p. 132.
17. Ibid., p. 133.
18. Ibid., p. 135.
19. Ibid., pp. 138–39.
20. Acknowledgment letter by William C. Pond to the AMA accepting his appointment as CCM superintendent. Quoted in *One Hundred Years of Leadership and Service, a Centennial Booklet of the San Diego Chinese Community Church (UCC) 1885–1985* (published by the church, 1985), p. 9.
21. Pond, op. cit., p. 143.
22. McCunn, op. cit., p. 71.
23. Ibid., p. 75.
24. Ibid., p. 77.
25. Woo, op. cit., pp. 143–44.
26. Lyman Abbott, "The Two Methods," *American Missionary* 24 (November 1880):373. Quoted in Woo, op. cit., p. 148.
27. *The Thirty-third Annual Report of the American Missionary Association and the Proceedings at the Annual Meeting Held at Chicago, Illinois, October 28–30, 1879* (New York: American Missionary Association, 1879), p. 16.
28. McCunn, op. cit., p. 84.
29. Ibid., pp. 87–88.
30. *California Chinese Mission Annual Report*, 1876, p. 9. Quoted in Woo, op. cit., p. 118.
31. Joseph Cook, *The Three Despised Races in the United States; or the Chinaman, the Indian, and the Freedman* (New York: American Missionary Association, 1878), p. 10. Quoted in Woo, op. cit., p. 118.
32. Woo, op. cit., p. 71.
33. Ibid., pp. 71–73.
34. Ibid., p. 72.
35. From the *San Diego Union*, March 23, 1899. Quoted in the centennial booklet of the *San Diego Chinese Community Church*, p. 12.
36. Woo, op. cit., pp. 154–62.
37. Ibid., p. 162.
38. Ibid., p. 170.

39. Ibid., p. 172.
40. Ibid., p. 173.
41. This list appears in a record book of the Berkeley Chinese Community Church dated February 19, 1900.
42. George W. Haskell, "The Southern California Story of Congregationalism." (Typewritten manuscript prepared for the seventy-fifth anniversary of the Congregational Conference of Southern California and the Southwest and the inaugural meeting of the United Church of Christ of Southern California, 1962), pp. 79–83. It is my understanding that the Los Angeles and Santa Barbara churches continue to exist outside the UCC.
43. From the *Directory of Oriental Missions*, ca. 1921, pp. 1, 14, 16. Quoted in Woo, op. cit., p. 104.
44. B. Y. Leong, "History of the Chinese Congregational Church," printed in the *80th Anniversary Booklet of The Chinese Congregational Church, San Francisco: 1873–1953* (published by the church, 1953), pp. 3–4. The number of members that were removed from the Bethany Church roll is cited in Bufford, op. cit., p. 12.
45. Florence Chinn Kwan, "Me and My Church: A Short Sketch," printed in the *80th Anniversary Booklet*, p. 10.
46. *The Chinese Congregational Church, San Francisco, 100th Anniversary 1873–1973* (published by the church, 1973), p. 5.
47. The *San Diego Union*, December 27, 1886. Reprinted in the centennial booklet of the *San Diego Chinese Community Church*, p. 10.
48. From an address of Chin Toy in San Diego, the fifth anniversary of the Congregational Chinese Mission of that city, February 9, 1890. Quoted in the centennial booklet of the *San Diego Chinese Community Church*, p. 11.
49. A complete history of the church, written by David Seid, Dorothy Hom, and Karl Fung, is found in the centennial booklet of the *San Diego Chinese Community Church*, pp. 6–28.
50. Handwritten minutes of the Women's Missionary Society of the First Congregational Church of Berkeley, 1894 and 1898.
51. Y. T. Dang, "My Life Work in Connection with the History of the Congregational Chinese Church of Berkeley, California." Typewritten manuscript in the possession of the author, dated 1954, p. 3.
52. "Berkeley Chinese Community Church, United Church of Christ." Typewritten statement prepared for the 125th anniversary of the Northern California Conference, United Church of Christ, 1983, 3 pp.
53. William C. Pond, *American Missionary* 32 (September and October 1878):281, 312. Quoted in Woo, op. cit., p. 114.

54. Kenneth Scott Latourette, *A History of Christian Missions in China* (New York: Russell and Russell, 1929), p. 365.
55. Leong, op. cit., pp. 5–6.
56. Ibid., p. 6.
57. William Edwin Hoy, *History of the China Mission of the Reformed Church in the United States* (Philadelphia: Board of Foreign Missions, 1914).
58. A fine treatment of the Chinese in Hawaii is Margaret C. Young, *And They Also Came* (Honolulu: United Church of Christ, 1976).
59. A brief history of *The First Chinese United Church of Christ in Hawaii* is found in its centennial booklet (published by the church, 1979), pp. 7–13. A longer version, originally written by Mrs. Ah Jook Ku, appeared in the ninetieth anniversary booklet (published by the church, 1969), pp. 7–23.
60. Young, op. cit., p. 12.
61. *The United Church of Christ, Honolulu 60th and 70th anniversary booklets (1975 and 1985).* Although they do not contain much early history of the church, they are excellent chronicles of recent history. The best history of the Beretania Church and the new church is in the *50th Anniversary Booklet of the Community Church of Honolulu: 1934–1984* (published by the church, 1984). See p. 5.
62. *50th Anniversary of the Community Church of Honolulu,* p. 5.
63. Young, op. cit., pp. 16–30.
64. A typewritten history of the Hilo Chinese Christian Church is available from the Hawaii UCC Conference (n.d.).
65. *United Church of Christ Yearbook,* 1986.
66. An anniversary booklet of the *Chinese Christian Union of San Francisco: 1916–1981* was published in 1981.
67. *Centennial Yearbook of the Chinese Christian Association of Hawaii: 1877–1977* (Honolulu, 1977).

Index

(prepared by Sharon Naylor)

Brueggemann, Walter A. 194
Bufford, Charles M. 209
Bulletin 89
Bultmann, Wilhelm Herrmann-Rudolf 69
Burlingame Treaty 174
Burnett, J. F. 112, 192, 199, 201
Burton, Charles E. 89-90, 99
Burton, Malcolm K. 109, 201

Calder, Helen B. 93-94, 199
California 9, 95, 169-72, 174-84, 188
California Chinese Mission (CCM) 10, 175-83, 210
    Addison Street 182
    Shattuck Avenue 182
Calvin, John 14, 116, 127
Calvin (Hungarian) Synod 44
Calvinism (Calvinist) 49-52, 68, 131, 137
Camp Fire program 160
Camp meetings 143
Canada 63
Cane Ridge, KY 139
Canton, China 169, 183
Cantonese language 185-86
Cape Cod, MA 191
Carlisle, PA 131
Carroll, Jackson W. 205
Casimir, John 15
Catechism of the Religion of Jesus Christ 190
Catholic (*see* Roman Catholic)
Catskill County, NY 18
Cave, Robert C. 194
CCM (*see* California Chinese Mission)
Centennial of Religious Journalism, The 103, 193
Central Pennsylvania Synod of the Lutheran Church 30
Channing, William Ellery 48
Charles II of England 18
Chavis, Benjamin 111
Chelsea, VT 54
Chen, Jack 209
Chicago Christian Training School for Women 153
Chicago Commons Settlement House 156
Chicago Congregational Training School for Women (*see*

Congregational Training School for Women)
Chicago, IL 81, 96, 149, 152-54, 156, 158, 163, 165-66, 180
Chicago Theological Seminary, The 9, 149, 153-54, 156-57, 163, 165
Chicago Training School for City, Home, and Foreign Missions 152
China 86, 168-69, 176, 182-84
    Manchu government 182
Chinatown, San Francisco, CA 172, 175, 178
Chinese 2, 9-10, 87, 168-71, 173-74, 176-77, 188, 209-10
    anti-Chinese sentiment 171
    California Chinese Mission (CCM) 10, 175-83, 210
        Addison Street 182
        Shattuck Avenue 182
    Christian education 182
    churches 178, 188
    Congregational (Congregationalism, Congregationalists) 2, 9, 176-77
    immigration 173-74
    in Hawaii 184-87
    labor (laborers) 173, 177
    language classes 182-83, 185
    missions 173, 175-77, 180-83
    prostitution 176, 184
    Sunday school 175, 182, 185
    women 175-76
Chinese Christian Association 185, 188, 212
Chinese Christian Church, Hilo, HI 212
Chinese Christian Union, San Francisco, CA 188, 212
Chinese Community (Congregational) Church, Berkeley, CA 168, 178, 181-83, 210-11
Chinese Community Church, Detroit, MI 188
Chinese Community (Congregational) Church, San Diego, CA 178, 180-81, 211
Chinese Congregational Church (UCC), San Francisco, CA 168, 178-80, 188, 211
Chinese Congregational Missionary Society 184
Chinese Evangelical Church, San Francisco, CA 181
Chinese Literary Club 182

Etna, PA 38, 191
Eureka, CA 176
Europe 103, 117, 119, 168-69
Evangelical (see Evangelical and
    Reformed Church, Evangelical
    Association, Evangelical
    Protestant Church of North
    America, Evangelical Synod of
    North America, Evangelical
    United Brethren Church)
Evangelical and Reformed Church 1, 3,
    32, 105-6, 109, 147, 190
Evangelical Association 136, 139
Evangelical Catechism 67
Evangelical Church, Darmstadt, IL 73
Evangelical Church, Eyota, MN 73
Evangelical Church, Germany 73
Evangelical Protestant Church of
    North America (German) 2-4, 32,
    38-45, 190
  Conference 44, 191
  Declaration of Principles 42
  Ministers' Association 40
  Pittsburgh Association 44
  Smithfield (Street) Church 3, 32,
    37-38, 41, 43, 45, 190-91
Evangelical Seminary, MO 70 (see
    also Eden Theological Seminary)
Evangelical Synod of North America
    (German) 4, 7, 32, 67, 70, 72-73,
    77-79, 101, 129, 152, 204
  Constitution 72
  General Conference 72, 74
  in Missouri 69-70
Evangelical United Brethren Church 7,
    123
Evangelion (gospel) 35
*Evangelische Kirchenverein des
    Westens* (Evangelical Church
    Society of the West) 66, 70
Evans, Letitia Thomas 88, 94-95,
    198-99
"Every Member Canvass" 84-86
Exclusion Act of 1882 (see Oriental
    Exclusion Act of 1882)
"Experience meeting" 133-34
Eyota, MN 73

Fagley, Frederick L. 197
Falkner Swamp, PA 19
Farnum, Douglas 60, 62
Federal Theology 116

Feminism 167
Fensham, Florence Amanda 9, 153-55,
    158, 163, 166, 206
Ferrier, Rosa B. 199
Fiebiger, Mary Denison 200
Filipino Church(es) 9
Finney, Charles G. 55, 133, 140-41
First Chinese Church of Christ in
    Hawaii, Honolulu, HI 185
First Chinese United Church of Christ,
    HI 212
First Congregational Church, Berkeley,
    CA 181, 211
First Congregational Church, Oakland,
    CA 170, 209
First Congregational Church, San
    Francisco, CA 170
First Lutheran Church of Pittsburgh,
    PA 37
First Presbyterian Church, Pittsburgh,
    PA 190
First Presbyterian Church, San Diego,
    CA 180
Flucke, John W. 195
Fong, G. L. 183
Fong, Matthew 168
Foot washing 137
Foreign institutes 162
Formosan United Church of Christ,
    Seattle, WA 188
Forney, C. H. 204
Fort Duquesne, PA 33
Fort Pitt, PA 33
Fort Street Chinese Church, Honolulu,
    HI 185-86
Foster, Robert 60
France (French) 16-17
Francke Orphan's Institute, Halle,
    Germany 69
Franco-Prussian War 41
Frantz, John B. 204
Frederick, MD 119, 131, 139
Frederick III 15
Free Religious Association 68
"Free will" 137
Free Will Baptist 50-51, 54, 56, 60, 136,
    192
French and Indian War 33, 119
French Huguenot(s) 119
Fresno, CA 176-77, 180
Friedensbote 66
Fundamentalism 68
Fung, Karl 211

Gam, Jee 170-71
Gates, Harriet E. 207
Geary Act 175
Gee, Gum 179
Geer, Curtis Manning 208
Geistliches Lustgartlein 116
Gemeinhaus 24
General Association of Congregational
  Churches of California 174
General Association of Illinois 152
"General Eldership" of the Church of
  God 138
German (Germany) 3, 14-16, 20, 23,
  32-43, 67-71, 73, 77, 101, 115-20,
  152-202
German Brethren (see United Brethren
  Church)
German Congregationalists 2
German Evangelical Protestant
  Church of North America
  (*Deutsche Evangelische
  Protestantische Kirche...*) 4, 33,
  35, 37-38, 42
  Smithfield (Street) Church 3, 32,
  37-38, 41, 43, 45, 190-91
German Evangelical Seminary, MO 68
  (see also Eden Theological
  Seminary)
German Evangelical Synod of North
  America 66-68, 79
German idealism 141-42
German language 3, 162
German Lutheran 2
German Lutheran deaconesses 152
German Mediating Theology 67, 195
German pietism 124, 132, 139 (see also
  Pietism)
"German Presbyterian Church" 20
German Reformed Church, The 33,
  115-16, 118, 120-23, 125, 128-32,
  134-36, 139-43, 147 (see also
  Reformed Church in the United
  States)
German Reformed Coetus of
  Pennsylvania 117-18, 120-22,
  124-26, 202-3
German Reformed Congregation,
  Hagerstown, PA 204
German Reformed Seminary,
  Mercersburg, PA 8, 67, 131, 141
German Reformed Synod 33-35 (see
  also German Reformed Church)
Get, Chui 184

Glades Valley Church, Frederick, MD
  131
Gloucester, England 26
Gobel, Max 189
Gold rush 169
Good, James I. 189, 204
Goodsell, Fred Field 196
Gospel Herald 106, 200 (see also
  Herald of Gospel Liberty)
Gospel Publisher 142, 146
*Gospel Publisher and Journal of
  Useful Knowledge, The* 146
Gossard, J. Harvey 130, 205
Graduate School of Theology, Oberlin
  College 162
Great Awakening, the 49, 55, 17 (see
  also Second Great Awakening)
Greek language 71, 73
Greek Orthodox Church 74
Greensburg, PA 34
Greep, Orpha 164, 208
Guangzhou (Canton), China 169, 185
Gunnemann, Louis H. 107, 191, 201

Haeberle, Louis F. 71
Hager, C. R. 183
Hager, John Frederick 18
Hagerstown, MD 135
Hakka(s) Chinese 185-86
Halstead, KS 73
Hampton, CT 60
Hampton, NH 106
Hanalei, HI 187
Hanapepe, HI 187
Handy, Robert C. 194
Hanko, Charles William 190
Hanover, NH 51
Harbaugh, H. 202-3
Hargrove, Barbara 206
Harkness, Georgia 164, 208
Harrisburg Anti-Slavery Society 145
Harrisburg, PA 130, 132-35, 138, 140,
  144, 146
Harrisburg Silk Agency 146
Hartford, CT 162
Hartford School of Religious
  Pedagogy 162
Hartford Seminary Foundation 208
Hartford Theological Seminary 162,
  208
Harvard University 49, 63

Mercersburg, PA 8, 67, 131, 141
Mercersburg Theology 8, 131, 141-42, 205
Merzdorf, Walter 195
Methodist(s) (Methodism) 7, 36, 45, 47-50, 55, 66, 68, 118, 121, 123, 125-26, 133, 138-39, 152, 164, 170, 177-78, 180, 184, 188, 196
  General Conference 197
  Woman's Foreign Missionary Society 197
Methodist Episcopal Church 123
Methodist's Chicago Training School for City, Home, and Foreign Missions 152
Methods 140
Mexico (Mexican) 9, 145, 169, 181
Michigan 138
Mickle, Jeffrey P. 203
Middle Atlantic states 139
Mid-Pacific Institute, Honolulu, HI 186
Midwest (Midwestern) 66, 157-58
Miller, William (Millerite Adventists) 48, 193
Mills School, Honolulu, HI 186
Milwaukee, WI 70
Ministers' wives 159
Minnesota 73
Mission (missionaries) 150-51, 161, 166, 176
Missionary Herald 89, 103
Missions 103
Missions Council 97
Mississippi River 38
Missouri 39, 44, 66-70, 191
Missouri Lutherans 66
Monongahela River 33, 36, 38
Montgomery, Helen Barrett 197
Montgomery, Martin L. 189
Moody Bible Institute 156
Moravian(s) 139
Morrill, Milo True 48, 55, 63, 191, 193
Mount Washington Church, Pittsburgh, PA 38, 42, 191
Muehlhaeuser, Pastor 70
Mueller, Julius "Sin" 69
Muhlenberg, Henry Melchior 117
Mulberry Street church, Harrisburg, PA 135, 146
Mulberry trees 147
Munter, Hermine 190-91
Mystical Presence, The 142

Nassau-Dillenberg, Germany 115-16
National Conference of Chinese Churches in America 10, 188
National Council of Congregational Churches 4, 32, 44, 85-86, 88-89, 94-98, 153
National Council of the Churches of Christ in the U.S.A. 101
Native American(s) 2, 9, 112 (*see also* American Indians)
"Neological Paragraph" 72, 76-78
Netherlands 16
Nettleton, Asahel 140
Nevin, John Williamson 8, 118, 131, 141-44, 147, 205
"New birth" 136-37
New Braunfels, TX 40
New Castle, NH 192
New England 4, 33, 46-47, 49-51, 53-56, 58-62, 64, 102, 106, 123, 192-93
New Hampshire 47, 51-52, 54-57, 59, 61, 102, 106, 192
New Lebanon, NY 140
"New Measures" 8, 130, 133, 138, 140-44, 147
New Richmond, OH 40
New World 17-18
New York 17-19, 22, 43, 56, 59, 61, 117, 140, 154, 172, 193
Newcomer, Christian 122, 125, 203
Newport, KY 39, 191
Newtown, NY 18
Nichols, James Hastings 194, 205
Nineteenth Amendment 99
Nollau, Louis 70
Nordbeck, Elizabeth C. 46
North Berkeley Congregational Church, Berkeley, CA 182
North Carolina 4, 22, 106, 110-11
North Dakota 158
Northampton, MA 123
Norwegian language 162

Oakland, CA 170, 176, 178
Oberlin College, Oberlin, OH 109, 162
Ockersdorf, Germany 117-18
Office of Communications, UCC 101
Ohio 4, 22, 36, 38-40, 43-44, 46, 63, 106, 108, 115, 130, 138, 162, 191, 201
Ohio Christian Book Association 106
Ohio Pastors Association 108

Ventura, CA 176, 178
Verdesi, Elizabeth Howell 208
Vermont 47, 50-52, 54-56, 59-60, 192-93
Vienna 16
Villars, Marshal 16
Virginia 4, 22, 47, 49, 51, 54, 110
Visalia, CA 176
Vlastos, Gregory 209
Voegtly, Mr. *(first name unknown)* 37
Voegtly Church, Allegheny, PA 37-38, 190
Volkskalender (People's Almanac) 42, 190
Voss, Carl August 43-44, 190
Voss, Carl Hermann 190
Voss, Eduard 43, 199

Wagner, James E. 147, 205
Wailuku, HI 187
Waimea, HI 187
War with Mexico 145
Washington, DC 44
Washington, George 74
WBM (see Woman's Board of Missions)
WBMI (see Woman's Board of Missions of the Interior)
WBMP (see Woman's Board of Missions for the Pacific)
WBMPI (see Woman's Board of Missions for the Pacific Islands)
WCTU (see Women's Christian Temperance Union)
Weare, NH 56
Weber, Johann Wilhelm 34-35, 45
Webster Groves, MO 67
Weekly Messenger, The 140, 142
Weeks, Thomas S. 201
Wellons, William Brock 110
Wesley, John 118, 126
West Camp, NY 18
West Covington, KY 39, 191
West End Church, Pittsburgh, PA 38, 191
West Virginia 22, 38, 43, 190
Westerly, RI 53
Western Theological Seminary, Allegheny, PA 141
Westminster Confession 131-32
Wheeling, WV 38, 43, 190
Wichita, KS 160
Wilbur, Isaac 103-4

Williams, Daniel Day 194
Wilmington, NC 111
Wilson, Woodrow 111
Windham, Connecticut 61
Winebrenner, John 8, 130-47, 204
Winebrenner, Philip 131
Winebrenner Theological Seminary, Findlay, OH 130
Wisconsin Synod (Lutherans) 69-70
Woman's Board of Missions (WBM) 81-82, 94, 96
Woman's Board of Missions for the Pacific (WBMP) 81-82, 86, 88-89, 94-97
Woman's Board of Missions for the Pacific Islands (WBMPI) 81, 196
Woman's Board of Missions of the Interior (WBMI) 81-82, 96
Woman's Boards 5, 80-99
Woman's Boards' Council 88, 90-91, 93-94, 198
Woman's Foreign Missionary Society of the Methodist Protestant Church 197
Woman's Home Missionary Federation 95
Women 2, 4-9, 41, 55-59, 80-100, 111, 149-66, 175-81, 196, 208
    as pastors, ordination of 154-55, 163-66, 197
Women's Christian Temperance Union (WCTU) 150
Women's International League for Peace and Freedom 161
Women's Missionary Society of the First Congregational Church, Berkeley, CA 181, 211
Wong, Dorothy 168
Woo, Wesley S. 209-11
Woodland, CA 176
Woodstock, VT 51, 54
Woolwich, ME 192
World War I 159
World War II 181
Worley, Minnie G. 176
Worthley, Harold F. 191
Wuerttemberg, Germany 41

Yale University 49
"Yee Jee Wui" (see Chinese Second Congregational Church)
YMCA (see Young Men's Christian Association)